ENVIRONMENTAL UNIONS
Labor and the Superfund

Craig Slatin
University of Massachusetts Lowell

Work, Health, and Environment Series
Series Editors: Charles Levenstein, Robert Forrant, and John Wooding

LONDON AND NEW YORK

First published 2009 by Baywood Publishing Company, Inc.

2 Park Square, Milton Park, Abingdon, Oxfordshire OX14 4RN
605 Third Avenue, New York, NY 10017

Routledge is an imprint of the Taylor & Francis Group, an informa business

First issued in hardback 2020

Library of Congress Catalog Number: 2008037371
ISBN 13: 978-0-89503-382-6 (hbk)

Library of Congress Cataloging-in-Publication Data

Slatin, Craig, 1951-
Environmental unions : labor and the Superfund / Craig Slatin.
p. ; cm. -- (Work, health, and environment series)
Includes bibliographical references and index.
ISBN 978-0-89503-382-6 (cloth : alk. paper) -- ISBN 978-0-89503-389-5 (pbk. : alk. paper) 1. United States. Comprehensive Environmental Response, Compensation, and Liability Act of 1980. 2. Hazardous waste site remediation--United States. 3. Labor unions--United States. 4. Environmental health--United States. I. Title. II. Series.
[DNLM: 1. United States. Comprehensive Environmental Response, Compensation, and Liability Act of 1980. 2. Occupational Exposure--prevention & control--United States. 3. Environmental Exposure--prevention & control--United States. 4. Environmental Pollution--prevention & control--United States. 5. Hazardous Waste--United States. 6. Health Policy--United States. 7. Labor Unions--United States. WA 400 S631e 2009]

HC110.W3S53 2009
331.7'62816830973--dc22

2008037371

Cover Photo: William E. Sauro/The New York Times/Redux

ISBN 978-0-89503-382-6 (hbk)

Dedication

To Louis E. Herman, my grandfather, who lovingly encouraged me to study.

Table of Contents

Acknowledgments

This book began as a dissertation under the encouraging advisement and mentoring of Charles Levenstein, along with critical support from John Wooding and Rafael Moure-Eraso. I had been directing one of the organizations funded through the Worker Education and Training Program (WETP) of the National Institute of Environmental Health Sciences (NIEHS) since the early 1990s. We were all curious to explore the program to better understand the political economy of regulating the U.S. work environment. At the same time, Eduardo Siqueira was conducting related dissertation research (which later became a book in this series), and we spent countless hours together in Cambridge, Massachusetts discussing our work. My dear friend Beth Rosenberg also helped me think through my research and later my writing.

Denny Dobbin, at NIEHS in North Carolina, who was directing the WETP, gave me a supportive go-ahead to conduct this research. Chip Hughes, who took over the WETP after Denny retired, helped me navigate my way through the data that so often had been moved just one too many times to be found easily. Then there were all the people involved in the WETP and its awardee organizations who gave me their time, information, stories, and documents. I am grateful to all of these people without whose support this work would never have been completed or published. Most of their names fill the list of interviews and correspondence found at the end of the book. One name not there is Patricia Thompson who as the WETP program analyst provided me with loving support and the most recent training program data available, every year when I thought I was asking for the last time. I am saddened that she did not live to see me finally complete this, and to live out her many dreams.

My thanks go to four people who helped me edit this work along the way. Greg DeLaurier and John Wooding helped me begin to shape the dissertation into a book. Mary Lee Dunn helped me to cut away so much of what I thought was essential at the time—and she even worked with me to get two articles published in the interim. Jim O'Brien, a keen editor and historian of progressive social movements generously worked with me to develop the text as it exists here. His sense of humor and steadiness were essential to my completing the book manuscript.

Lastly, Ruth Brownstein, my wife, and Rebecca Slatin, my daughter, gave me their time and confidence in my ability to complete this work, and more often than they probably cared to—their ears. Not only can't I thank them enough, I probably don't. And my thanks to my parents, Martin and Myrna Slatin whose love I carry with me and share in this world.

The hazardous mess left behind by industrial production and the subsequent consumption endemic through the twentieth century's last half needs to be cleaned up. I hope that these lessons are useful for movements seeking safe environmental remediation and establishing just and sustainable ways to produce what we need to live comfortably on this planet.

List of Abbreviations and Acronyms

AFSCME American Federation of State, County, and Municipal Employees
AGC Associated General Contractors
AHER Asbestos Hazard Emergency Response Act
AOEC Association of Occupational and Environmental Clinics
ATSDR Agency for Toxic Substance and Disease Registry
BCTD Building and Construction Trades Department (AFL-CIO)
CAA Clean Air Act
CAC California Consortium
CACOSH Chicago Area Committee on Occupational Safety and Health
CAT curriculum action team
CDC Centers for Disease Control
CEP Council on Economic Priorities
CERCLA Comprehensive Environmental Response, Compensation, and Liability Act of 1980
CIH certified industrial hygienist
CMA Chemical Manufacturers Association
CNI Committee for Nuclear Information
ConnectiCOSH Connecticut Committee for Occupational Safety and Health
COSH coalition (or committee or council) on occupational safety and health
CSI Clean Sites, Inc.
CSP certified safety professional
DHHS Department of Health and Human Services
DOD Department of Defense
DOE Department of Energy
DOL Department of Labor
DOT Department of Transportation
DSCEJ Deep South Center for Environmental Justice
EPA U.S. Environmental Protection Agency
EPCRA Emergency Planning and Community Right-to-Know Act
ER emergency response
ERCs educational resource centers
ERG Eastern Research Group, Inc.
ERT Environmental Response Team
FDA Food and Drug Administration

FEMA Federal Emergency Management Agency
GAO General Accounting Office
H&S health and safety
HASP Health and Safety Plan
HAZMAT hazardous materials
HAZWOPER hazardous waste operations and emergency response
HEW Department of Health, Education, and Welfare
HHE Health Hazard Evaluation
HSWA Hazardous and Solid Waste Amendments of 1984
IAFF International Association of Fire Fighters
IBT International Brotherhood of Teamsters
ICWU International Chemical Workers Union
IDP Instructor Development Program
IUD Industrial Union Department (AFL-CIO)
IUOE International Union of Operating Engineers
LACOSH Los Angeles Committee on Occupational Safety and Health
L-AGC Laborers—Associated General Contractors
LECET Laborers-Employers Cooperation and Education Trust
LHSFNA Laborers' Health and Safety Fund of North America
LI Labor Institute
LIUNA Laborers International Union of North America
LOHP Labor Occupational Health Program
MASSCOSH Massachusetts Coalition for Occupational Safety and Health
MSDS material safety data sheet
MSHA Mine Safety and Health Administration
MWTP Minority Worker Training Program
NACOSH National Advisory Committee on Occupational Safety and Health
NCI National Cancer Institute
NCP National Contingency Plan
NEC New England Consortium
NEJAC National Environmental Justice Advisory Council
NFPA National Fire Protection Association
NIA National Institute for Arthritis
NIEHS National Institute of Environmental Health Sciences
NIH National Institutes of Health
NIOSH National Institute for Occupational Safety and Health
NLRB National Labor Relations Board
NPRM notice of proposed rulemaking and public hearings
NSWMA National Solid Waste Management Association
NTP National Toxicology Program
NYCOSH New York Committee for Occupational Safety and Health
OCAW Oil, Chemical, and Atomic Workers International Union
OMB Office of Management and Budget
OSHA Occupational Safety and Health Administration
OSH Act Occupational Safety and Health Act of 1970

OSHECS occupational safety and health education coordinators
OSWER Office of Solid Waste and Emergency Response
OTA Office of Technology Assessment
PELs permissible exposure levels
PHS U.S. Public Health Service
PPE personal protective equipment
RCRA Resource Conservation and Recovery Act of 1976
RFA request for applications
RICOSH Rhode Island Committee for Occupational Safety and Health
RTP Research Triangle Park, Raleigh/Durhan, N.C.
SARA Superfund Amendments and Reauthorization Act of 1986
SEIU Service Employees International Union
SEMCOSH Southeast Michigan Coalition on Occupational Safety and Health
SFBR Superfund Basic Research Program
SGAM small group activity method
SWTP Superfund Worker Training Program
TOP Triangle of Prevention
TSCA Toxic Substances Control Act of 1976
TRI Toxics Release Inventory
TSDF treatment, storage, and disposal facility
TUC British Trades Union Congress
UAW United Auto Workers Union
UBC United Brotherhood of Carpenters
UCLA University of California at Los Angeles
USCG United States Coast Guard
USWA/USW United Steel Workers of America
WETP Worker Education and Training Program
WHF Workplace Health Fund
WISH Workers' Institute for Safety and Health
WMDs weapons of mass destruction
WTC World Trade Center

CHAPTER 1

Cleaning Up the 20th-Century Mess: Protecting the Workers Who Do It

In the movie *Ghostbusters,* New York City is gradually covered by green, oozing slime. Dripping out of building cracks, slipping down into sewer catch basins, even going up library shelves, the slime is the advance party of a force that is going to destroy human life as we know it. Someone must be called to eradicate the slime and the evil force it portends. The Ghostbusters come onto the scene: three guys in hazardous materials suits with sci-fi weapons who zap the slime and turn back the destructive force—and life in the city resumes its happy path.

The story is a lot of fun to watch on the big screen, but perhaps more realistic than it may seem. A slime is creeping across the land and seeping into our water, even polluting the air we breathe. Hazardous wastes, sitting in a great variety of regulated or abandoned sites, harm not only human beings but many other forms of life. Nearly half of all Americans live within 10 miles of a federally listed hazardous waste site (Sapien, 2007)—and that doesn't include the thousands of other sites identified by states or the thousands expected to be found over the next several decades. It all has to be cleaned up, and it is going to take more than three guys in suits with sci-fi guns. It's inherently dangerous work, because the toxic and hazardous substances cannot be made safe. Those who clean them up are providing a national service. They require training and equipment that protects their health and safety while doing the work and enables them to enjoy their lives after that work. Who you gonna call?

THE 20TH-CENTURY MESS

In the 20th century we learned new ways to use our world's many resources, finding new ways to process materials, manufacture goods for production and commerce, and energize our machines. Learning a multitude of ways to synthesize chemicals was one of the most remarkable technological advances of the period. The basis for our modern modes of industrial production was transformed over a few short decades from biophysical to chemical resources. Oil and coal became the basis for new hydrocarbon-based chemicals that opened up a world of new materials, from plastics to chemical solvents to poisons once used to slaughter prisoners in concentration camps and later refined to slaughter insects and plants.

The synthetic chemistry revolution created materials and substances that had never been in the ecosystem before and that often persist in that environment rather than decomposing rapidly. No life form on the planet has had time to adapt to exposure to these substances. In the case of eradicating unwanted plants, insects, and even other humans, the intention was that the materials would be potent poisons that would do the job. The vast majority were not designed to bring about disease and death, yet many of them cause harm to the life processes that establish healthy organisms, including human beings. Nor were they designed with the intention of causing physical destruction, but it was known that they were often highly acidic, caustic, flammable, and/or explosive.

Related to these technological advancements were advances in the human organization of industrial production and wealth management. Unfortunately, systems of waste management did not advance as rapidly as did the systems for creating waste; by the 1970s, the world faced a hazardous waste crisis that would become so enormous that no planetary region, including the poles, is free of toxic pollution and contamination. Similar advances in nuclear technologies and the military and industrial capacity to use them resulted in an enormous radioactive waste problem. Around the world, the failure of industrial and governmental leaders to appropriately address all the waste related to industrial, commercial, and military activities established the web of poisoned ground, water, and air that surrounds us.

The work of tens of millions of U.S. workers across industrial sectors involves making, using, managing, or moving hazardous materials. Many of them clean up hazardous wastes or respond to accidents and disasters involving these materials and what's left of them after their use in production and consumption. Those workers engage in *H*azardous *W*aste *OP*erations and *E*mergency *R*esponse—HAZWOPER work in the industry's lexicon.

The health and safety of HAZWOPER workers must be protected—whether they are cleaning up abandoned waste sites, managing hazardous wastes at industrial facilities, hauling such wastes from one location to another (as we move them around to try to make it appear that they don't exist), or dealing with a catastrophe such as a chemical plant explosion or the derailment of a train with tanker cars filled with pesticides. Sometimes the industrial accidents are less spectacular and more commonplace, things that the public never hears about, such as a pipeline breaking and leaking in a facility or a mechanical process breaking down and causing workers to be overcome by fumes that may kill them. Sometimes workers find themselves exposed to hazardous wastes in jobs that no one thought would present such exposures, as, for example, in the case of a New York City sanitation worker who was killed when the crushing arm of a garbage truck caused a 1-gallon container of hydrofluoric acid to pop and spray the worker's face with the acid (Slatin & Siqueira, 1998; Van Gelder, 1996). Sometimes school janitors are exposed to asbestos from deteriorating pipe insulation or from PCB dust resulting from deteriorating caulking. As our industrial processes contaminated our environments, both outdoor and indoor, more and more workers were being exposed to hazardous waste materials on the job.

By the late 1970s, it was becoming obvious that at least those workers with the most obvious exposures—clean-up workers, workers who treat, store, and dispose of hazardous wastes, those who haul them, the firefighters who have to respond to the chemical fires, and the manufacturing and processing workers who make the hazardous chemicals—all needed protection from the inherent dangers of work with toxic and hazardous substances.

All of this work needs to be healthy and safe. Regardless of the inherent dangers in this work, workers should not have to sacrifice themselves, their families, and their communities in exchange for their jobs. Societies advanced enough to create and use such technologies and organize the enormous related systems of production, distribution, consumption, and disposal can and should fulfill internationally agreed-upon principles of human rights and not force the abandonment of health for a job.

This book is about workplace health and safety and environmental protection. Its theoretical framework is that the prevention of workplace injuries, illnesses, and fatalities can be maximized, even for inherently dangerous work. Further, it holds that the failure to implement measures to prevent these adverse health effects of work results from a system in which, in the words of Tony Mazzocchi, one of the early labor leaders of the modern health and safety movement, workers "essentially give a subsidy" (quoted in Isaac, 1995) to employers who generate profit and productivity at the expense of workers and their communities. Workplace injuries and environmental pollution result from deliberate financial practices and organizational priorities that shift resources toward corporate wealth accumulation and away from the optimization of workplace health and safety and environmental protection.

THE SUPERFUND WORKER TRAINING PROGRAM

There was a moment at which the strength of the environmental movement, the sharp political eye of labor lobbyists, and the commitment of dedicated labor leaders and public health professionals converged, producing the most extensive government-subsidized worker health and safety training program in U.S. history. This was the Superfund Worker Training Program (SWTP), subsequently named the Worker Education and Training Program (WETP). And this occurred in the face of a rightward shift in American politics that, for the most part, undermined the hard-won (if incomplete) social safety net and abandoned the "environment" to the mercy of the market.

The program's history is important, not because we can assume that the coalition politics that once worked can be duplicated in these days of "the death of environmentalism" and fragmented "tiny labor"[*1] but because we require a clear, unflinching eye with which to survey the social and political tasks facing those concerned about worker and community health as well as environmental protection. And we need to understand the importance of political economy and economic policy as constraints on public health success. Lessons can be learned from one of the last great worker health and safety/environmental protection victories of the 1960s–1980s reform era, a victory that came on the cusp of the end of the golden age of regulation and the beginning of the new era of deregulation and the dominance of the market, referred to as neoliberalism.[2]

[*] All footnotes are at the end of each chapter under Endnotes.

By the late 1970s, the legacy of decades of chemical-based production and consumption had created a pollution crisis so monumental in its proportions that more than a decade's worth of public health laws had been passed to protect occupational and environmental health. When the Thatcher and Reagan governments called for an end to liberalism and its attempts to regulate capitalism by command and control, these laws and the agencies they mandated came under attack. In the United States, failing to gain public support for their elimination, the Reagan administration quickly learned to implement stealth measures that left the facade of government programs standing, while gutting them and disabling their capacity to engage in effective law enforcement.

Yet, grassroots organizing and pressure not only forced reversals of these strategies but succeeded in passing the Superfund Amendments and Reauthorization Act (SARA) of 1986. Extending the reach and goals of the national Superfund program for hazardous waste cleanups, the legislation was passed one and a half years into President Reagan's second term. The legislation included the Emergency Planning and Community Right to Know Act (EPCRA), which required the public reporting of hazardous materials and toxic chemical releases. No less than a year later, Reagan would succeed in getting tax code overhaul legislation passed, ending the remnants of the New Deal compact and setting the stage for an era of privatization and downsizing of government functions at all levels of government.

A small section of SARA was a measure pressed for by labor and won on the coattails of this major environmental victory. It included mandates for a training grant program to protect U.S. workers who engage in hazardous waste operations and hazardous materials incident emergency response, and for the Occupational Safety and Health Administration (OSHA) to promulgate a regulation to protect such workers and require the health and safety training specifically described in the legislation. This book presents the history of how labor unions won those mandates in SARA and worked to give them real meaning.

THE LABOR MOVEMENT, THE FOLKS WHO BROUGHT YOU THE WETP

What does it mean to be part of a union—part of a labor movement? How do most citizens learn about trade unions these days, when our schools teach children little about labor unions and our newspapers no longer have labor sections? With fewer than 13% of the U.S. workforce belonging to unions, most children don't grow up learning anything about unions at home. And even most union members don't know much about what their unions and the labor movement do to improve the quality of life for the working class.

This book presents the story of how union leaders, staff, and allied professionals worked to secure health and safety protections for HAZWOPER workers. These efforts create potential for improving the working conditions of all workers, not just union members. But they may never directly increase anyone's take home pay. Rarely will workers, even union members, know that labor unions were responsible for the legal requirement for employers to better protect their employees or for the worker-oriented health and safety training that would not be available otherwise.

The goals of the building trades unions that worked to secure HAZWOPER worker protections were as much about creating a way to open the hazardous waste remediation sector to union contractors as they were about creating safer work. There again, though, most union workers on these sites will never know that their union worked to create the work opportunities for them. It's just like the bumper sticker I sometimes see: "The Labor Movement, The Folks Who Brought You the Weekend." It probably doesn't make much sense to most people who see it. Perhaps we should have another slogan: "Workplace Health and Safety, Brought to You by the Labor Movement."

THE CASE STUDIES

Between 1997 and 1999, I conducted the research necessary to write the history of how the WETP came to be and the first 5 years of the effort to establish a sustainable national worker health education program. This involved learning about the origins of the idea and how labor was able to get Congress to pass the measures as part of the Superfund Amendments and Reauthorization Act of 1986 (SARA). Labor worked for legal measures—legislation, regulations, and administrative measures— for a period of 8 years, between 1979 and 1986. I studied many volumes of legislative history and interviewed many people involved in the efforts to get the law passed and to develop the program. I conducted three case studies. One focused on the Worker Education and Training Program (WETP) administration within the National Institute of Environmental Health Services (NIEHS), while the other two examined two union programs funded by the WETP—one operated by the Oil, Chemical, and Atomic Workers International Union (OCAW) and one by the joint labor-management trust fund of the Laborers Union and the Associated General Contractors (the Laborers—Associated General Contractors [Laborers-AGC] Education and Training Trust Fund). Both of the union programs provided strong leadership in the national program and both represented workers in key hazardous waste sectors: OCAW members produce hazardous materials and waste, and the Laborers clean it up. Each union was focusing on worker health and safety in the context of increased management resistance to joint labor-management cooperation alongside decreasing job security. The union case studies provided an opportunity to explore how health and safety struggles are shaped by industry-specific contexts as well as by the overall political economy.

The research included reviews of documents related to each organization. It also included observations of each program's activities as well as participation in program events. At the time, I directed a university-based WETP awardee organization and was actively involved in WETP meetings and discussions. As an insider-researcher I was able to access my own notes and the notes of others in the national program. Throughout the book I include quotations from people who were interviewed during the research. Quotations that are not otherwise cited resulted from these interviews.

The book is primarily about the first 5 years of the WETP and each union's program. In 2007, however, the WTEP was in its 20th year of operation, with the strong likelihood that it would continue. I have included updates on the WETP and the two union programs in order to provide a fuller picture of the WETP's successes, its constraints, and the context within which it operates. On September 15, 1987, NIEHS awarded 11 grants to nonprofit organizations (unions and university programs) so that they could develop and deliver training to targeted worker populations. By 2007, the agency's WETP was funding 18 awardees representing more than 80 organizations.

The WETP's boundaries have been established by multiple forces. Certainly most powerful has been the turn to free-market fundamentalism (neoliberalism) coupled with a conservative political consensus in Washington, DC. The greatly weakened labor movement largely withdrew from its never-too-strong platform on worker health and safety. The weakened environmental movement had largely abandoned hazardous waste issues to pursue sexier issues that would recruit more members, donations, and foundation dollars. Often this has taken the form of looking toward a sustainable future without sufficiently addressing the past-to-present environmental destruction and its ever mounting legacy of degradation and disease, which disproportionately burdens people of color and the working class. As this history will demonstrate, the WETP has steadfastly and successfully pursued its collective goal of developing excellent worker health and safety training and using HAZWOPER worker protections as a focus for addressing hazardous waste management and remediation and hazardous materials incident prevention and response issues.

LAYOUT OF THE BOOK

To provide the historical context for the WETP story, chapter 2 discusses the hazardous waste management industry, a regulated private-sector answer to the hazardous waste crisis. This chapter also provides a short history of the OSHA New Directions training program, an earlier national health and safety training grant program that helped to build an active health and safety movement but was dismantled by the Reagan administration. Chapters 2 and 3 present the history of labor's involvement in obtaining federal government resources to protect HAZWOPER workers, looking at the efforts of the American Federation of Labor—Congress of Industrial Organizations (AFL-CIO), the International Association of Fire Fighters, and the building trades unions. The work spans the 9 years between the community uprising at Love Canal in Niagara, NY, that put the hazardous waste crisis on the national agenda and led to the passage of the Superfund law and to the signing of the reauthorization of the Superfund law in 1986.

Chapters 4 and 5 present the process of developing and implementing the WETP within NIEHS. The various actors and their major concerns are considered in detail as they build its architecture and begin training workers. The early concerns of WETP leaders were to establish cohesion across the different awardee organizations, excellence in training and program management, and measures to sustain the program beyond the initial funding cycle. Conflicts arose among the awardees and between the awardees and NIEHS. The skillful conflict management and the willingness of awardees to engage in dialogue and compromise present a glimpse of the sometimes delicate balancing of commitment to coalition building and individual organizational goals.

Chapters 6 and 7 present the case studies of the two labor union programs. Each adopted an emphasis on program excellence that was framed in part within the boundaries set by employer control of the workplace and the industry. Each also intended to use the training to strengthen the union and its capacity to increase workers' ability to secure healthier and safer working conditions and to build confidence from those actions to create stronger unions.

Chapter 8 presents an actor analysis of the political economy of the efforts by labor and its allies to establish and build a national HAZWOPER worker health and safety training program. The analysis assumes that economic forces shape the political decisions arising from and used to engage in class struggle (with worker health and safety protection and environmental quality being aspects of class struggle). An analysis of the roles played by five broad sets of social actors (unions, management, professionals, the state, and social movements) in this history sheds light on the arenas of conflict and cooperation in the political economy of the work environment and the ways in which existing corporate hegemony influences those arenas. This analysis of a social history provides a window into how the existing capitalist state operates, how unions and corporations relate to the state and to each other, and how professionals within labor, corporations, and the government influence these dynamics while also pursuing their own interests. It demonstrates how divisions within social sectors (corporate or labor, for example, as well as social movements) provide points at which temporary alliances can be forged to leverage opportunities for victories—whether they be regulating industrial practices or gaining ideological hegemony through threats of scarcity and competitive weakness. Exploring the interplay between these actors in the political economy of the work environment provides a valuable tool for mapping directions for creating future changes (see Figure 1).

Chapter 9 concludes the book, looking at the hazardous waste crisis today and the limitations of reforming capitalism at the expense of the ongoing degradation of human health and environmental sustainability.

MOVING FORWARD

The history of the Worker Education and Training Program and an analysis of its political economy provide a window into worker health and safety at the end of the 20th-century U.S. liberal reform era. The history demonstrates the limits of public health and labor strategies that have not challenged the mode and control of production, particularly in the face of free market ideology. It can help us gauge the successes and limitations of past strategies as we pursue new strategies for navigating the role of the state and achieving fair and just trade and market systems, the advancement of workers' rights, and global democracy.

United fronts of labor and environmentalists are now needed to fight against the corporate elite's assault on the working class, its health, and the environment. The assault's global dimension has had a core goal of dismantling the capacity and role of the state as a tool for broadening the rights and living standards of the working

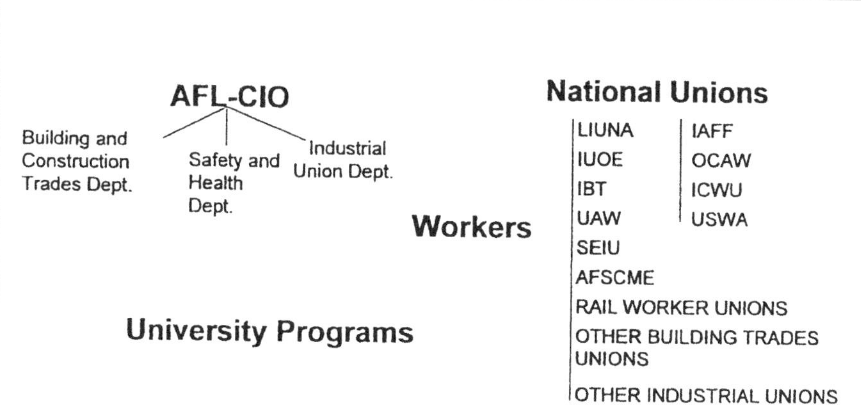

Federal Government

Agencies

Congress
Politicians
Staff

Research
NIEHS
NIOSH

Regulatory
OSHA
EPA
DOT
FEMA

President
OMB

Judicial Branch

Other
DOE
DOD

Movements
Labor
Environmental
Health and Safety
Public Interest

Employers & Industries
Hazardous Waste Mgt. Industry
Oil/Petrochemical
Manufacturing
Construction
Public Sector
Service Sector
Insurance
Smaller Employers

Professionals/Scientists

Health & Safety
Attorneys
Medical
Economists
Educators
Toxicologists
Legislative Coordinators
Engineers

Figure 1. Actors in the political economy of the WETP.

class. The liberal reform strategies of the 1960s and 1970s probably are not replicable in this new era of diminished and less democratic governments—particularly in the United States.

Yet, OSHA, the National Institute of Environmental Health Sciences (NIOSH), the WETP, and the U.S. Environmental Protection Agency (EPA)—the bodies providing the public health regulation and police functions of the state—have made a substantial difference for many workers. These reforms have been successfully used to make work safer and healthier and to make health and safety an issue of greater social concern. The EPA's regulation and enforcement of environmental protection has produced a cleaner environment than most people had 50 years ago. Agencies like these will not by their existence alone result in a transformation to environmentally clean and socially just and equitable production, but they certainly could be used to do that if it were the national intention. For now, though, OSHA has played only a timid role and, as already stated, the EPA has not prevented the continuing spread of hazardous waste sites. Hopefully, an examination of the WETP can help us to consider whether we want our great-grandchildren to spend their working lives in and among industrial poisons.

ENDNOTES

1. To better understand these references, see Shellenberger and Nordhaus (2004), and Ehrenreich (2005).
2. In his book, *A Brief History of Neoliberalism,* David Harvey describes neoliberalism as,

> a theory of political economic practices that proposes that human well-being can best be advanced by liberating individual entrepreneurial freedoms and skills within an institutional framework characterized by strong private property rights, free markets, and free trade. The role of the state is to create and preserve an institutional framework appropriate to such practices. . . . There has everywhere been an emphatic turn towards neoliberalism in political-economic practices and thinking since the 1970s. Deregulation, privatization, and withdrawal of the state from many areas of social provision have been all too common. (Harvey, 2005, pp. 2-3)

REFERENCES

Ehrenreich, B. (2005, August). Tiny Labor. *The Progressive, 6.* Retrieved July 7, 2007, from http://www.progressive.org/?q=mag_tinylabor

Harvey, D. (2005). *A Brief History of Neoliberalism.* New York: Oxford University Press.

Isaac, K. (1995). *The Cold War's Continuing Victims.* Retrieved July 8, 2007, from http://multinationalmonitor.org/hyper/mm1095.06.html

Sapien, J. (2007, April 26). *Superfund Today: Massive Undertaking to Clean Up Hazardous Waste Sites Has Lost Both Momentum and Funding.* Retrieved July 7, 2007, from http://www.publicintegrity.org/Superfund/report.aspx?aid=851

Shellenberger, M., & Nordhaus, T. (2004). *The Death of Environmentalism: Global Warming Politics in a Post-Environmental World.* The Breakthrough Institute. Retrieved July 7, 2007, from http://www.thebreakthrough.org/images/Death_of_Environmentalism.pdf

Slatin, C., & Siqueira, E. (1998). Does a Collateral Duty Require Less Protection: Workers, Hazardous Materials Emergency Response, and OSHA's Failure to Protect. *New Solutions, A Journal of Environmental and Occupational Health Policy, 8*(2), 205–219.

Van Gelder, L. (1996, November 13). Trash Collector Dies After Inhaling Discarded Acid. *The New York Times,* p. B1.

CHAPTER 2

Workers on Poisoned Ground

The 1970s were a decade of environmental and occupational health activism energized by the struggles and successes of the labor, civil rights, student, antiwar, women's, and environmental movements. The emergence of the new left provided fertile ground for some activists who used health and safety issues as a link to labor and the old left (Wooding, 1994). The United States had been moved to better protect workers' health and safety after national news coverage of the suffering and vigilance of mine workers in West Virginia and other states who staged massive walkout strikes to protest conditions that were killing and maiming mine workers—from explosions and cave-ins to black lung (Derikson, 1991; Kerr, 1990; Nyden, 2007; Smith, 1981). In 1969, responding to the strikes and coalitions of labor and public health advocates and a public outcry, the U.S. Congress passed the Mine Safety and Health Act, a forebearer to the Occupational Safety and Health Act (OSH Act), which was passed in 1970.

On the environmental side, two decades of outrage over industrial pollution had resulted in early environmental protection laws aimed at protecting the quality of air and waters. President Richard Nixon signed the National Environmental Policy Act in 1970, and then established the Environmental Protection Agency (EPA). The year 1970 saw the first Earth Day event. Industrial hazardous wastes were becoming a critical environmental concern.

The political and economic system that spawned social unrest and protest also spawned environmental destruction and its subsequent consequences for ecological and human health. The chemical soup was boiling, making a mess that was going to have to be cleaned up. Steadily, individuals in the communities living with these hazardous wastes, in the chemical soup line, would organize others to protest against the health consequences that seemed so obvious to them. Workers and their unions would also raise concerns about exposure to these chemicals, at work and in their communities, and some began to understand that hazardous waste workers needed effective health and safety protection measures.

WORKPLACE AND HAZARD ARE "ONE AND THE SAME"

The hazardous waste crisis of the late-20th-century United States had its origins in a transition from a biophysical economy to a chemical economy.[1] By the late 1970s, nearly 70,000 chemicals were used in U.S. industries, with approximately

1,000 new chemicals entering commercial markets annually. The introduction of new chemicals, often hazardous and toxic, shaped new production processes and methods that greatly changed the nature and levels of production throughout industry. This resulted in unimagined quantities of hazardous industrial waste. In their history of the management of industrial waste before the EPA was established, Colten and Skinner note:

> Except for plating, smelting, and certain refinery wastes . . . most persistent and toxic industrial wastes were manageable, at least until the 1930s—largely because the volumes produced were relatively small. During the 1930s and 1940s, the organic chemicals industry flourished and created a new spectrum of wastes whose quantities, toxicity, and persistence took quantum leaps. (Colten & Skinner, 1996, p. 5)

Colten and Skinner provided substantial evidence of industry's awareness of the environmental and public health risks posed by the hazardous wastes it was generating. By the late 1930s, the increase in the volume of industrial effluents and toxic discharges was of particular concern to industry toxicologists. They saw that such wastes constituted serious environmental and, likely, public health threats. "Finding ways to secure or sequester toxic wastes without causing environmental damage had become particularly vexing, especially with the introduction of new, more complex, and environmentally persistent chemicals, and in the absence of a universal waste treatment method" (Colten & Skinner, 1996, p. 53). Companies were increasingly using lagoons and ponds for disposal, for example, but that tactic further raised the concerns of industrial hygienists and toxicologists. In 1951, the American Petroleum Institute warned against dumping caustics into ponds (Colten & Skinner, 1996, p. 41), and the Manufacturing Chemists' Association issued guidelines for abating water pollution. Still, the elaboration of new industrial processes, together with their legacy in the form of hazardous wastes, was far outpacing the ability of even well-intentioned efforts by industry groups to regulate themselves. With the postwar expansion of synthetic chemicals into most industrial sectors, the problem continued to worsen.

Colten and Skinner observed that, unlike urban garbage, for which government had assumed collection and disposal responsibilities, the management of industrial wastes—particularly hazardous wastes—was left to the private responsibility of industrial firms. Firms commonly employed three approaches in waste disposal. First, they isolated the manufacturing process by siting plants away from populated areas. Second, they compensated neighbors for hazardous waste damage. Their third and most widely used method between the 1940s and 1970s, especially by large manufacturers, was to dispose of wastes on-site to "provide physical isolation and long-term trusteeship" (Colten & Skinner, 1996, p. 50). The overriding goal however, was to limit costs. Low-cost, low-control technologies for industrial waste management practices, Colten and Skinner argue, led to the waste crisis of the late 20th century. This was due to three causes: "1. inadequate stewardship and engineering, 2. deviance from industry or government guidelines, and 3. transfer of trusteeship" (Colten & Skinner, 1996, p. 147).

THE EPA STUDIES THE PROBLEM

Soon after the EPA was founded, in 1970, Congress required the agency to prepare a report on the storage and disposal of hazardous wastes, with a plan "for the creation of a system of national disposal sites" (U.S. EPA, 1974, p. 1). The charge for the report was to identify the materials that could be disposed of at the sites, describe the methods of hazardous waste disposal at that time, recommend hazardous waste reduction and management methods, inventory possible sites, and estimate the cost of developing and maintaining the sites.

In order to comply, the EPA conducted five studies between 1970 and 1973. It found that the hazardous waste problem was much greater than had been anticipated. Ten million tons of nonradioactive hazardous waste were generated annually, 90% of it in liquid form, and 60% organic. Hazardous waste generation was increasing at 5–10% a year. The EPA also found that manufacturers were paying only about 5% of the costs of environmentally adequate waste management and disposal. Overall, the EPA found that management of toxic, chemical, biological, radioactive, flammable, and explosive wastes was "generally inadequate" (U.S. EPA, 1974, p. ix).

Surveying existing federal and state legislation on hazardous waste disposal, the EPA learned that the Clean Air Act (CAA), the Federal Water Pollution Control Act, and the Marine Protection, Research, and Sanctuaries Act addressed the incineration and water and ocean dumping of hazardous wastes, but not land disposal. Fourteen other federal laws peripherally addressed hazardous waste management, while

> approximately twenty-five States [had] limited hazardous waste regulatory authority. Given this permissive legislative climate, generators of waste are under little or no pressure to expend resources for the adequate management of their hazardous wastes. There is little economic incentive . . . for generators to dispose of wastes in adequate ways. (U.S. EPA, 1974, p. ix)

The EPA predicted that regulatory controls on air and water pollution would push generators of hazardous wastes to seek land disposal options. It foresaw a hazardous waste crisis, noting that

> In order to forestall the type of environmental degradation likely to occur from the uncontrolled use of the land as an ultimate sink for the nation's ever-increasing supply of hazardous wastes, the focus of any hazardous waste regulatory program must first be on land disposal activities and those who provide and utilize land disposal services. (U.S. EPA, 1974, p. 20)

Seeking Private Sector Approaches

Significantly, the EPA sought primarily to force waste recovery and recycling rather than to challenge industrial production methods and force the development and adoption of technology that would prevent hazardous waste generation. That choice was fraught with consequences. In the EPA's rather sunny view, "treatment and disposal technology is available for most hazardous wastes" (U.S. EPA, 1974, p. 2), and the public was not opposed to regional locations for waste-processing facilities since they would "increase environmental protection and stimulate the economy of the region" (U.S. EPA, 1974, p. 2).

The EPA found that a hazardous waste management industry was developing, and that this new industry already had the capacity to handle about 25% of the required national capacity. But the industry was grossly underutilized, managing only about 6% of the national total, and the EPA believed that this resulted from "the absence of regulatory and economic incentives for generators to manage their hazardous wastes in an environmentally sound manner" (U.S. EPA, 1974, p. x). The agency sought to encourage private-sector investment in hazardous waste management capacity creation, and it believed that regulations would not only prod large-quantity waste generators to seek appropriate off-site disposal options but would also stimulate the major solid waste management "conglomerates" that had emerged since the 1960s to acquire the technology and skills necessary for the successful expansion of their services into hazardous waste management and disposal.

"The private sector, following a profit motive, has incentives to run only as good a hazardous waste management operation as it takes to obtain and keep business and to comply with governmental regulations," the EPA said (U.S. EPA, 1974, p. 33). Accordingly, the agency presented four sets of governmental and citizen activities necessary to pressure the private sector into appropriate hazardous waste management and disposal practices:

- Standards and regulations;
- Criteria for facility licensing;
- Vigorous inspection and enforcement by government, "with the attendant threat of licensing suspension or revocation actions"; and
- Legislation providing for citizen suits, facilitating the ability of citizens to "bring legal pressure to bear on both the government and private industry to force compliance with . . . regulations." (U.S. EPA, 1974, p. 34)

As for labor requirements, the EPA noted that hazardous waste management was a "capital intensive" process: "A significant increase in capacity will require only a limited expansion of labor" (U.S. EPA, 1974, p. 33). Labor unions would not agree with this assessment when they addressed this issue a decade later.

FEDERAL LAW AND A NEW INDUSTRY

As a partial response to the problem, Congress passed the Resource Conservation and Recovery Act of 1976 (RCRA), which vastly expanded the regulation of hazardous and solid wastes. RCRA established a "cradle-to-grave" system for tracking and manifesting industrial hazardous wastes, and a permit system for facilities that would treat, store, and/or dispose of hazardous wastes. It included requirements for the on-site management of hazardous wastes and the management of controlled hazardous waste sites. Additionally, all the emergency contingency plans and equipment were required for all regulated facilities. Gottlieb has noted that RCRA helped to

> stimulate a pollution control industry. Though sometimes in conflict over implementation issues, the triad of mainstream environmental group, government regulator, and pollution control or waste management industry promoted these hazardous waste management laws and regulations as an effective way to deal with the growing problem of toxics in society. (Gottlieb, 1993, p. 186)

The Council on Economic Priorities (CEP), a nonprofit public research group, has discussed the way in which the hazardous waste management industry differs from most other industries, in that it is "largely a product of environmental regulations" (Goldman, 1986, p. 37). Where many industries fight government regulation as interference with free enterprise, the council noted, the hazardous waste management industry has protested government efforts to weaken environmental regulations that force stricter waste management.

Grassroots environmentalists, however, did not consider the hazardous waste management industry well regulated. A demand of the environmental movement, "not in my backyard" (NIMBY), resisted the new industry, believing that it neither would nor could properly manage hazardous wastes. Significant and successful opposition was organized against the siting of hazardous waste treatment, storage, and disposal facilities (TSDFs).[2] Nonetheless, the EPA reports showed that between 1971 and 1980, the "revenues of the U.S. hazardous waste management industry had grown at a rate of approximately twenty percent per year—from $60 million to $315 million" (Goldman, 1986, p. 39).

An engineer employed by CH2M Hill, an engineering firm that was an early entrant into the remediation industry sector, described seven general types of contractors or companies involved in hazardous waste site investigation and remediation. They are surveyors (topographical and geophysical), test boring contractors, water well construction contractors, excavation contractors, "clean-up" contractors, consulting engineers/environmental firms, and analytical laboratories (Walker, 1987). The range of workers in these operations stretched from skilled engineers and technicians to laborers and exhibited "widely diverse educational levels" (Hughes, 1991). The workforce was generally young, particularly for those designated as hazardous waste workers (Gochfeld, Campbell, & Landsbergis, 1990; Hughes, 1991).

THE PROBLEM TAKES CENTER STAGE

With the passage of RCRA in 1976, the country began to address the problems of industrial hazardous waste generation. The EPA, for instance, was told to develop a hazardous waste program. But several RCRA problems nagged at Congress. First, the EPA was mandated to regulate the proper disposal of hazardous materials, but the agency missed an important April 1978 deadline and predicted a two-year delay. Second, RCRA did not address inactive or abandoned hazardous waste sites.

The links between hazardous chemical exposures and health problems were becoming obvious to all. In 1977, for example, the media reported on sewer workers in Lowell, Massachusetts, who were overcome by toluene fumes that had leaked from some 15,000 corroded drums stored at the site of a waste disposal company named Silresim Chemical Corp.

In 1978, a group of families in Niagara Falls, in western New York, learned that their neighborhood had formerly been a toxic waste dump for Hooker Chemical Co., which had buried 21,000 tons of nearly 400 chemicals in what were now their yards. Parents worried about their children's illnesses; they could not sell their homes, whose market value eroded steadily. Nor did they know much about the chemicals, except that many of them were dangerous. Media reports produced a national sensation and the alarms raised caused families elsewhere to question the histories of their own properties. Meanwhile, the EPA announced that "as many as 30,000 to 50,000 [hazardous waste dump sites] existed, of which between 1,200–2,000 present a serious risk to public health" (U.S. Code. 96th Congress, 1980, p. 6120). Across the country, U.S. Rep. Robert Eckhardt (D-TX) warned that "approximately ninety billion pounds of toxic wastes are generated each year." At hearings in 1979, Eckhardt probed, "[H]ow many other past dump sites are time bombs of hazardous materials ticking toward catastrophic health and property damage?" (U.S. Congress. House of Representatives, 1979, p. 2) Answering his own question, Eckhardt cited EPA data: 90% of hazardous waste disposal threatened public health and the environment.

In 1979, the Valley of the Drums was discovered near Louisville, Kentucky, where 17,000 containers of unidentified hazardous wastes were leaking into a branch of the Ohio River. That year, a consulting group, Fred C. Hart Associates, told the EPA that 1,200 to 34,000 hazardous waste sites across the United States might present serious hazards to public health and the environment (U.S. EPA, 1979). The very uncertainty of the numbers made the problem all the more frightening.

Unions Weigh In

Many labor and government figures confronted the realization that, as International Union of Operating Engineers (IUOE) President J. C. Turner said, the hazards were part of the workplace. But it was not a brand new concept for union leaders. The AFL-CIO's attention was focusing worriedly on the emerging hazardous waste management industry (Seminario, 1997). At the same time, community activists were organizing around their fears of adverse health effects related to the Love Canal hazardous waste site near their neighborhood. Their efforts alerted the nation to the threat of hazardous waste "ticking time bombs" around the country. The United States was compelled to acknowledge its hazardous waste crisis.

Testimony from workers and unions was presented at 1979 Congressional hearings on hazardous waste disposal (U.S. Congress. House of Representatives, 1979).[3] The United Steel Workers of America (USWA) and the Oil, Chemical, and Atomic Workers Union (OCAW) each sent officials of locals in Niagara, New York, who represented workers at three facilities—National Lead (NL) Industries, Greif Brothers, and Niagara Steel Finishing Co.—near the Hyde Park landfill there. The landfill was contaminated with many of the same chemicals that tainted Love Canal. Greif Bros., for example, manufactured 50-gallon steel drums, 90% of which were sold to Hooker Chemicals, whose wastes were dumped at Love Canal. The facilities' workers were concerned about health hazards from exposures to hazardous wastes from such dump sites. The exposures came from pollution overflows from man-made waste collection lagoons into streams and creeks as well as air pollution from fumes that emanated from the sites.

International representatives of both OCAW and USWA had met in December 1978 to discuss the health problems of workers at Niagara Steel Finishing. Local union members from all three facilities attended. OCAW sent occupational physician Christine Oliver to investigate the health problems.[4] The locals surveyed their members for detailed information.[5]

Occupational health and safety issues related to the hazardous waste sites were described in the survey. Also disclosed were the waste management practices employed and their impact on health and safety. At the hearings, Carl Sabey, president of USWA Local 12230, described the practices used at a Hooker landfill "just over the fence from N.L. Industries." He saw Hooker dump drums into the pit and only partially cover them with dirt. The drums later exploded. Shortly after the drums' burial, fumes wafted through NL Industries. When workers complained, NL managers called Hooker, which then threw more dirt on the drums. NL workers had respiratory illnesses, cancers, and heart trouble. Sabey began to hear of diagnoses of cancer in the 1970s.

Labor was primed to take action when complaints that clean-up workers at Love Canal were not properly protected reached the AFL-CIO early in 1979 (Seminario, 1997). In November, George Taylor of the AFL-CIO wrote to OSHA, the EPA, and NIOSH. He asked OSHA for regulations and enforcement. Taylor wanted the EPA to devise a system to identify operations where cleanup was planned or underway and notify OSHA and NIOSH; he also wanted the EPA to develop a hazard alert system and ascertain that federal site clean-up contract awards would be based on the "demonstration that proper and adequate protective measures" would be followed. He asked NIOSH to conduct on-site health hazard investigations of major clean-up operations, to determine the type and extent of exposures and the adequacy of protections (U.S. Congress. House of Representatives, 1985b, pp. 9-11). In 1980, AFL-CIO staff met with the agencies. They sought action by Congress in both the Superfund law and amendments to RCRA.

In another area at the same time, the International Association of Fire Fighters (IAFF), an AFL-CIO affiliate, worried about firefighters' exposures to hazardous wastes at fires, chemical transport vehicle accidents (truck or rail), and other hazardous materials (HAZMAT) emergencies. The union asked NIOSH to investigate incidents to determine whether waste exposures threatened firefighters. The IAFF wanted a study of the "current physiological and psychological effects in firefighters who were present at a fire in Alliance, Ohio, at the Universal Cooperatives, Inc. pesticide warehouse in July 1974" (U.S. DHHS-CDC-NIOSH). After looking into it, NIOSH concluded that exposures to the chemical by-products released from burning pesticides accounted for an excess of adverse health effects in exposed firefighters. It was the beginning of IAFF's effort to secure legal protections and training for firefighters in such work situations.

The problems in Niagara suggested that hazardous waste sites could be an environmental issue around which labor and citizens who had environmental concerns could build coalitions. In February 1979, the three locals, residents, politicians, and members of the Love Canal Homeowners Association formed the Bloody Run Area Association, named for a creek that ran through the industrial facilities. During Congressional hearings, the union officials spoke as concerned environmentalists. Dennis Virtuoso, president of USWA Local 12256, said, "There have been no criminal charges yet to any Hooker official. I feel like this is a crime. They are polluting our air. They are ruining our environment. They are killing our people. If that is not a crime, I do not know what is" (U.S. Congress. House of Representatives, 1979, p. 35). Carl Sabey, President of USWA Local 12230, urged that if hazardous waste sites do pose public health threats, "laws [should] be passed to stop this nightmare. You must do something to make this great country of ours a safe place for our grandchildren and our great grandchildren" (U.S. Congress. House of Representatives, 1979, p. 50). U.S. Rep. Al Gore (D-TN) asked Virtuoso, "How do you balance the age-old conflict or the recent conflict between jobs and cleaning up the environment?" Virtuoso replied, "No job is worth your life" (U.S. Congress. House of Representatives, 1979, p. 51).

"It was clear," AFL-CIO health and safety staff told Congress in 1985, "that hazardous waste clean-up would be a growing industry, with thousands of workers exposed to toxic chemicals" (U.S. Congress. House of Representatives, 1985a, p. 3).[6] This was perhaps the first opportunity for the AFL-CIO to address the health and safety impacts of a new, emerging industry. They sought federal worker protections to "get ahead of it. . . . Unlike the EPA, which did not foresee a need for labor in these operations, the ALF-CIO correctly foresaw that this would be labor intensive work that was inherently dangerous" (Seminario, 1997).

A TRAINING PROGRAM FOR WORKERS

By the mid-1970s, a new U.S. health and safety movement was emerging. The existence of OSHA, a federal regulatory structure with enforcement capability, however limited, supported the expansion of the pool of union activists and health and safety professionals. Most of the expansion was among professionals who worked either for large businesses or for the government. Steadily, however, health and safety activists and union-based and other concerned public health professionals saw health and safety training as a mechanism to enlarge their movement and give it a more balanced impact. A report prepared by a university labor education program for the Department of Labor in 1977 outlined the reasons for the generally inadequate health and safety training and the perceived need for federal support. The report cited the following:

- Inadequate government or private funding for health and safety education;
- A lack of programs providing health and safety training directly to workers and their representatives;
- Existing occupational health educators having insufficient experience of, or insensitivity to, effective training and educational methods for health and safety

training, particularly for workers, resulting in ineffective materials development and delivery;

- An inadequate data base on the nature and severity of occupational hazards, limiting the information available to workers;
- Substantial and increasing threats from employers that the regulation of job health and safety risks would cause catastrophic economic consequences and increased unemployment (job blackmail);
- Concerted campaigning by employers and employer associations denying the existence of occupational diseases and their importance in the realm of public health. (Freedman, 1978, pp. 2-3)

OSHA, under Section 21(c) of the OSH Act, had been funding limited worker health and safety training since 1972.[7] OSHA significantly expanded this effort during the Carter administration (1977-1980) when Dr. Eula Bingham, Assistant Secretary of Labor, was its director. Bingham created a training program that was administered to provide competitive access to nonprofit organizations. It was named New Directions and began in 1978. It provided funding to nonprofit organizations to develop and deliver a wide array of health and safety training and education. Applicants could be labor or employer organizations, institutions of higher education, or other nonprofit organizations that "could provide training and related service for employers or workers with unique needs" (U.S. DOL, 1978). The original target populations were high-hazard industries and small employers. Other populations were targeted later; these included "organizations serving minorities, women, federal government workers in high-hazard occupations, and organizations assisting workers and employers in establishing joint labor-management safety and health committees" (Brown, 1981, p. 4).

New Directions was organized by Basil J. Whiting, who was brought to OSHA by Bingham. Whiting came from the Ford Foundation, where he had established a grant program for the support of occupational safety and health. The foundation supported such efforts as Nicholas Ashford's book, *Crisis in the Workplace* (1976), and projects conducted by the University of California at Berkeley's Labor Occupational Health Program (Whiting, 1989, p. 87).

In assessing the need for an OSHA grant-funded health and safety education program, the existing resources of labor, management, and educational institutions were reviewed. One motivating finding was that only six industrial hygienists were employed on the staffs of U.S. unions.[8] To Bingham and Whiting, this fact suggested "the degree of competence and expertise at that time in the labor movement in this field" (Whiting, 1989, p. 88). Larger companies had programs that "varied in orientation and commitment" and small businesses generally lacked adequate information. Trade associations also lacked competence in the area. Forty-two poorly funded labor education programs existed then, and technical institutes and community colleges "lacked competence in occupational safety and health" (Whiting, 1989, p. 89).

In view of this "imbalanced and incompetent institutional context," they decided to establish a grant program to fund health and safety education (Whiting, 1989,

p. 89). Here, then, was a federal government agency, staffed by occupational health professionals, developing a program to extend competence in all areas of the field of occupational safety and health. Within the health and safety movement, anecdotal explanations have claimed that Bingham viewed such training as a way to make workers the eyes and ears of OSHA. Whiting and Bingham also perceived a strong need to increase the competence of both academic labor education programs and management programs in the areas of occupational safety and health. Another important New Directions goal was to build a committed constituency for both OSHA and, more broadly, occupational safety and health.

New Directions was designed to support planning grants and developmental grants. Planning grants were 1-year awards for programs demonstrating the potential to meet certain objectives. The developmental grants were given for up to 5 years to organizations requiring support so that they could become "effective, self-supporting centers of competence" (Brown, 1981, p. 2). Institutional competency included the concept of developing financial self-sufficiency. It was a way of addressing the Office of Management and Budget's (OMB's) concerns about extensive federal support through long-term contracts (Powers, 1997). The notion of financial self-sufficiency was also incorporated to prevent awardees from becoming dependent on OSHA funding, which was as vulnerable as the agency. The National Cancer Institute (NCI) collaborated with OSHA and supplied funds for programs that addressed occupational cancer hazards. NIOSH contributed some funding in 1980, and the Federal Emergency Management Agency (FEMA) provided some funds for the IAFF (Powers, 1997). The total amount of funds awarded between 1979 and 1984 was $56.8 million: $42.8 million from OSHA and $14 million from NCI (Whiting, 1989, p. 92). At its peak in 1982, New Directions gave out $18.7 million.

New Directions was innovative in supporting occupational health and safety education. It was a mechanism for funding organizations to develop and deliver training, and it also supported increased advocacy for occupational health and safety. It incorporated some key components that brought professional credibility to occupational health and safety education and encouraged stronger integration of scientific and professional approaches with labor approaches to health and safety.

Key aspects of the program, as described by Tobey and Revitte and others, included the following:

- OSHA provided strong administrative support and made efforts to develop a sense of collectiveness among grantees, including the organizing of annual meetings at which they addressed program business and shared the lessons learned, and distributed a newsletter that informed grantees and others of the efforts and educational materials, curricula, and so forth, of grantees.[9]
- OSHA facilitated the peer review of both the applications and the programs that were funded.[10]
- New Directions' awardees stimulated peer training: that is, within a particular population—workers, unions, supervisors, employers—members of that group would provide the training, or be involved in the training program, that reached others in the organization.

- New Directions helped develop institutional competency, building support and capacity for occupational safety and health programs within the organizations receiving awards.
- New Directions enhanced the evaluation of worker health and safety education and training; emphasis was placed on supporting the effectiveness of the training and the evaluation of training outcomes.[11]
- New Directions supported innovative educational methods and materials, including audio-visual presentations (e.g., films), newsletters, fact sheets, hands-on training and walk-arounds, participatory training methods, problem-solving exercises, small-group exercises, and nonlecture formats.
- New Directions supported advanced training for workers. The curriculum addressed technical issues such as hazard recognition, health effects, control technologies, understanding regulatory standards, and so forth.
- Emphasis was placed on instructor competence. One aspect of this was to provide support for instructors in understanding both the technical aspects of health and safety and appropriate training methodology for adult workers.
- Emphasis was placed on addressing workers' and unions' rights. New Directions encouraged and supported education and training that addressed these issues—although the manner of inclusion was not mandated, since employer organizations and labor-based programs had differing approaches to this matter.
- The program supported the development of materials and curriculum that addressed labor-management relations. (Tobey & Revitte, 1981, pp. 49-51)

New Directions had a powerful impact on the health and safety and labor movements. OSHA documented the training of 570,000 individuals. By 1981, the national unions had nearly 100 full-time health and safety staff, and 19 university-based health and safety programs for workers existed, supporting 125 health and safety professionals (Deutsch, 1981, p. 4). New Directions fostered the development of the current leaders of the health and safety movement, many of whom participated in its programs (Powers, 1997). It also nurtured the coalitions on occupational safety and health (COSH) movement[12] by expanding the available network of labor-friendly experts and building the technical competence of COSH staff and volunteers.

SUPERFUND BECOMES LAW IN CERCLA, 1980

Momentum was building for a law that would bring the federal government's authority to bear on the "polluter pays principle": that those who created a hazardous waste problem should pay to clean it up. Going into the 1980 presidential elections, however, success seemed unlikely. Disagreements over the extent of liability, funding mechanisms, and the identification of which industrial sectors would bear the brunt of the costs stalled progress. Then, Republican Ronald Reagan won the presidency, beating Democratic incumbent Jimmy Carter. Republicans also won 12 Senate seats, giving them a majority (55–53) for the first time since 1955. The Superfund bill, the Comprehensive Environmental Response, Compensation, and Liability Act (CERCLA), was passed "in secrecy and confusion in the waning moments of the lame-duck, Democratic-controlled 96th Congress" (Greenberg, 1993, p. 14), but not without conflict.

The legislative history of the bill gives background and discloses the perceived inadequacies of the earlier RCRA law. House Report No. 96-1016, Part I, pointed out that RCRA "provided a prospective cradle-to-grave regulatory regime governing the movement of hazardous waste in our society" (U.S. Code. 96th Congress, 1980, p. 6120). It discussed "the tragic consequences of improperly, negligently, and recklessly [employing] hazardous waste disposal practices known as the 'inactive hazardous waste site problem.'" The report called for action, noting that there were too few waste disposal sites, a problem that would only worsen with increased hazardous waste generation (U.S. Code. 96th Congress, 1980, p. 6120). Carter's EPA had estimated that "77.1 billion pounds of hazardous waste are produced each year but only ten percent are disposed of in an environmentally sound manner" (U.S. Code. 96th Congress, 1980, p. 6124). Eighteen months after its Congressionally set deadline, the EPA had failed to promulgate RCRA-mandated regulations for managing hazardous wastes. Further, what had been proposed was inadequate, since comprehensive testing was not required and small-quantity generators were exempted. Finally, RCRA insufficiently addressed the management of past waste sites, active and inactive.

The Senate sent a bill to the House on November 24, 1980. The bill was moved by the Senate's Environmental and Public Works Committee, chaired by Jennings Randolph (D-WV) and with Robert T. Stafford (R-VT) as the ranking minority member. The panel had assumed that the passage of the Superfund bill was a dead issue for that Congress, according to Curtis Moore, former Republican counsel to the committee. When the Republicans took the Senate, Stafford, a moderate and a strong environmentalist, was the "sort of chairman-designate" (Moore, 1998). Stafford returned from a reception with new Republican senators-elect and told Moore, "I just had cocktails with a U.S. senator-elect who believes that adultery should be a capital crime. We'd better get what we can on Superfund, now" (Moore, 1998). The bill that went to the House required members to accept it as the Senate passed it; there would be no conference committee. It was the last major piece of environmental legislation to pass Congress for several years.

Unsurprisingly, the CERCLA bill met serious opposition, especially from House Republicans. Some opposed taxing industry for cleaning up and argued for leaving the problem of hazardous waste management to the ingenuity of the private sector—firms could burn it in incinerators and use it for fuel. Others argued that the private sector required government support for technological development and that the EPA would serve industry better by providing such services rather than carrying out enforcement. The bill disturbed many people particularly because it maintained strict, joint, and several liability against responsible parties and applied liability retroactively (Klees, 1996).

> We do not quarrel with the proposition that a responsible party should have to pay. The problem is that this legislation goes much further. It is intended to give access to the "deep pockets" of whatever company has the money to pay [,]

> regardless of the degree of culpability. This concept may be expedient, but it certainly flies in the face of fundamental fairness and equity. . . . This bill imposes both a fee and strict liability on private parties without relieving them of any legal liability. (U.S. Code. 96th Congress, 1980, p. 6144)[13]

The Republican representatives who made this statement objected to the lack of due process against an EPA clean-up order and to the fee structure for its inflationary impact. Some of the sharpest criticism found in the legislative history is written by Rep. David Stockman (R-MI), who later became the OMB director under Reagan. Through that office, in conjunction with Reagan's EPA appointees, Stockman thwarted the intent of Congress in CERCLA.

Representatives Stockman and Tom Loeffler (R-TX) asserted that the provisions of H.R. 7020, a predecessor to the final bill, were

> a replay of the patented formula for environmental legislation developed over the past decade. . . . an implicit cost of billions in national economic resources for marginal or non-existent social benefits. Having established this pattern of regulatory overkill in the 1970s, the nation is now paying the price in the form of worsening economic conditions, stagflation, collapsing productivity and international competitiveness, declining living standards, and rising welfare costs. The bill as reported inadvertently embodies an anti-industrial, zero-discharge mentality. . . . the bill is motivated by a sweeping environmental ideology that views the by-products of industrial activity as inherently malign—a blight encapsulated in thousands of ticking time bombs capable of releasing a torrent of poisons, toxins, carcinogens, fires, and explosions on an unwary public at any moment. (U.S. Code. 96th Congress, 1980, p. 6145)

These representatives said that the continuing discovery of hazardous waste sites posing public health threats "does not establish a systematic, generalized, and perilous pattern. . . . the former situations are aberrant rather than pandemic" (U.S. Code. 96th Congress, 1980, p. 6146). Their dissent claimed that there were in existence adequate legal and regulatory structures supporting appropriate waste management practices throughout industry. Despite these criticisms, CERCLA was passed by Congress and was signed into law by President Carter on December 11, 1980, 3 weeks before the end of his presidency.[14]

Three sections of CERCLA were secured by the AFL-CIO: sections 301(f), 104(f), and 104(g). NIOSH also helped to win the first two of these sections. Section 301(f) mandated that, within 2 years of the law's enactment, the EPA, the Department of Transportation (DOT), OSHA, and NIOSH must study and modify "the National Contingency Plan (NCP) to provide for the protection of the health and safety of employees involved in response actions" ("Environmental Responses Act, Comprehensive Environmental Response, Compensation and Liability Act," 1980).[15]

The AFL-CIO's Health and Safety Department proposed and supported 301(f) and 104(f). At the time, though, not enough was understood about the work hazards to support a call for a single standard or program. In 1980, Margaret Seminario of the AFL-CIO talked with OSHA about standards for hazardous waste workers. The labor request was intended to generate information to support either the development of one or more standards or a protective program based on existing standards. The strategy seemed adequate, since nobody could foresee the pending weakening of regulatory support for occupational safety and health or the expansion of the hazardous waste site remediation program that came under Reagan.

NIOSH, led by Dr. Anthony Robbins, began to investigate the hazards for workers at hazardous waste operations and in emergency response (ER) actions. Dr. James Melius was brought aboard to direct its Health Hazard Evaluation (HHE) program, which became the effort's main arm. Responding to requests from the firefighters' union, the HHE program established two new policy directions: attention to public employee requests and investigation of hazardous waste sites and responses at them. NIOSH was the only agency to act before the mandate from 301(f) (Melius, 1998).

RCRA Amendments, 1980

Information was required about the nature of the hazards and risks posed to workers, in order to formulate policy initiatives. A month before the passage of CERCLA, Congress amended RCRA when it approved the Solid Waste Disposal Act Amendments. The AFL-CIO won worker protection language in that law as well. Section 7001(f) called for the EPA to supply information to OSHA and NIOSH. It demanded the identification of all hazardous waste operations sites where cleanup was planned or underway; the identification of all exposures at hazardous waste operations, the nature and extent of exposures, and the methods of worker protection in place; all incidents of worker injury or harm at hazardous waste operations; and notifications or reports filed in compliance with RCRA provisions. But the mandated systematic approach to gathering the information was never implemented.

A SHIFTING POLITICAL TERRAIN

Starting with Nixon's administration, the labor and environmental movements had had many victories, but their successes evoked a strong response from corporate America, whose leaders began to organize against what they saw as losses. In 1972, they formed the Business Roundtable, "the first new inter-industry organization since the 1940s" (Noble, 1986, p. 101). In the mid-1970s, small businesses were represented by two strong national organizations—the National Federation of Independent Businesses and the Chamber of Commerce. Organizations such as the National Legal Center for the Public Interest (created by conservative industrialists) took the "ideological offensive" in opposing movements for social justice. They supported "free enterprise" and "limited government." "Employers," Noble observed, "attempted to identify their particular interests in lower costs and higher profits with a general societal interest in jobs, economic growth, and capital investment. Economic growth, business suggested, was not only as important as protection but was the precondition for it" (Noble, 1986, p. 101).[16]

Ronald Reagan's election in 1980 represented in part a triumph of the corporate and conservative backlash against governmental regulation of business. Moreover, Reagan's terms in office (1981–1989) were concurrent with significant changes in U.S. industry and the national economy. Inflation was soaring; U.S. industries were losing market share to foreign competitors. Trade unions had steadily lost membership and represented a smaller percentage of the workforce due to corporate restructuring. The Reagan years had a profound, negative impact on worker health and safety.

Targeting the Agencies

Reagan's 1980 campaign pledge of widespread "regulatory reform" especially targeted environmental and occupational health protections.[17] The EPA and OSHA under Reagan applied consistent strategies: deregulation; oversight and interference from the OMB; withdrawal of standards and policies established under the Carter administration; drastically reduced budgets, which, in turn, forced reductions in inspections and enforcement; weakening of the scope of enforcement; and the appointment of pro-industry administrators, division directors, and managers. By Reagan's second term, the strategies included the continual shifting of agency heads, which blocked consistency and internal competence and interfered with the availability of the agencies to their constituencies.

At the EPA, Anne Gorsuch was named administrator and the White House appointed Rita Lavelle to direct the Superfund. Gorsuch had a reputation in Colorado as a legislator who espoused "laissez faire economic policies" (Greenberg, 1993, p. 22). Lavelle had formerly worked for AeroJet General, Inc., a major party responsible for the hazardous waste site at the Stringfellow Acid Pits in Riverside, California. In a memo to the EPA's general counsel, Lavelle said that the administration saw the "business community" as its main constituency (Greenberg, 1993, p. 23). Both Gorsuch and Lavelle were forced out of service in 1983 as a scandal dubbed "Sewergate" threatened to derail the Reaganites' deregulatory agenda. The Reagan administration not only mismanaged the Superfund program but also mismanaged its response to the Democratic Congress's investigations of allegations of "political manipulation of clean-up timetables, financial mismanagement, use of government resources for personal use—[which] were added to old allegations of nonimplementation, conflict of interest, and sweetheart deals" (Szasz, 1994, p. 127).[18]

NIOSH was also weakened. It was part of the Centers for Disease Control (CDC), and Reagan moved much of the institute from Cincinnati to CDC's offices in Atlanta to better assure compliance with his administration. The leadership had to "bend" to CDC, which enforced administration policy (Randall, 1998; Samuels, 1998; Seminario, 1997). The changes restricted NIOSH both fiscally and politically. As for OSHA, its new director came into office sharing the administration's goal of effectively dismantling the agency. He was Thorne Auchter, a construction contractor whose firm had been cited by OSHA for "48 different safety violations, including six serious ones" (R. Gottlieb, 1993, p. 293). Labor's and the health and safety movement's cherished New Directions program was now under his jurisdiction.

Crippling of the New Directions Program

At Auchter's Congressional confirmation hearings and in statements as director, Auchter suggested that New Directions' work had not been reviewed against appropriate criteria and that he intended to carefully examine the problem (Business

Publishers Inc., 1981). Auchter significantly reduced the funding available to unions, COSH groups (which were grassroots labor-based coalitions for occupational safety and health), and the university labor education programs, as well as the trade associations. By financial year (FY) 1982, funds were cut by nearly two-thirds; hardest hit were "various non-profit organizations," especially the COSH groups. Whiting has suggested that they in particular "were simply not acceptable, ideologically, to this administration" (Whiting, 1989, p. 94). Auchter told the Philadelphia COSH, PhilaPOSH, that because of its activism, future New Directions funding was in jeopardy. "Shortly thereafter, PhilaPOSH's grant was cut from $119,488 to $10,000" (Lawrence & Mager, 1982). University labor-education funding was cut by 75% and grants to unions were reduced by 54% (Lawrence & Mager, 1982). By January 1982, labor-oriented grantees were forced to eliminate 23.5 positions, a 41% reduction. Delivery of training was curtailed (Lawrence & Mager, 1982).

Auchter moved much of the New Directions funding to the state government OSHA consultation programs that had been established in compliance with the OSH Act. He also instituted regulations requiring awardees to submit all of their educational materials for OSHA review, whether they had been developed through OSHA funds or otherwise. Formerly, New Directions awardees submitted any materials developed through OSHA money for a review for technical accuracy. The new rules focused on technical accuracy and objectivity, which, as reported by *Labor Notes,* was defined by OSHA as the intent to "stimulate cooperative effort on the part of employers and employees . . . and to encourage joint labor-management efforts to reduce injury and diseases" (Lawrence & Mager, 1982). The measures either blocked pro-labor programs from applying for funds or established a way for OSHA to turn down proposals from such organizations.

Noble has argued that "The labor movement lobbied for enforcement of the OSH Act but did not seek to mobilize workers in politics or at the workplace" (Noble, 1986, p. 14). The New Directions program, to some degree, contradicts this view. Here was a program largely initiated and shaped by health and safety professionals. It was used by some unions, academic programs, and COSH groups to mobilize workers to develop health and safety strategies. The effort was inadequate for success on its own and was drastically reduced in funding and scope by the hostile Reagan administration. By 1987, New Directions was barely functioning.[19]

NOT A COMPLETE HALT

To some extent, despite the Reagan administration's intentions, there was a degree of continuity as the federal agencies with a role in dealing with hazardous wastes followed the logic of their mandates. NIOSH's role in conducting health hazard evaluations (HHEs) is an example of this.

On Earth Day in April 1980, the Chemical Control dump in Elizabeth, New Jersey, exploded. As many as 45,000 55-gallon drums of chemical waste burned for most of the day (Freudenberg, 1984, p. 21). Local firefighters fought the blaze. Richard Duffy, director of health and safety for IAFF and a New Jersey native, hurried from Washington, DC, to Elizabeth to investigate. He saw firefighters bring hoses back from the site by rolling them and putting them in the backs of their trucks. In the decontamination area, they used a mechanical cleaner to wash down their contaminated hoses. The runoff "runs down the middle of the floor inside the fire house, runs out the street and runs down the street" (Duffy, 1997).[20] The firefighters who washed the hoses suffered chemical burns and later developed dermatitis. Because no one knew what chemicals were stored at Chemical Control and firefighters quickly developed adverse effects, Duffy requested a NIOSH investigation.

NIOSH began a health hazard evaluation, under Dr. Melius. A mobile laboratory-clinic was sent to Elizabeth, and pulmonary function and other tests were conducted on the exposed firefighters. These tests showed a "high prevalence of respiratory problems among the firefighters exposed at that fire" (U.S. DHHS-CDC-NIOSH, 1984). By 1984, NIOSH had conducted many more HHEs in situations where firefighters were exposed to hazardous chemical wastes.

NIOSH also assisted the few remediation contractors working at Superfund sites during this time. The primary companies were OH Materials, IT, and Ecology and Environment. Melius wrote the medical screening guidance for Superfund responses. Very few firms were engaged in hazardous waste site remediation work then, so there were no professionals developing safety protocols. The larger firms—BFI, Chemical Waste Management, and Rollins—were just starting their hazardous waste response businesses. They called Melius to figure out what they needed to do if they entered the field. Rollins may have been the only firm that even had an industrial hygienist at that time (Melius, 1998).

After CERCLA became law in December 1980, Carter's heads at NIOSH, OSHA, the EPA, and the DOT, represented by the U.S. Coast Guard (USCG), agreed to work under NIOSH to protect hazardous waste and ER workers. They outlined three tasks: (1) to develop a comprehensive manual of procedures to protect workers; (2) to establish mechanisms to give occupational safety and health information to workers and their supervisors; and (3) to find ways to transmit field experiences in occupational health and safety practices to federal agencies (U.S. Congress. House of Representatives, 1985b, pp. 165-167).[21]

NIOSH led in developing technical guidance.[22] The agency "visited twenty-three Superfund clean-up sites to evaluate the EPA safety plans" (U.S. Congress. House of Representatives, 1985a, p. 141).[23] NIOSH also gauged workers' exposures at several sites and researched ways to improve protections. The agency improved the ways to rapidly measure air concentrations of toxics, including the adaptation of direct reading instruments. NIOSH's laboratory in Morgantown, West Virginia, investigated the personal protective equipment (PPE) used by workers, upgraded selection methods, and studied means to better estimate heat stress when PPE was used.

The EPA was the second most active in the group. It developed protection protocols for EPA staff assessing and testing sites and established safety plans for employees conducting the few emergency cleanups that the EPA then had underway. NIOSH assisted in this. The EPA also amended the National Contingency Plan (NCP), to require compliance with all OSHA general industry and construction standards and other rules. It called for the development of a health and safety plan for each site and held employers responsible for the well-being of their employees. However, as late as March 1985, the amendments remained only "proposed" changes to the NCP (50 Federal Register, 1985). In addition, the EPA established a national training center in Edison, New Jersey (U.S. Congress. House of Representatives, 1985a, p. 121).[24] Still, the agency largely left the protection of site remediation workers to NIOSH. It did not publish its own health and safety manual for hazardous waste operations until December 1984 (U.S. Congress. House of Representatives, 1985a, p. 121).[25]

The agencies developed two publications. The first was a guidance manual, the *Worker Bulletin: Hazardous Waste Sites, and Substance Emergencies.* When NIOSH finally published it, though, it was "so general that it offers virtually none of the specific and technical information" (U.S. Congress. House of Representatives, 1985a, pp. 29-30)[26] that the AFL-CIO wanted to come out of the effort. The second publication was released in October 1985. Whatever its possible drawbacks, the *Occupational Safety and Health Guidance Manual for Hazardous Waste Site Activities* (U.S. DHHS-NIOSH-OSHA-USCG-EPA, 1985), commonly called the Four-Agency Manual, became the primary health and safety text for several years. Soon afterward, the EPA published an interim manual for chemical emergency preparedness. It gave meager guidance on the protection, training, and preparation of the ER workforce (U.S. EPA, 1985, pp. 4-20).[27]

Of the four agencies assigned to protect workers, OSHA was "the least responsive." It had made "no attempt since 1980 to draft regulations" and had not established "any real enforcement program to inspect hazardous waste sites" (U.S. Congress. House of Representatives, 1985b, p. 5).[28] OSHA took a year to develop a field directive (issued at the end of 1983) for enforcement activities at hazardous waste sites. The agency saw primary responsibility for administration of the Superfund law as resting with the EPA and USCG. The field directive did not target sites for inspections, although OSHA did offer technical assistance and enforcement on referral by the EPA and responded to accidents and complaints.

If Superfund contractors did not follow EPA procedures, John Miles, OSHA director of field operations, indicated that OSHA could cite them under the General Duty Clause of the OSH Act. U.S. Rep. Joseph Gaydos (D-PA) retorted, "General duty clause. We haven't had a general duty clause fine stand up as long as I can remember" (U.S. Congress. House of Representatives, 1985b, p. 22).[29]

LEGISLATIVE STRUGGLES IN THE MID-1980s

Passing environmental and occupational health and safety legislation during the first Reagan term was extremely difficult. Under Republican control, the Senate was far more conservative than its predecessor. Its Environment Committee was headed by Stafford, who took the chairmanship to protect the legislative gains of the 1970s and guide whatever legislation was possible. Although the House remained under Democratic control, "Philosophically, the House, for at least a couple of years, became Republican too. . . . They shift[ed] because of Reagan. They also shift[ed] because they were responding to business saying 'We've got to restructure everything. . . . We've got a global economic crisis on our hands and we're not competing'" (Moore, 1998). No attempt was made to amend the Clean Air Act to protect it.

Concern over the health impacts of hazardous wastes increased, however, and neither politicians nor industries could ignore it. New waste sites were discovered, some created by past practices, but many by industry's ongoing disposal methods. W. M. Bulkeley, in *The Wall Street Journal,* said that "a four-million-ton-a-year shortage of disposal sites could develop by the end of the decade" (Bulkeley, 1980, p. 48).

The High-Risk Worker Notification Bill

During the mid-1980s, the AFL-CIO worked to pass the High-Risk Occupational Disease Worker Notification and Prevention Bill, which it had sought for a decade.[30] The effort began as an outgrowth of the fight for asbestos victims' benefits, according to Sheldon Samuels, then director of the Industrial Union Department (IUD) of the AFL-CIO. NIOSH had taken steps toward notification during the Nixon years when the director at the time, John Finklea, told a Senate hearing that the government had an obligation to inform exposed workers who were at risk for disease (Mallino, 1997). Between 1977 and 1979, NIOSH even started two pilot projects that gave workers such information and evaluated the impact of doing so (U.S. Congress. Senate, 1986, pp. 46-55).

By 1986, it appeared that the High-Risk Occupational Disease Worker Notification and Prevention Act (S. 2050) would pass (U.S. Congress. Senate, 1986, pp. 46-55). Written to include former and current employees, the bill required that workers be notified of prior exposures that might threaten their health and be informed that they might wish to receive a physical exam and establish an exam regimen. The key AFL-CIO staff members working to win its approval were Samuels and David Mallino, deputy director for legislation. Mallino had secured the support of the Chemical Manufacturers Association (CMA), which was unprecedented. The bill encountered intense opposition from the Chamber of Commerce, the National Association of Manufacturers, the National Federation of Independent Businesses, the steel industry, and others (Connor, 1989; Mallino, 1997; Samuels, 1998). The Reagan administration opposed it. Employers who were against it feared that notification would promote litigation and that courts could find employers liable for workers' occupational illnesses (Connor, 1989; Ringen, 1989, pp. 136-138).

NIOSH submitted written testimony by its director, J. Donald Millar, which was presented by Melius. NIOSH shared the sponsors' concerns, Millar said, but "we do not support S. 2050. We do not believe that additional notification is needed for worker notification efforts to proceed" (U.S. Congress. Senate, 1986, p. 47). His testimony described NIOSH's efforts and aspects of the bill that he believed were not feasible. A primary complaint was about cost; Melius said that locating and notifying only the workers who had been exposed to lead would cost as much as $20 million.

While NIOSH's opposition was not decisive, the bill failed to secure the vote of even one third of the Senate. Nonetheless, for at least Samuels and Mallino, who were also working to secure worker protection and training language in SARA, Millar's role in its defeat only exacerbated their frustrations with NIOSH. There were significant consequences for the WETP.

RCRA AMENDMENTS, 1984—A RESPONSE TO A STEADILY WORSENING HAZARDOUS WASTE CRISIS

RCRA was passed in 1976 and amended several times, for example, in 1980, when the AFL-CIO secured language covering worker health and safety. RCRA was amended again in the Hazardous and Solid Waste Amendments of 1984 (HSWA) (PL 98-616). Reagan opposed HSWA, but it passed, even as other environmental laws stalled.[31] Section 1002 of the original RCRA lists Congress's findings on solid waste (Resource Conservation and Recovery Act, 1976). HSWA amended these to state that improper hazardous waste management would result in "substantial risks to human health and the environment." Actions to correct improper hazardous waste management were "likely to be expensive, complex, and time consuming," and land disposal, which was inappropriate for many hazardous wastes, "should be the least favored method for managing hazardous wastes" (Hazardous and Solid Waste Amendments, 1984). HSWA also established a new national policy stating that, wherever feasible, the generation of hazardous waste was to be reduced or eliminated as expeditiously as possible. Waste that was nevertheless generated should be treated, stored, or disposed of so as to minimize the present and future threat to human health and the environment (Hazardous and Solid Waste Amendments, 1984, Sect. 1003(b)).

Environmentalists had organized in 1984 to help pass the Hazardous and Solid Waste Amendments (HSWA), which included nearly 80 statutory deadlines. "Hammer provisions" were built into 8 of them, directing actions in case the EPA failed to meet the schedule.[32] The legislation also banned the land disposal of "non-containerized" liquid wastes (Truax, 1989), which clearly responded to the Sewergate scandal that grew out of Ann Gorsuch's initial decision to permit sanitary landfills to accept liquid waste.

HSWA moved beyond RCRA's limitations toward a new set of national policies aimed at pollution prevention rather than management and control. HSWA strengthened the legal requirements for controlling hazardous waste disposal and preventing hazardous waste generation. Still, the nation faced a growing burden of abandoned hazardous waste sites. CERCLA best captured the national response to the crisis, but this law was due to expire in 1985. The next effort to pass environmental legislation was the reauthorization of Superfund, or, as some were calling it, Son of Superfund.

An April 1984 study commissioned by the EPA and conducted by Westat, Inc., reported on the hazardous waste generators and TSDFs that were regulated under RCRA during 1982 and 1983. The Westat survey found that 90% of generated wastes were disposed of on-site, but that the 10% taken off-site represented over 20 million metric tons. Westat also found another worrisome fact: at least one-third of wastes taken off-site were unaccounted for (Goldman, 1986, p. 46). In 1984, in an investigation commissioned by the EPA, Fred C. Hart Associates studied 927 industrial sites suspected of hazardous waste mismanagement. "The Hart report identified documented or suspected contamination . . . at . . . ninety percent of the [generator and disposal facility] sites evaluated" (Goldman, 1986, p. 48). The U.S. Office of Technology Assessment (OTA) found that "some of the facilities that received Superfund wastes were leaking" (Goldman, 1986, p. 50). In 1984, Lee Thomas, then the EPA assistant administrator in charge of the hazardous waste program, issued several memos revealing that nearly 25% of "the RCRA facilities that had received Superfund wastes were deficient" (Goldman, 1986, p. 52).

Girding Up for Superfund Renewal

By 1985, the Republicans were vulnerable to the public's discontent over environmental issues. The administration was viewed as willing to sacrifice the environment to support business interests. Although Reagan won reelection in 1984, the Democrats planned to fight hard to retake the Senate in the 1986 elections. Superfund reauthorization was an important campaign issue. Democrats and Republicans alike wanted to be able to argue that they had helped to pass a strong Superfund bill.

COMMUNITY PROTECTION ISSUES AND CITIZEN SUITS—EVENTS OVERTAKE WASHINGTON

In December 1984, a Union Carbide facility in Bhopal, India, released methyl isocyanate in the middle of the night, killing more than 2,500 people and injuring more than 200,000. Watching the news that day, Curtis Moore and Phil Cummings, the Republican and Democratic counsels, respectively, on the Senate Environment and Public Works Committee, realized that "on the strength of Bhopal, we could get some strengthening amendments in Superfund" (Moore, 1998). In both chambers, legislators were drafting measures to go beyond remediation—to build a legal and organizational framework and an information base that would support public action opposing the generation and incidental environmental release of hazardous materials.

On New Year's Eve 1984, 3,000 gallons of ethylene oxide escaped from a Union Carbide rail tank car in Little Rock, Arkansas. Nine months later, U.S. Rep. Henry Waxman (D-CA) held a House subcommittee hearing on health and the environment in Institute, West Virginia, which was home to a Union Carbide facility. Company representatives testified at the hearing. As they declared that "there could never be a methylene isocyanate release in the U.S. like Bhopal, the sirens went off" (Moore, 1998). Aldicarb oximine, a toxic chemical used to make pesticides, had been released, sending more than 150 people to seek medical attention (Wolf, 1996).

The incidents only added to the concerns raised by the IAFF over the protection of firefighters who responded to such incidents. They also gave rise to another set of hazardous waste sites that required remediation or "response" (as CERCLA and the EPA had termed it)—the sites created instantly by the unplanned incidental release of hazardous materials into the environment. Hazardous materials accidentally released qualify as hazardous wastes. The issue significantly affected the policies established to protect workers in hazardous waste operations because it extended the program to emergency responders. The impact on Superfund reauthorization immediately became clear.

On January 3, Senators Stafford and Frank R. Lautenberg (D-NJ) introduced the Superfund Improvement Act of 1985. Lautenberg was a proponent of environmental and health protections. He cited the "tragedy in Bhopal" and asked, "In the wake of the worst industrial accident in history, citizens and officials around the globe are asking, 'Could it happen to us?'" (U.S. Congress. Senate, 1990, vol. 2, p. 409). Congress, he said, had to include Superfund terms that would establish nationally the capability to adequately respond to emergency hazardous materials (HAZMAT) incidents. He gave the grounds for establishing a community right-to-know program when he said, "To respond to leaks and spills of chemicals (used in production), we need to know what chemicals they use or produce, and in what volume these chemicals are released on a routine basis" (U.S. Congress. Senate, 1990, vol. 2, p. 409).

The public fear and concern raised by the Bhopal and West Virginia events, along with others, moved Congress to enact community right-to-know legislation. "Who the hell was going to stand up and say you don't need a community right-to-know provision[33] after 20,000 people have been killed?" Moore asked. "There ain't no way on earth they're going to stand up in public and say that" (Moore, 1998).

Nearly 50 organizations mobilized urgently, coalescing to secure community rights to know (U.S. Congress. Senate, 1990, vol. 5, p. 4347). They capitalized on Congress's difficulties in its reauthorization bill. They built momentum on real-world events. Their efforts, with Congressional support, led to the passage of Title III of the Superfund law, the Emergency Planning and Community Right-to-Know Act (EPCRA).

The Environment, Labor, and Public Health Coalition

During these years, the AFL-CIO interacted with movements that addressed health issues, such as those dealing with environmental, civil rights, public health, and consumer protection matters. Beginning with the earliest moves to pass the OSH Act of 1970, a coalition of advocacy organizations at times operated as a lobbying force in the capital. In the early 1980s, the coalition assumed various forms. For the passage of the OSH Act, OCAW and USWA took the lead for labor. Another early effort was called the Urban Environmental Coalition, supported by the American Federation of State, County, and Municipal Employees (AFSCME). By the mid-1970s, the IUD of the AFL-CIO led the coalition, calling the effort the OSHA Environment Network or the Labor/Environment Coalition. This was founded to help pass the Toxic Substances Control Act in 1976.

Its success kept labor in the coalition to help pass environmental laws, including RCRA, CERCLA, amendments to the Clean Air Act, and other legislation (Elisburg, 1997; Mallino, 1997; Samuels, 1998; Seminario, 1997). Although it is not a focus of this book, in the 1980s the coalition committed extensive resources and time to the passing of the Emergency Planning and Community Right-to-Know Act, Title III of SARA. This law included, among other measures, the Toxics Release Inventory (TRI) provisions, which would provide the public with annual reports of toxic industrial releases. These have been used to identify workplace exposures and support calls for cleaner production processes. In addition to labor unions, coalition members working on this included the Sierra Club, the National Audubon Society, Citizen Action, and Environmental Action.

CONCLUSION

The emerging hazardous waste management sector had an expanding workforce engaged in inherently hazardous work involving hazardous waste materials—the hazard and the workplace were one and the same. Health and safety measures were needed to protect these workers, and the OSHA New Directions program, developed in the Carter administration, provided a worker training model. The national divide over the Viet Nam War, the emergence of the new left, and the Watergate scandal brought in the Carter administration, preserving liberal governance for just a little bit longer before Reagan's election secured the capacity to ensure a full shift to the neoliberal era. Eula Bingham's OSHA worked on a New Deal liberal model with a taste of the neoliberal budgets to come. New Directions was established to encourage the building of a national movement that could successfully organize and advocate for the protection of worker health and safety. This was the last liberal reform from OSHA, and it was smashed as quickly as possible by Reagan.

Less easy to dismantle, though, were the multiple environmental protection and control laws that imposed stern regulatory requirements on U.S. corporations. Environmental damage, an increasingly visible hazardous waste crisis, and exposed corruption in the federal executive branch fueled the growth in the environmental movement. Demands for a stronger Superfund law were strong. Labor would be able to piggyback on the rising tide for environmental protection to get a new worker health and safety program, but OSHA would no longer be its home.

ENDNOTES

1. For discussions of the transition from a biophysical economy to a chemical economy, see (Commoner, 1972; Epstein, Brown, & Pope, 1982; Gottlieb, ed., 1995; Jackson, Costanza, Overcash, & Rees, 1993).
2. See (Freudenberg, 1984) for a discussion of the environmental movement in the early 1980s. Also see (Barnett, 1994; Dowie, 1997; Gottlieb, 1993) for more in-depth discussions of these issues.
3. Testimony of Dennis Virtuoso, president, Local 12256, USWA, National Lead (NL) Industries and Greif Bros.; Clifton Van Epps, vice president, Local 8-778, OCAW, Niagara Steel Finishing Co.; and, Carl Sabey, president, Local 12230, USWA, NL Industries.
4. NIOSH had investigated these issues at the request of USWA. In 1978, NIOSH began its first investigations of the potential for health hazards posed by exposures from hazardous waste sites adjacent to manufacturing facilities (this was confirmed through an interview with Dr. James Melius, formerly director of health hazard evaluations for the agency). However, NIOSH had not gone into the facilities. Dennis Virtuoso testified that "the only help we have received is from OSHA. . . . They were testing the air at the plant site. What we want is NIOSH into our plants. We feel that they are much more equipped to handle the situation than OSHA is" (U.S. Congress. House of Representatives, 1979).
5. In testimony to Congress, Dennis Virtuoso, president of Local 12256, USWA, listed the results of the surveys at Greif Bros. and NL Industries. Health problems included cancers (primarily nasal and facial), respiratory illnesses, cardio-vascular diseases, skin ailments (rashes), reproductive problems (birth defects and miscarriages), headaches, and eye-nose-throat irritations. Virtuoso reported that "The percentages [of] these health

problems are much too high for the number of people we are talking about" (U.S. Congress. House of Representatives, 1979).

6. OSHA estimated that its HAZWOPER rule would cover nearly 2 million workers. Hughes noted that OSHA had made an underestimation because it excluded workers at generating or transport facilities. He further noted that NIEHS estimated that "an additional 110,000 workers are employed in RCRA-regulated hazardous waste generator operations and another 92,000 workers are involved in transporting hazardous wastes and hazardous materials" (Hughes, 1991 p. 115). He pointed out that steadily increasing rates of HAZMAT spills and releases involved a vast population of workers in HAZMAT ER. This population included not only public-sector ER personnel, such as firefighters, but also people in a range of job categories in most sectors of industry.
7. Per an unpublished report by Michael Brown, prior to the New Directions program less than 1% annually of the OSHA budget had been allocated for worker training (Brown, 1981).
8. In 1981, Steven Deutsch reported that "before 1978 there were fewer than 15 health and safety staff persons in unions, only one-half of whom had professional training" (Deutsch, 1981). He credited the New Directions program with much of the responsibility for the increase by 1989 to nearly 100 union staff members.
9. Bingham and others involved in the administration of the New Directions program believed that a sense of collectiveness was not successfully developed among the grantees.
10. Peer review activities were discontinued by Reagan appointee Thorne Auchter (Powers, 1997).
11. A utilization analysis of the New Directions program (Reesman & Jordan, 1980) includes comments obtained during interviews with New Directions awardees about evaluation issues. Awardees addressed many issues that they believed were barriers to the appropriate evaluation of worker education and training. Central were questions about how to evaluate the impact of training on the reduction of injury and illness rates. Overall, little literature about the effectiveness of worker health and safety training resulted from New Directions-funded programs. Later, when the WETP administrators reviewed the New Directions program, they concluded that OSHA had not succeeded in promoting strong training evaluation.
12. COSH groups are coalitions, committees, or councils for occupational safety and health formed by health and safety and labor activists and occupational health and other professionals. For further discussion of the COSH movement, see (Berman, 1981; Kazis & Grossman, 1991; Wooding, 1994).
13. The comments concern H.R. 7020, a House bill that was largely incorporated into the Senate bill. Since neither a conference committee nor a floor debate occurred, House members' comments from earlier procedures were included in the limited legislative history. The quotation is from a statement prepared by Reps. Broyhill, Devine, Collins, Loeffler, and Stockman.
14. A final aspect of the CERCLA story that bears on the subsequent effort to protect workers in SARA was the role of the Chemical Manufacturers Association (CMA). The petrochemical industry organization had negotiated with House legislators over the language of CERCLA's predecessor bills. An earlier House bill had CMA's support, but after Reagan's election, Bob Roland, then CMA president, announced that the association would not support any effort to pass Superfund. His stand cost CMA credibility with Congress, whose members had worked with CMA so long as it agreed to language that was acceptable to environmentalists and the public. Republicans were put " in an untenable public position: if they did not . . . support Superfund, it would appear that they were merely servants of the chemical industry" (Barnett, 1994). The reversal

so angered many House members that it was likely one reason why the leadership agreed to Stafford's condition that the House accept the bill without modification or lose Superfund for that term. In consequence, CMA's impact on the subsequent reauthorization of Superfund was also weakened (Moore, 1998).

15. U.S. PL95-510, Comprehensive Environmental Response, Compensation, and Liability Act of 1980 (CERCLA), December 11, 1980, 42 USC 9601 et. seq., amended by PL 96-561, December 22, 1980. Section 104(f) of the law requires that contractors and subcontractors awarded clean-up contracts pursuant to the act must comply with any standards that OSHA promulgated under its mandate in Section 301(f). This was included so that failure to comply with OSHA worker protection measures would be grounds to discontinue the contract. It provided a financial as well as a legal incentive for compliance (interview with Margaret Seminario, 1997): Section 104(g)(1) mandated that all laborers and mechanics employed by the contractors and subcontractors be paid the prevailing wage in accordance with the Davis-Bacon Act. This section most likely was secured by the Building Trades Department of the AFL-CIO, which had been paying attention to much environmental legislation passed in recent years. The health and safety language was a new consideration for these laws. Probably few individuals in the AFL-CIO other than George Taylor, director of the Department of Safety and Health, Margaret Seminario, and some legislative staff, were aware of the effort at the time.
16. See *A Brief History of Neoliberalism* (Harvey, 2005) for a discussion of these integrated efforts as critical steps toward implementing a shift to the neoliberal era.
17. For discussions of the Reagan administration's efforts and the historical policy development leading toward that administration, see (Dowie, 1997; Gottlieb, 1993; Greenberg, 1993; Kazis & Grossman, 1991; Noble, 1986; Wooding, 1990).
18. On December 1, 1983, Lavelle was convicted of four felony charges related to her activities at the EPA, for which she was imprisoned in 1985. See (Greenberg, 1993), for a fuller description of the corruption and abuse in the Reagan EPA and Superfund programs.
19. Substantial funding for worker training was not resumed through OSHA until the 1990s, when its Targeted Training Grant Program was set up. This initiative did not restore funding for worker training to the level provided at the peak of New Directions. It was not until 1998, under the direction of Charles N. Jeffress, that OSHA restored its former levels of funding for worker-oriented training with its Susan B. Harwood training grants.
20. Richard Duffy. This quotation and other information in this section came from an interview by the author.
21. Memorandum of Understanding [MOU]: NIOSH, OSHA, USCG, EPA, *Guidance for Worker Protection During Hazardous Waste Site Investigation and Clean Up and Hazardous Substance Emergencies,* signed December 18, 1980. A copy is found in (U.S. Congress. House of Representatives, 1985a). The MOU does not state that the activities would lead to the development of OSHA standards.
22. Information about NIOSH's role in addressing the mandate of CERCLA section 301(f) is from interviews with Dr. James Melius, Sheldon Samuels, Margaret Seminario, and Richard Duffy, and from Congressional hearings.
23. Testimony of James Melius, MD, NIOSH.
24. Testimony of John H. Skinner, director, Office of Solid Waste, U.S. EPA. The EPA was training more than 1,000 of its employees annually, as well as employees of other agencies and of private employers. Seven courses were offered.
25. Testimony of John H. Skinner, director, Office of Solid Waste. Skinner defended the actions of the EPA, but the agency's general disregard for worker protection at the time

was suggested in interviews with James Melius, Denny Dobbin, Sheldon Samuels, and Richard Duffy.

26. Testimony of Margaret Seminario.
27. The document indicates that ER activities require prior training, but does not list the job titles of such workers. It only instructs to contact the EPA for training programs; it makes no mention of the worker protection requirements of the NCP and does not direct readers to the four-agency worker protection manual published earlier.
28. Testimony of James Ellenberger, AFL-CIO Department of Safety, Health and Social Security.
29. John Miles explained that new guidelines for section 5(a)(1) citations had led to OSHA winning the cases. However, he never spoke to the issue of actually being able to collect on the issued fine.
30. For a review of the issues related to the bill, see (Needleman, 1990).
31. For discussions of HSWA and RCRA, see (Fortuna & Lennett, 1987; Goldman, 1986).
32. The incineration sector of the hazardous waste management industry worked closely with environmentalists and government regulators to achieve environmental policy changes in both HSWA and SARA. In the former, land disposal of hazardous wastes was banned, forcing incineration. In the latter, an emphasis on permanent solutions to uncontrolled hazardous waste sites also strongly supported the incineration of remediated wastes. For an overview and analysis of RCRA and HSWA, see (Fortuna & Lennett, 1987). Richard Fortuna was the director of the Hazardous Waste Treatment Council, an incinerator sector group, in 1990. He is an example of the links between the hazardous waste management industry and the mainstream environmental organizations. For criticisms of these links, see (Dowie, 1997).
33. For a history of workplace right-to-know laws, as OSHA regulation and municipal and state laws, see (Morse, 1998).

REFERENCES

50 Federal Register. (1985). Environmental Protection Agency. 40 CFR Part 300. National Oil and Hazardous Substances Pollution Contingency Plan. Proposed Rules. *Section III, Other Revisions. Subpart C, Section 300.38. (Proposed New) Worker Health and Safety. Discussion.* (Tuesday, Feb. 12, Vol. 50, 29, pp. 5876-5877). Washington, DC: GPO.

Ashford, N. (1976). *Crisis in the Workplace: Occupational Disease and Injury.* Cambridge, MA: MIT Press.

Barnett, H. C. (1994). *Toxic Debts and the Superfund Dilemma*. Chapel Hill: UNC Press.

Berman, D. (1981). Grassroots Coalitions in Health and Safety: The COSH Groups. *Labor Studies Journal, 6*(1), 104-113.

Brown, M. (1981). *History of New Directions Program.* (Unpublished report discovered within a file of materials regarding the New Directions Program, either written or collected by Mr. Brown. The file is now in the possession of the author.)

Bulkeley, W. M. (1980, Tuesday, Nov. 18). Dearth of Dumps: EPA's New Rules on Hazardous Wastes Don't Solve Problem of a Scarcity of Sites. *WSJ,* 48.

Business Publishers Inc. (1981, March 22). Auchter Says He Supports New Directions Program—But Changes Seem Certain. *Occupational Health and Safety Letter,* 2-4.

Colten, C., & Skinner P. (1996). *The Road to Love Canal: Managing Industrial Waste Before EPA.* Austin: University of Texas Press.

Commoner, B. (1972). *The Closing Circle: Nature, Man & Technology.* New York: Alfred A. Knopf.

Connor, M. F. (1989). The Politics of the Worker-Notification Bill. *Annals of the New York Academy of Sciences, 572,* 126-129.

Derikson, A. (1991). The United Mine Workers of America and the Recognition of Occupational Respiratory Diseases, 1902-1968. *AJPH, 81*(6), 782-790.

Deutsch, S. (1981). Introduction—Theme Issue on Occupational Safety and Health. *Labor Studies Journal, 6*(1), 3-6.

Dowie, M. (1997). *Losing Ground: American Environmentalism at the Close of the Twentieth Century.* Cambridge, MA: MIT Press.

Duffy, R. (1997). Interview by author, tape recording, Washington, D.C. (December 9).

Elisburg, D. (1997). Interview by author, tape recording, RTP, North Carolina (October 21).

Environmental Responses Act, Comprehensive Environmental Response, Compensation and Liability Act, U.S. Public Law 96-510. 96th Congress, 2nd Session. (1980).

Epstein, S., Brown, L., & Pope, C. (1982). *Hazardous Waste in America.* San Francisco: Sierra Club Books.

Fortuna, R. C., & Lennett, D. J. (1987). *Hazardous Waste Regulation, The New Era: An Analysis and Guide to RCRA and the 1984 Amendments.* New York: McGraw-Hill Book Co.

Freedman, F. (1978). Report On Worker Education On Health and Safety Issues Sponsored By the Occupational Safety and Health Administration. U.S. DOL contract # B-9-F-8-0721.

Freudenberg, N. (1984). *Not In Our Backyards!: Community Action for Health and the Environment.* New York: Monthly Review Press.

Gochfeld, M., Campbell, V., & Landsbergis P. (1990). Demographics of the Hazardous Waste Industry. *Occupational Medicine: State of the Art Reviews, 5*(1), 9-23.

Goldman, B. (1986). *Hazardous Waste Management: Reducing the Risk. Council on Economic Priorities.* Washington, DC: Island Press.

Gottlieb, R. (1993). *Forcing the Spring.* Washington, DC: Island Press.

Gottlieb, R., ed. (1995). *Reducing Toxics: A New Approach to Policy in Industrial Decision Making.* Washington, DC: Island Press.

Greenberg, E. J. (1993). *Toxic Temptation: The Revolving Door, Bureaucratic Inertia and the Disappointment of the EPA Superfund Program.* Washington, DC: Center for Public Interest.

Harvey, D. (2005). *A Brief History of Neoliberalism.* New York: Oxford University Press.

Hazardous and Solid Waste Amendments, U.S. Public Law 98-616. (1984).

Hughes, J. T. (1991). An Assessment of Training Needs for Worker Safety and Health Programs: Hazardous Waste Operations and Emergency Response. *Applied Occupational and Environmental Hygiene, 6*(2), 114-118.

Jackson, T., Costanza, R., Overcash, M., & Rees, W. (1993). The 'Biophysical' Economy—Aspects of the Interaction Between Economy and Environment. In T. Jackson (Ed.), *Clean Production Strategies: Developing Preventive Environmental Management in the Industrial Economy.* Boca Raton, FL: Lewis Publishers.

Kazis, R., & Grossman, R. L. (1991). *Fear at Work: Job Blackmail, Labor and the Environment* (New Edition ed.). Santa Cruz, CA: New Society Publishers.

Kerr, L. (1990). Occupational Health: A Classic Example of Class Conflict. *Journal of Public Health Policy, 11*(1), 39-49.

Klees, A. A., JD. (1996). The Interface of Environmental Regulation and Public Health. *Occupational Medicine: State of the Art Reviews, 11*(1), 173-192.

Lawrence, A., & Mager, S. (1982, February 24). Cuts in New Directions Grants Cripple Health and Safety Training. *Labor Notes, 37.*

Mallino, D., Sr. (1997). Interview by author, tape recording, Washington, DC. (December 10).

Melius, D. J. (1998). Melius, Dr. James, former Director of the NIOSH Health Hazard Evaluation Division. Telephone interview by author. Notes. (February 18).

Moore, C. (1998). Interview by author, tape recording (January 15). McLean, VA.

Morse, T. (1998). Dying to Know: A Historical Analysis of the Right-To-Know Movement. *New Solutions, A Journal of Environmental and Occupational Health Policy, 8*(1), 117-145.

Needleman, C. (1990). High-Risk Notification: Avoiding Adverse Effects for Workers. *New Solutions, A Journal of Environmental and Occupational Health Policy, 1*(1), 25-31.

Noble, C. (1986). *Liberalism at Work: The Rise and Fall of OSHA*. Philadelphia: Temple University Press.

Nyden P. (2007). Rank-and-File Rebellions in the Coalfields, 1964-80. *Monthly Review, 58*(10), 38-53.

Powers, M. (1997). Interview by author, Denver, CO (July 19).

Randall, J. (1998). Telephone interview by author (March 27).

Reesman, C. J., & Jordan, R. (1980). Issues and Recommendations for the Design of an Evaluation of the OSHA 'New Directions' Program (December 1980): OSHA Directorate of Policy, Legislation and Interagency Programs.

Resource Conservation and Recovery Act, U.S. Public Law 94-580. (1976).

Ringen, K. (1989). *The Case for Worker Notification.* Unpublished manuscript.

Samuels, S. (1998). Interview by author, tape recording, Solomon's Is., MD (January 16).

Seminario, M. (1997). Interview by author, tape recording. Washington, D.C. (December 10).

Smith, B. E. (1981). Black Lung: The Social Production of Disease. *International Journal of Health Services, 11*(3), 343-359.

Szasz, A. (1994). *EcoPopulism: Toxic Waste and the Movement for Environmental Justice.* Minneapolis: University of Minnesota Press.

Tobey, S., & Revitte, J. (1981). Building Worker Competence. *Labor Studies Journal, 6*(1), 41-52.

Truax, H. (1989). The Birth of a Waste Law. The Resource, Conservation, and Recovery Act: Managing the Nation's Waste, Part I, *Environmental Action, March/April*, 26-27.

U.S. Code. 96th Congress. (1980). Legislative History: U.S. Public Law 96-510. Environmental Responses Act, Comprehensive Environmental Response, Compensation and Liability Act of 1980 (Vol. 5, pp. 6119-6150). Washington, DC: Congressional and Administrative News.

U.S. Congress, House of Representatives. 1979. Committee on Interstate and Foreign Commerce, Subcommittee on Oversight and Investigations. *Hazardous Waste Disposal Hearings: Part 1*. 96th Congress. March-June. Washington, DC: U.S. GPO.

U.S. Congress, House of Representatives. 1985a. Committee on Government Operations. Subcommittee on Employment and Housing. Hearings: OSHA and Hazardous Waste Sites. 1st sess., 99th Congress. March 27. Washington, DC: U.S. GPO.

U.S. Congress. House of Representatives. 1985b. Committee on Education and Labor. Subcommittee on Health and Safety. *OSHA Oversight—Worker Protection at Superfund Sites*. 99th Congress, 1st sess. May. Washington, DC: U.S. GPO.

U.S. Congress. Senate. (1986). Hearing: High Risk Occupational Disease Notification and Prevention Act of 1986., *Committee on Labor and Human Resources, Subcommittee on Labor, 99th Congress, 2nd sess.* (May 15). Washington, DC: U.S. GPO.

U.S. Congress. Senate. (1990). A Legislative History of the Superfund Amendments and Reauthorization Act of 1986, Public Law 99-499 (1990, Vol. 1-7). Washington, DC: U.S. GPO.

U.S. DHHS-CDC-NIOSH. (1984). *Health Hazard Evaluations of Fire Fighting*. Cincinnati.

U.S. DHHS-NIOSH-OSHA-USCG-EPA. (1985). Occupational Safety and Health Guidance Manual for Hazardous Waste Site Activities (Publication No. 85-115). Washington, DC: DHHS (NIOSH).

U.S. DOL. (1978). *OSHA Announces Major New Job Safety and Health Training Program* (Press release). Wednesday, April 12. Washington, DC: Occupational Safety and Health Administration.

U.S. EPA. (1974). *Report to Congress: Disposal of Hazardous Wastes* (No. Publication # SW-115). June 30, 1973. Washington, DC: U.S. Environmental Protection Agency.

U.S. EPA. (1979). Preliminary Assessment of Cleanup Costs for National Hazardous Waste Problems (draft version). Washington, DC: U.S. Environmental Protection Agency.

U.S. EPA. (1985). Chemical Emergency Preparedness Program: Interim Guidance (November, 1986-619-194:40439). Washington, DC: U.S. GPO.

Walker, K. D. (1987). Letter of support for a Superfund Worker Training Program grant proposal from the University of Lowell, to Chuck Levenstein (March 11).

Whiting, B. J. (1989). Early Worker and Employer Training Initiatives at OSHA. *Toxicology and Industrial Health, 5*(4), 87-95.

Wolf, S. M. (1996). Fear and Loathing About the Public Right to Know: The Surprising Success of the Emergency Planning and Community Right-to-Know Act. *Journal of Land Use & Environmental Law, 11,* 217-260.

Wooding, J. (1990). *Dire States: Workplace Health and Safety Regulations in the Reagan/ Thatcher Era.* University Microfilms International Dissertation Services, Ann Arbor. 366 pages; AAT 9017977.

Wooding, J. (1994). *Labor and the Legacy of the New Left: The Impact on the Conditions of Work.* Paper presented at the 1994 Annual Meeting of the American Political Science Association. New York.

CHAPTER 3

Moving Congress to Mandate Worker Protection

Corporations and their allied politicians can easily manipulate social decision making regarding the organization and regulation of production, simply by threatening to eliminate jobs if they don't get their way. Congressional Superfund reauthorization debates often pitted demands for corporate responsibility to ensure the members of the working class a clean environment in which to live and raise their children and grandchildren against the jobs the corporations could provide for workers.

For example, Rep. Jack Fields (R-TX) worried about the 74,000 people "directly and indirectly" employed by his state's petrochemical industry. He wanted Congress to ensure that the industry was "not taxed out of competition with foreign petrochemical importers. We need a clean environment and I am committed to that goal. But I'm also committed to protect the jobs of Houston-area workers" (U.S. Congress. Senate, 1990, vol. 3, p. 1537).

Similarly, Rep. Fred J. Eckert (R-NY) represented a district in which 60,000 people worked for petrochemical companies—Eastman Kodak, Du Pont, Olin Corp., Jones Chemical, and Dow Chemical. He worried that they would be "thrown out of work as a result of being taxed out of business" (U.S. Congress. Senate, 1990, vol. 5, p. 4079). No congressperson from a state that was predominantly either petrochemical producing or petrochemical using wanted a policy that might cause political dissatisfaction among the state's employers or jeopardize jobs in their districts. Nonetheless, the public demanded cleanups. The driving force remained the need to pass a bill providing a balanced funding mechanism. Rep. Eckert concluded, "The bottom line is a . . . bill that moves the clean-up of hazardous waste forward without costing thousands of workers their jobs" (U.S. Congress. Senate, 1990, vol. 5, p. 4080).

Beyond the "job blackmail" used against the working class, members of Congress referred to the hazardous waste crisis and the widespread use of hazardous materials in industry and commerce as a collective responsibility—not just that of the industries that were profiteering from having externalized hazardous waste management costs, but also the public's. Rep. Tauzin, then a Democrat from oil- and chemical-producing Louisiana, observed:

> The truth is, we all are [responsible]. We have benefited from the products of our great manufacturing establishments in America. . . . We have all caused each other harm and neglect because we have not taken care of the wastes that have

> been produced in the manufacture of those products. (U.S. Congress. Senate, 1990, vol. 5, p. 4030)

We may have "all caused each other harm," but we weren't all reaping the financial profits from the harmful modes of production. In addition, the health consequences of exposure to hazardous wastes were devastating and/or frightening communities around the country. The pressure was on Congress to end the hazardous waste crisis. Ronald Reagan's Republican Party, which worked with the president to undermine hard-won environmental protection measures, was scrambling to show that its members were protectors of the environment while they were also strengthening the economy. The party was facing U.S. voters who thought that the Reagan administration's attack on workers' jobs, the government safety net, public health, and environmental and consumer protection had gone too far. The Republicans' control of the Senate for the first time since the 1950s was probably going to be lost, as well as House seats, and the Superfund law was seen as one way to cut their losses.

Within this setting, the AFL-CIO and some of its affiliated unions coordinated a successful effort to win strong worker health and safety protection and training language in an environmental protection law, the Superfund Amendments and Reauthorization Act of 1986 (SARA). It brought together, somewhat serendipitously but mostly in a well-organized way, labor's various strategies of 1979 through 1985 to get federal agencies to establish protections for HAZWOPER workers, as well as the building trades' desire for hazardous waste worker health and safety training for their members. Labor understood that the hazardous waste remediation and management industries were emerging in direct relationship to the hazardous waste crisis that was steadily unfolding in the United States. Labor urged that Congress not ask American workers to put their lives on the line cleaning up and responding to hazardous materials/waste sites and incidents without being provided with essential measures of protection.

This is a history of action "within the beltway," of the lobbying potential available through labor's collective resources. Although a relatively small network of individuals understand how to maneuver the political/legal system of Washington, it is their position as representatives of a movement that facilitates their access to the apparatus.[1] What follows is a description of how labor unions, having sufficient economic, political, professional, scientific, and grassroots resources, were able to win government measures to improve working class life—in this case, workplace health and safety protections and environmental protection and quality.

THE AFL-CIO AND THE SUPERFUND REAUTHORIZATION EFFORT

The legislative process to reauthorize the Superfund law began in the Senate in April 1984,[2] and it climaxed in Reagan's signing SARA into law on October 17, 1986.[3] The tax that supported the Superfund, established under CERCLA, was set to expire in September 1985. In light of that deadline, and mobilizing against the subversion of Congressional intentions by the Reagan administration and the EPA, environmentalists and key members of Congress began to work in earnest on bills to reauthorize CERCLA. The Democratic congressmen addressing these issues were Florio and John Dingell (D-MI). Both had helped pass CERCLA, but they had disagreed vehemently over some central issues. The contentious aspects mostly related to rights that the law would establish for citizens interested in challenging the production and waste management practices of industrial facilities within their communities or states. Florio was a primary supporter of environmentalists' concerns. Dingell backed a range of other concerns, including those of manufacturers. He spoke up particularly for the priorities of automakers, as automaking was an industry that was based in his home state. In 1984, Florio was preparing for a renewed fight over Superfund, particularly with Dingell. Both were members of the House Committee on Energy and Commerce, which had prime jurisdiction over environmental legislation. Dingell chaired the committee and Florio chaired an important subcommittee. Florio hoped that his role as a leader on environmental concerns would help make him the next governor of New Jersey.

Florio came to Howard Samuel and asked for support from labor on Superfund. Samuel assigned David Mallino, Sr., to work on it. Mallino was a policy analyst who had worked for the AFL-CIO and affiliated unions for years, and had previously lobbied Congress for a federalized workers compensation program. He knew influential members of Congress. As Mallino (1997) immersed himself in Superfund issues, he realized that "there was absolutely no concern in that bill over the health and safety of the people who were going to do the clean-up work." Mallino decided that he would push to have "a health and safety program as an integral part" of the Superfund bill. At that point, Mallino the policy specialist wanted to see the development of a health and safety program with an appropriate set of corresponding standards. "I hadn't even thought about a training program at all," he said.

Mallino discussed the idea with IUD staff at the AFL-CIO. The lobbyist for the IUOE told him that J. C. Turner, the union's president, was "potentially interested" because he saw hazardous waste site clean-up work as a "jobs opportunity." Turner was a member of the AFL-CIO Executive Committee and chaired its standing committee (an executive policy panel) on health and safety. When Mallino sought a formal mandate to pursue the inclusion of worker protection language in the Superfund bill, Turner backed him to secure legislation that would protect workers engaged in hazardous waste operations. Interestingly, Mallino was unaware of the language that had been written and included in CERCLA (Section 301[f]) by Seminario (1997). Also, it seemed that no one with whom Mallino spoke was familiar with the letters that Taylor of the AFL-CIO had sent to agency heads in November 1979 or with the interagency effort on hazardous waste worker protection.

Mallino had talked with Donald Elisburg, an attorney and former assistant secretary of employment standards in the Department of Labor (DOL) during the Carter administration. Elisburg had worked as counsel to the Senate Labor Committee and addressed health and safety issues. After leaving government in 1981, Elisburg represented the Laborers International Union of North America (LIUNA) and other building trades unions on health and safety. He worked with the IUD on high-risk worker notification and asbestos matters. Elisburg and Mallino were associated with Robert Connerton, general counsel for LIUNA. Elisburg, Warren Anderson, director of the L-AGC Education and Training Fund, and James "Mitch" Warren (who became the fund's director), shared ideas about Mallino's effort to secure worker protections in the Superfund reauthorization. They realized that a worker training grant program could be incorporated into the legislation (NIEHS, 1997).

At the same time, Ben Hill, the IUOE's director of health and safety, discussed the legislative effort with Turner, also of the IUOE. Hill believed that worker training was needed. The union already had a facility in New Jersey that was training some hazardous waste workers.

Mallino soon learned about labor's earlier efforts: Seminario explained the history to him. Mallino and Seminario agreed to work together on the issue. Mallino would coordinate primarily the political effort and Seminario would develop the substance of the legislative language they would propose.[4] Key union players met regularly to devise their plan. They included Sheldon Samuels from the IUD, Duffy, Hill, Seminario, and Elisburg. No industrial unions were involved at that point, but Samuels represented their interests. Some industrial unions became involved later when the need for a community right-to-know law was discussed. According to Duffy,

> This is the first time that public employees, with us, the building trades, and the IUD, were actually working on an issue. We had the insight that we knew we had a window of opportunity to do this, if we could do it quietly, and could make a big difference. [We picked] an amount [of money] that would be palatable [to] Congress and wouldn't stick out like a sore thumb. There was no backstabbing or cutting up the pie beforehand.

Mallino understood that as long as a Superfund reauthorization bill was debated, a solid argument could be made for protecting the clean-up workers. He was aware that Dingell and Florio were fighting heatedly over what a Superfund bill would say. Mallino calculated that bringing worker protections into the struggle could greatly diminish the chances of passage, so he sent the provisions through a different set of committees.

While Mallino represented the IUD, he was close to the building trades and stayed in contact with Turner. The building trades had a "long-standing and good relationship" with House and Senate members of both parties in the public works committees. So Mallino worked with the House Committee on Public Works and Transportation and the Senate Committee on Environment and Public Works, as well as the Subcommittee on Health and Safety of the House Committee on Education and Labor. The last-mentioned was chaired by Rep. Joseph Gaydos (D-PA), who had not only a longstanding interest in worker health and safety but also a close working relationship with Mallino.

Mallino understood committee jurisdiction issues and made certain that the authority and jurisdiction of those responsible for occupational health and safety were not usurped.

1985 CONGRESSIONAL HEARINGS: THE ISSUES AND ACTORS

In spring 1985, Congress held hearings on the health and safety of hazardous waste workers. The House Committees on Public Works and Transportation and on Education and Labor took testimony about worker protection at Superfund sites

(U.S. Congress. House of Representatives, 1985b, 1985c). The House Committee on Government Operations held a hearing to investigate OSHA's role in protecting hazardous waste workers (U.S. Congress. House of Representatives, 1985a). Finally, although this was not directly related to waste sites and Superfund, the House Committee on Education and Labor looked into "Worker Health and Safety in the Manufacture and Use of Toxic and Hazardous Substances," an inquiry that addressed related issues (U.S. Congress. House of Representatives, 1985d).

The hearing transcripts and a hearing-based committee report facilitated an examination of the social "actors" involved and a review of the contentious aspects of the bill. The primary actors were union representatives. In the case of construction, each union represented a specific trade or craft and not the industry as a whole. The unions, although sharing common concerns, offered different ideas about addressing workplace hazards and government protections.

The industrial unions had limited participation in the hearings. The IUD was represented, but its representatives focused mostly on building trades issues.[5] First, Turner, as head of the IUOE and chair of its standing committee on health and safety, assumed leadership on this issue. Second, Mallino worked closely with Turner and other building trades representatives and saw it largely as a building trades issue.[6] Third, because of CERCLA's focus on hazardous waste sites, most union representatives assumed that the issues were primarily those of the building trades. Finally, the IUD's role was more closely allied with efforts by the labor and environment coalition in securing provisions for communities' right-to-know and chemical emergency preparedness. Even within the building trades, though, not all unions were interested in the work. It was viewed as in the jurisdiction and interest of the operating engineers, the laborers, and the teamsters.

The IAFF was the main other union that pushed for worker protections. Duffy had worked on these issues since 1979. Because of the incident in Elizabeth, New Jersey, in 1980, he had worked with New Jersey's Congressional delegates, four of whom had key committee positions with jurisdiction over Superfund reauthorization. Duffy's efforts greatly influenced the process of securing worker protections. The concerns of the IAFF and the building trades unions coincided, but the IAFF was unable to get what it wanted most, which was OSHA protection for municipal firefighters (government workers). The IAFF's interests collided with those of another set of actors—Congressional representatives who defended the interests of government employers. Government employers who were not yet required to comply with OSHA regulations did not want such a mandate. Unless a state had a state OSHA plan that covered public workers, these workers did not fall under OSHA's protections.

Employers at the hearings were primarily involved in site remediation and mostly focused on winning protections from the potential liabilities of the work. The members of Congress who testified largely supported labor's needs. The House was controlled by the Democrats, who traditionally supported worker protections. No Republican committee members were overtly hostile to providing protections, but some wanted a more limited approach. Some congressmen testified or commented in support of labor's arguments. Florio spoke in support of protecting waste site workers (U.S. Congress. House of Representatives, 1985a, p. 2).

Several House committees held hearings that addressed hazardous waste worker protections or included them among other issues. Gaydos decided that the House Committee on Education and Labor would hear worker protection issues. His goal was to develop a record of support for protective provisions. The House Committee on Public Works and Transportation hosted Superfund hearings. Its chair was Rep. James Howard (D-NJ), and the hearings subcommittee's chair was Rep. Robert Roe (D-NJ). Much attention was given to the needs of workers in Superfund site remediation. Mallino worked closely with Roe.

The House Committee on Government Operations conducted hearings because of the interests of key members. Rep. Barney Frank (D-MA), chair of the Subcommittee on Employment and Housing, wanted to hold OSHA accountable to its mandate. According to Stuart Weisberg,[7] former staff director of Frank's subcommittee, and Rep. Tom Lantos (D-CA), this subcommittee probably conducted more oversight of OSHA in the late 1980s than any other committee of Congress (Weisberg, 1998). It ensured that language supported by the hearings was part of the bill.

The role of the Committee on Government Operations was to create a bully pulpit to raise issues and build momentum for legislative action. Even the committee Republicans supported protections, according to Weisberg. The committee's report, for instance, was unanimously approved (U.S. Congress. House of Representatives, 1985e; Weisberg, 1998).

Cleanup of the average toxic waste site, said the IUOE's Turner, required "at least fifty highly trained and skilled workers . . . [demanding] at least one million jobs for the 20,000 or more sites involved . . . [and] other jobs will be created in the engineering, design, and equipment production sectors" (U.S. Congress. House of Representatives, 1985a, p. 15). The IAFF counted "170,000 paid professional fire service employees in the U.S. and Canada" (U.S. Congress. House of Representatives, 1985b, p. 45).

The focus of the hearings included the following: (1) the health and safety hazards of hazardous waste operations; (2) the failure of OSHA and the EPA to address worker health and safety; (3) the need for an OSHA standard; (4) health and safety training; (5) ER in HAZMAT incidents; and (6) health and safety protection for government workers.

1. The Health and Safety Hazards of Hazardous Waste Operations

The unions and associated professionals testified to the range of risks faced by site workers. Dr. Ruth Ruttenberg, an OSHA economist under Carter who testified for a nonprofit public research group, explained the results of a study of the eight largest publicly owned hazardous waste management companies at that time.[8] Her data concerned OSHA's inspections and enforcements at sites operated by the firms. The OSHA citations for exposures to hazardous substances indicated either incomplete OSHA data or inconsistent inspection patterns for the companies. "I think probably what we are faced with is a serious gap between what the OSHA record shows in terms of inspections and the actual risks that workers are facing in hazardous waste sites," she observed (U.S. Congress. House of Representatives, 1985a, p. 173).

Ruttenberg pointed to the inadequacy of air monitoring at hazardous waste facilities. She told the story of a 17-year-old employee at a North Carolina waste site who had died in minutes after suffering an acute exposure. The youth was a summer employee whose employer did not require him to wear the necessary personal protective equipment. "When one looks at some of the deaths that have occurred from acute exposure, [they] are temporary workers [and] summer teenage employees" (U.S. Congress. House of Representatives, 1985a, p. 190). Suzanne Kossan of the International Brotherhood of Teamsters (IBT) described site workers' increased risks, stating that "The lost workday injury rate for hazardous waste operations is 11.4 cases per hundred workers versus 4.3 cases for the national average" (U.S. Congress. House of Representatives, 1985a, p. 60).

Duffy explained the hazards for firefighters and the lack of protection afforded to them. He showed a slide of a front-page photograph from the *New York Times,* taken at the site of the Chemical Control fire at Elizabeth, New Jersey. It showed a

> firefighter rowing a boat for a federal investigator. The federal investigator is taking water samples . . . in full protective garment. No part of his body is

Responders at the Scene of the Chemical Control Corp. Fire, photo that Rich Duffy Presented at Congressional Hearings.

> exposed whatsoever. . . . [The firefighter] . . . has a pair of polyester pants on; his boots are rolled down; he has an open turnout coat on and a dress hat and the only hand protection he has is the calluses on his palms. (U.S. Congress. House of Representatives, 1985a, p. 46)

For Duffy, showing the picture was a tactical act. The unions and members of Congress repeatedly referred to it as the justification for legislating worker protection and training. The unions' main demand was that workers should get the same protection that EPA employees got.

> Duffy had this wonderful picture that they had blown up on posters. It probably was the thing that made our case. . . . When they testified, they said, here is our problem. . . . This EPA guy knows that he is going to go on a very hazardous island. The guy taking him to the island is a worker that happens to be a firefighter. He has no goddamn idea, and he is going out there essentially in this blue collar. This is why we need a training program and OSHA standard. . . . [The firefighters'] take on this was that their people absolutely needed to have high quality training, and there was no provision in the current bill to do that. (Mallino, 1997)

In testimony, the Associated General Contractors (AGC) supported worker protections. The AGC delivered the position of both union contractors and the building trades unions: prevention of occupational injuries and illnesses was necessary in order to conduct the work in the most efficient manner.

> It is paramount in cleaning up these sites that no additional safety or health problems be created for the surrounding communities and that the clean-up workers are protected from safety and health hazards that are inherent in this type of work. [It is necessary] to ensure that the work is performed as economically as possible. . . . Safety and economy are not competing goals but in fact complement one another because the more economically the work is performed, the more funds will remain available for future clean-ups. (U.S. Congress. House of Representatives, 1985b, p. 1719)

Federal support for health and safety protection in the construction industry was a basis for union contractors' successful competition against nonunion contractors. For the building trades, it meant more jobs for their members.[9]

2. The Failure of OSHA and the EPA to Address Worker Health and Safety Issues

The AFL-CIO Safety and Health Department and the IUD, the unions, and Democratic members of Congress who were friendly to labor all used the hearings to document the failures of the Reagan administration's OSHA and EPA when it came to protecting workers. While Congress debated the EPA's failures with regard to implementing the CERCLA and RCRA programs, the unions focused on OSHA's failures as well.

The Teamsters brought T. Louis Brown Jr., a shop steward in Local Union Number 270, to testify. Brown worked at a facility that processed petrochemical wastes. His plant had never received OSHA inspections, he said, even when the government knew of potentially hazardous conditions, as when 80 tons of waste asbestos from the military were brought there. Since 1984, OSHA had done only six inspections at Superfund sites and 11 inspections at licensed disposal sites, the Teamsters said (U.S. Congress. House of Representatives, 1985a, pp. 54-56).

Seminario used the hearings to gain support for mandates to force OSHA to make stronger efforts to protect waste workers. She assailed the agency's failure to comply with the mandate established in Section 301(f) of CERCLA. The agency had failed to draft regulations or establish an enforcement program for hazardous waste operations. Seminario criticized OSHA for omitting most waste sites from targeted inspection programs. "There has been no leadership asserted by OSHA in this particular area," she said (U.S. Congress. House of Representatives, 1985a, p. 85).

The AFL-CIO described the responsibilities that OSHA had failed to meet after CERCLA passed. Union representatives criticized OSHA, the EPA, and the Coast Guard for weak efforts under the interagency memorandum of understanding. The agencies, they said, had spent most of 4 years arguing over jurisdiction and the content of protection provisions. They criticized OSHA for being the least responsive agency: "OSHA has taken the position that since EPA is the lead Superfund agency, OSHA will not schedule routine inspections at sites cleaned up under the Superfund, even though these represent the most dangerous sites" (U.S. Congress. House of Representatives, 1985b, p. 5).

Duffy criticized the EPA's lack of support for worker protection. He described the union's experience at the American Electric Corporation warehouse in Jacksonville, Florida, where firefighters had responded to a HAZMAT fire that involved large quantities of PCB oil. At the site, EPA personnel failed to warn firefighters of potential health hazards. The EPA disregarded

> obvious unsafe actions by not only the firefighters, but the private clean-up contractor and the workers they hired for site mitigation. . . . The EPA personnel on-scene decided . . . to follow the administration's policy, which is to get big government off industry's back and allow for the industry to clean up by themselves. (U.S. Congress. House of Representatives, 1985b, p. 44)

OSHA and the EPA were represented at the Government Operations and Education and Labor Committee hearings. Robert A. Rowland, an assistant secretary of labor, said the agency had a field directive instructing inspectors to enforce existing standards at waste sites. OSHA had also trained 100 compliance officers to respond in emergencies. The EPA paid for the training (U.S. Congress. House of Representatives, 1985a, pp. 96-102).

John Miles, then Director of Field Operations for OSHA, made points for the agency. OSHA saw worker protection at hazardous waste sites as the responsibility of the EPA and the Coast Guard. OSHA was part of the interagency National Response Team and followed the terms of the National Contingency Plan established pursuant to CERCLA. The plan called for contractors to comply with existing OSHA standards for industry in general and construction. The standards for chemical exposures were difficult to enforce because hazardous waste site work was conducted outdoors, where ambient conditions generally prevented the kinds of exposure levels that could develop indoors. Miles asserted that OSHA could investigate only workplaces where there were employees. Since Superfund cleanup was a slow process, with only 300 sites under response actions at the time, OSHA had little opportunity to investigate sites. But OSHA might have visited hazardous waste facilities as part of targeted inspections in the chemical industry, he said.

Miles and Rowland presented the agency's opinion that a new standard was unnecessary (U.S. Congress. House of Representatives, 1985b, pp. 146-164).

OSHA was criticized by the committees but argued that OMB had restricted its budget. Gaydos was frustrated by the frequent changes in OSHA's leadership. Hearing the argument about budget restrictions, he growled angrily,

> I don't know if it is attributable to lack of funds or the lack of will, or is it a changing of the Director too often? . . . Granted you have limited funds. But I don't see the Secretary of Labor . . . kicking and screaming and asking for more funds down there at the OMB. . . . I have asked ... do you need more money? And they said no. (U.S. Congress. House of Representatives, 1985b, p. 158)

3. The Need for an OSHA Standard

The unions pushed to persuade Congress that an OSHA standard was necessary to protect hazardous waste workers. Robert A. Georgine, of the AFL-CIO, called for the enforcement of existing OSHA industrial and construction standards at waste sites, but did not call for a new OSHA standard. Ruttenberg explained why a standard was needed:

> Hazardous waste management regulations are led by environmental politics, even though worker exposure is usually far more intense, extensive, and hazardous than community exposure. It is not only the employees at hazardous waste sites, but transportation workers, emergency personnel, including firefighters, etc., who need adequate protections. We know that significant health risks exist. (U.S. Congress. House of Representatives, 1985a, p. 188)

The AFL-CIO Safety and Health staff urged Congress to order OSHA to promulgate a "comprehensive, permanent standard, within a specified period of time, for example, two years" (U.S. Congress. House of Representatives, 1985b, p. 6). The department, the IBT, and the IUOE detailed a nine-point program of needed protections. The IUOE wanted the EPA to administer the training program. It also wanted rules addressing the risks of continuous handling and transport of hazardous waste materials and the introduction of new technologies and equipment. The IBT wanted NIOSH to administer the training and called for the extension of the OSHA Hazard Communication Standard to cover hazardous wastes. The AFL-CIO included rules for ER operations and decontamination and sought site hazard analyses and health and safety plans.

Duffy demanded a standard to protect firefighters and additional research into the types of protective clothing needed, and he also covered other aspects of ER work. He cited the experience of firefighters at a particular incident:

> So what that particular company did, they went downtown to day workers and hired the people you see here on my right. They had absolutely no training on chemical site mitigation, no training in site clean-up, and were allowed to go on-scene to perform this clean-up without any protection. (U.S. Congress. House of Representatives, 1985b, p. 44)

The Committee on Government Operations issued a report that recommended action by OSHA. Drafting substance-specific exposure standards for hazardous waste operations and ER was not possible, members noted, but more was needed than existed at that time. They called for prompt action to develop a comprehensive rule, an accelerated OSHA enforcement program, "serious consideration" of extending OSHA coverage to municipal firefighters, and a broader scope for the Hazard Communication standard to include the hazardous waste industry. The committee stressed that coverage of firefighters for response at hazardous waste sites was a separate matter from coverage of public workers in general (U.S. Congress. House of Representatives, 1985e, pp. 12-13).

A final point that was significant for the WETP was a comment from the IUOE. John Brown said that strong federal standards would "drive the fly-by-night contractor away from this [, a contractor] . . . who will do a lousy job . . . [and contaminate] the soil that he is removing and the soil where he is going to, and the worker himself, and the community as a whole" (U.S. Congress. House of Representatives, 1985b, pp. 123-124).

4. Health and Safety Training

The building trades unions and the firefighters were the strongest advocates for a government grant–funded training program. Seminario certainly supported the concept, but the strategy was put forward by various unions. The IBT called for a training grants program that would award $2 million to universities and $8 million to labor organizations to train workers and other public groups (U.S. Congress. House of Representatives, 1985a, p. 73). Ben Hill of the IUOE asked that Congress amend the Superfund law to require health and safety training. He supplied legislative language that he had developed by modifying language in the Mine Safety and Health Act of 1977. It included minimum amounts of training and 8 hours of annual refresher training. Training should be conducted during working hours, he said, with full pay for employees, and employers should certify that they had properly trained each worker (U.S. Congress. House of Representatives, 1985a, pp. 70-71).

Duffy testified that firefighters needed training and that adequate ER training did not exist in the United States. Firefighters needed certificates to document minimum classroom and field training that was specific to their HAZMAT ER roles. Duffy called for general site worker training specific to each trade, on-scene training specific to each site, and ER training for firefighters. Duffy discussed the success of the training developed by unions, worker representatives, and employers under the OSHA New Directions program and said the Superfund ought to support similar work (U.S. Congress. House of Representatives, 1985b, p. 121).

Gerard Gallagher, Jr., the vice president of Ecology and Environment, Inc., a remediation firm, reported that the company's worker protection costs "run about $15,000 to train and equip an individual" (U.S. Congress. House of Representatives, 1985a, p. 189). Gallagher's firm gave 5 days of training, which covered multiple topics, including protective respiratory instruction and practice in several levels of chemical protective clothing. Gallagher said that others in the industry considered the worker protection provided by his firm to be "state of the art . . . in the private sector . . . [and] the minimum that you can provide" (U.S. Congress. House of Representatives, 1985a, p. 191). When training and protection carry such high costs, Ruttenberg said later, a stable workforce is required to secure the investment.

5. ER to HAZMAT Incidents

The decade of the 1980s was a time when previously disposed of hazardous wastes were discovered as they exploded, caught fire, or caused adverse health outcomes in humans, plants, and animals. Catastrophic accidents had occurred at petrochemical facilities. The circumstances led to an increase in the number of workers involved in HAZMAT incidents. Industrial unions, such as OCAW and the International Chemical Workers Union (ICWU), testified in favor of what later were called process safety management regulations (U.S. Congress. House of Representatives, 1985c).

Duffy was the most vocal advocate for emergency responder health and safety protections and certainly the only person asking for these protections for emergencies at hazardous waste operations. Firefighters were exposed to HAZMAT risks through a lack of concern or knowledge among private employers. During one emergency, an EPA hazardous waste site response contractor's employee identified himself to firefighters as an EPA toxicologist. He advised that medical exams would not be necessary and that no decontamination of clothing or equipment, other than normal washing, was needed. The incident occurred at the second worst hazardous waste site in Michigan, where a range of toxic substances had been stored (U.S. Congress. House of Representatives, 1985b, p. 42).

Firefighters usually responded to HAZMAT incidents in their normal fire gear, Duffy said. But firefighter protection required research on the types of materials that would provide adequate safeguards against chemical exposure and the effects of multiple chemical exposures on protective clothing (U.S. Congress. House of Representatives, 1985b, p. 44). Duffy also pointed out that the lack of training of ER personnel, firefighters in particular, could put the public at significant risk.[10]

6. Health and Safety Protection for Government Workers

Above all else, Duffy strongly believed that firefighters' health and safety would not be adequately protected unless employers were required to comply with the OSH Act and OSHA regulations (Duffy, 1997). Often at hearings, he urged Congress to extend OSHA protection to public employees. He testified that a recent Supreme Court decision (*Garcia v. San Antonio Transit Authority*) had determined that all of the Fair Labor Standards Act applied to public employees who had previously been excluded. He asked the committee to investigate whether that decision could support changes in the OSH Act to protect "firefighters and other public employees" (U.S. Congress. House of Representatives, 1985a, p. 84).

THE UNIONS REPRESENTING HAZARDOUS WASTE OPERATIONS WORKERS

At the time of the hearings, only three unions were aware that they represented members who worked in the hazardous waste management or remediation industries.[11] The three unions mentioned or testifying at the hearings were the IUOE, LIUNA, and IBT.

The Teamsters were not then part of the AFL-CIO but participated in the legislative effort. Only the Teamsters, according to Seminario, had a good relationship with the Reagan administration. They were given a position on the National Advisory Committee on Occupational Safety and Health (NACOSH), which represented labor in an advisory capacity to OSHA), by the administration in the same period when the AFL-CIO was taken off the committee. "So, for things like getting a standard, they could get support that the rest of the unions could not. They always worked collaboratively with the AFL-CIO and the other unions," Seminario said.

The IUOE had the only hazardous waste worker training center among the unions. LIUNA was not listed in the contents of these hearings, but its viewpoints likely were represented by Mallino, who worked closely with Elisburg and LIUNA's general counsel, Connerton. LIUNA had trained laborers for hazardous waste work in Iowa. By November 1984, it had developed a resource and information manual for the courses (Iowa Laborers' Heavy Highway Training Fund, 1980). From the start, the IUOE, LIUNA, and IBT were strong proponents of what became Section 126 of SARA, which developed into the WETP.

OCAW had brought the issue of hazardous waste site exposures to the AFL-CIO in 1979 but was not involved in the SARA effort. OCAW, Sheldon Samuels said, supported the IUD's work to secure protections, but it was not engaged in independent action (Samuels, 1998).

THE LEGISLATIVE HISTORY OF WORKER PROTECTION PROVISIONS IN SARA

By the end of the hearings, the members of a core group of union representatives was developing the language that they wanted secured in the Superfund reauthorization bill. Seminario, Hill, Elisburg, Mallino, Samuels, and Duffy were the main drafters. The group decided to include a training program plan and $10 million to support it. Its members pursued a single OSHA standard for the health and safety protection of hazardous waste employees, which would include ER workers.

Eleven mandatory worker protection provisions were established for inclusion in the OSHA standard. The group set a timetable for the issuance of an interim standard and then a final standard. The standard would apply to government employees engaged in ER and hazardous waste operations. Specific requirements were set, including the number of hours of training. The group also included training certification requirements.

Most of the draft language concerned hazardous waste operations, but some of it was broader. The broader terms affected workers involved in HAZMAT ER and concerned the scope of the training program. The training standards would apply to ER personnel—"workers who are responsible for responding to hazardous emergency situations who may be exposed to toxic substances in carrying out their responsibilities" (U.S. Congress. Senate, 1990, vol. 4, pp. 227-228). Grants would cover "the training and education of workers who are or may be engaged in activities related to hazardous waste removal or containment or emergency response" (U.S. Congress. Senate, 1990, vol. 4, p. 228). While only hazardous waste operations were covered, the term was not defined, leaving it open to interpretations set within the context of the new Superfund bill. For the most part, the language that was signed into law was the same as the draft language.

Mallino followed Congress's progress toward passing a bill. The Republicans had controlled the Senate since 1980 and it was now a year before the 1986 elections. The Reaganites' poor performance on environmental issues was a looming campaign issue that the Democrats intended to use to their advantage. That summer, a bill, S-51, which had been introduced on January 3, 1985, by Senator Stafford as the Superfund Improvement Bill of 1985, began moving quickly. By September, Republicans were eager to pass a bill to show that the party had moved from the positions it had taken during Reagan's first term. Mallino shifted his attention to the Senate.

Senator Metzenbaum's Role

Mallino went to Senator Howard Metzenbaum (D-OH) and his staff for support in securing worker protections in S-51. Mallino presented the draft language. He had missed the marking up of the bill, so he asked Metzenbaum to offer the language as an amendment from the Senate floor. Metzenbaum's staff and Mallino discussed the difficulty of presenting it this way and worked out a plan. The problem was that the Democrats were the minority party and did not chair committees. They assumed that Senator Orin Hatch (R-UT), then chair of the Senate Labor Committee, would object to the language and prepared for that likelihood. Metzenbaum and his staff discussed the matter with key Senate committee chairs before offering the amendment, and Hatch did object. An agreement was made with Hatch that much of the language would be removed, except for a few provisions.[12]

Amendment No. 677 (submitted on September 24) to S-51 called for OSHA to promulgate standards for the health and safety protection of employees in hazardous waste operations, which included ER. The standards were to be issued within a year of the enactment of the Superfund Improvement Act. The amendment also authorized "The cost of training such employees, in an amount not to exceed $10 million per year" (U.S. Congress. Senate, 1990, vol. 2, p. 1221). Metzenbaum discussed the need to protect clean-up workers and firefighters. He criticized OSHA for its failure to establish "any enforcement program to inspect hazardous waste sites . . . [or to] develop regulations on environmental monitoring, medical surveillance or the training of workers involved in hazardous waste operations" (U.S. Congress. Senate, 1990, vol. 2, p. 1222). Metzenbaum said that clean-up workers should receive the same level of protection that the EPA gave its own personnel on waste sites. He used the same arguments that labor had presented at the hearings.

The ranking members of all pertinent committees, including the Labor Committee, had indicated their support for the legislation, Metzenbaum said. Stafford then noted that the mandate in CERCLA to develop worker protection standards had not been met, even though 5 years had elapsed. Deadlines must be set, he argued, for proposing and promulgating standards for appropriate worker protections.

Before the vote on the bill, Hatch explained that he was "sympathetic with the need to protect employees involved in hazardous waste operations . . . [but maintained] . . . unqualified opposition to any amendment which would expand the scope of the OSH Act or goes beyond the Senate position," and asked that the House uphold the Senate's positions "in the conference committee" (U.S. Congress. Senate, 1990, vol. 2, pp. 1286-1287). It was important, he stressed, to the Senate Labor and Human Resources Committee and the Department of Labor. Hatch may have communicated with the administration, or at least the secretary of labor, over the matter.

Nonetheless, Mallino wanted something to pass that "smelled like a health and safety program" (Mallino, 1997), so that if and when a Superfund bill went to the conference committee, he could get Senate members to agree to the House's language. Once S-51 contained protection provisions (Section 121 [g]), Mallino worked with House members on the language he wanted.

The Eckart-Lent Bill in the House

On June 20, 1985, a bill (H.S. 2817) to amend CERCLA was introduced to the House by Reps. Dennis Eckart (D-OH) and Norman Lent (R-NY). By November, the bill contained several sections that were part of the policy initiative to secure worker protections, create a health and safety training program, and support the expansion of construction union employment in the remediation industry. A major fight over other provisions had taken place in the House Energy and Commerce Committee. As a result, the bill lacked a consensus that was adequate to make it law. The bill moved to the next committee with jurisdiction, the House Committee on Public Works and Transportation. Rep. Roe became the chair of the committee during the deliberations on H.R. 2817. Mallino worked closely with Roe to include the protections and training that labor sought.

On November 12, 1985, the Committee on Public Works and Transportation submitted its report; it was the last House committee to do so. During the first session of the 99th Congress, other House committees worked on the bill: Energy and Commerce, Ways and Means, Judiciary, Merchant Marine and Fisheries. Committees have specific jurisdictions, which provide power for their chairs. Mallino respected these jurisdictions. The problem was that he was "inserting OSHA into an environmental bill." The Education and Labor committee handled matters involving OSHA, but neither Gaydos nor Mallino wanted that committee to get involved in the Superfund bill. Mallino suggested to Gaydos that after the hearings, letters asserting the Education and Labor Committee's jurisdiction might be exchanged between Rep. Augustus Hawkins (D-CA), Education and Labor chair, and Rep. Howard, Public Works and Transportation chair.

The November 12, 1985, reporting of H.R. 2817 by the House Committee on Public Works and Transportation opened with the letters. Hawkins and Gaydos said that

> Since the Occupational Safety and Health Act is within the exclusive jurisdiction of the Committee on Education and Labor, the [worker protection] provisions thereby fall exclusively within our committee's jurisdiction. In order to preserve and protect this jurisdiction, we respectfully request that you insert a copy of this letter in your committee report on H.R. 2817, acknowledging that we continue to have such jurisdiction. (U.S. Congress. Senate, 1990, vol. 4, pp. 2512-2513)

Howard indicated his agreement.

H.R. 2817 was the first House Superfund reauthorization bill that contained the new protection and training provisions. They appeared in two sections—Section 111 of CERCLA, subsequently H.R. 2817—and were titled "Uses of the Fund." They authorized Superfund to pay the costs of the worker training and education grants, up to $10 million annually for 5 years. (The two sections of CERCLA were section 111(c)(6) which provided funds to support the worker protection activities in Section 301[f].) Section 128 established the worker protection and training provisions, including the training grants program.

The language of Section 128 was specific and represented a substantial departure from what the AFL-CIO Safety and Health Department wanted in terms of OSHA standards. Since 1970, labor had supported the proposal and promulgation of standards through the process established in Section 6 of the OSH Act. Through the provisions of the various Superfund reauthorization bills, labor pressed Congress to mandate an OSHA standard. This fact concerned Hatch, since a Congressional mandate amounted to a change in the scope of the OSH Act. The AFL-CIO, for the most part, had held consistently to the provisions that labor had fought for and won in the OSH Act. It was industry that had vigorously fought to change the OSHA legislation, either directly or through appropriations riders. Now, with a recalcitrant administration, a half-decade of noncooperation and hostility from OSHA, an emergent and dangerous industry, and the allure of job expansion for building trades workers, the AFL-CIO attempted to secure a Congressional mandate for OSHA.

Section 128 included the issuance of a standard, pursuant to Section 6 of the OSH Act. In addition, minimum general requirements addressed the following aspects of hazardous waste operations: site analysis, training, medical surveillance, protective equipment, engineering controls, maximum exposure limits, an informational program, handling, a new technology program, decontamination procedures, and ER. Specific training standards for off-site training (40 hours and a minimum of 3 days of field experience) were set up. Also included were training for supervisors, certification and enforcement of training requirements, and training of ER personnel (broadly defined as "workers who are responsible for responding to hazardous emergency situations who may be exposed to toxic substances in carrying out their responsibilities" (U.S. Congress. Senate, 1990, vol. 4, p. 2736); a deadline for interim regulations (the issuance of interim final rules within 60 days of the enactment of the Superfund legislation); and a grant program. Section 128 listed the grant purposes, the grant program administration, and the eligible grant recipients:

> nonprofit organizations which demonstrate experience in implementing and operating worker health and safety training and education programs and demonstrate the ability to reach and involve in training programs target populations of workers who are or will be engaged in hazardous waste removal or containment or emergency response operations. (U.S. Congress. Senate, 1990, vol. 4, p. 2736)

The bill also stipulated that CERCLA would be amended by the new section.

The 99th Congress was unable to pass the legislation by the end of its first session. On December 5, 1985, the House passed a resolution to substitute H.R. 3852 for H.R. 2817. The new bill was a compromise. Four hours of debate were permitted; amendments were limited. Each of the four committees that had jurisdiction controlled an hour of debate. Only two representatives commented on the worker protection and training provisions in Section 128.

Rep. Thomas Petri (R-WI), a member of the committees on Education and Labor and Public Works and Transportation, raised questions about amending the "OSHA statute by extending its jurisdiction to cover local and state workers" (U.S. Congress. Senate, 1990, vol. 5, p. 4107). Coverage should be extended only through a statutory process, he said, not by regulation, especially since it would have a "potential fiscal impact on all levels of local government" (U.S. Congress. Senate, 1990, vol. 5, p. 4108). Petri also opposed mandating the terms of a regulation and cited the requirement to set maximum levels of exposure.

Rep. Rod Chandler (R-WA) raised the same issues later in the day. Mandating the terms of an OSHA standard was, he said, in "direct contradiction to the OSH Act" (U.S. Congress. Senate, 1990, vol. 5, p. 4343), by circumventing the rulemaking process set forth in Section 6 of the OSH Act. "A Superfund bill is not the appropriate place to amend OSHA," he said (U.S. Congress. Senate, 1990, vol. 5, p. 4343). He honored the agreement to limit amendments, but asked that the conference committee members use the Senate language for this section. These concerns were the ones first voiced by Hatch.

House action continued on the bill until December 16. On December 10, the House agreed to a bill that included the House bill with Senate amendments. It also included additional House amendments. It became H.R. 2005. The final comment on the House floor about Section 128 came from Rep. Gaydos, who said that the section was so important that if it had not been included in the bill, he would have added it as an amendment. He restated that the Committee on Education and Labor and the Subcommittee on Health and Safety maintained jurisdiction over the matter. Although the EPA had responsibility for Superfund site remediation and had established elaborate protection measures for its employees, OSHA had failed to apply them for the protection of remediation workers. Section 128 was "a major step forward in ensuring that those workers handling and being exposed to toxic and hazardous substances at Superfund sites be offered every possible safeguard" (U.S. Congress. Senate, 1990, vol. 5, p. 4356).

The amendments in H.R. 2005 renumbered the sections, and the worker protection requirements became Section 126 and applied to state and local government employees. NIOSH would run the grants program, which would receive $10 million a year for 5 years.[13]

WORKER PROTECTION LANGUAGE THROUGH THE CONFERENCE COMMITTEE

The second session of the 99th Congress convened on January 21, 1986. One major bill that had bipartisan support was Superfund. The taxing authority for the Superfund had expired in September 1985. Until the passage of the act, $198 million in emergency appropriations kept the program active (Barnett, 1994, p. 200). The Senate bill included a broad-based tax, which the House would not accept. Therefore, action on H.R. 2005 remained stalled until summer.

Expansion of OSHA

Though the bill was stalled, various interests were jockeying for different provisions to be included in or removed from the bill. The worker protection and training provisions in H.R. 2005 came under pressure from the Republicans on February 10, when the conference committee received a letter from eight minority members of the House Committee on Education and Labor (Jeffords et al., 1986). They called the expansion of the OSH Act to state and local employees "egregious" and strongly opposed it. They supported the need for an OSHA standard but opposed mandating the terms of a standard. "This specificity effectively denies the public their right to participate in the development of standards in the rulemaking process" established in the OSH Act. They urged that the conference committee adopt the Senate's language.

On March 5, Secretary of Labor William E. Brock sent a letter to Stafford, calling on him to support the administration's opposition to what it saw as objectionable provisions in the Senate and House versions of the worker protection language (Brock, 1986). Brock opposed any "statutory requirement to develop specific health and safety rules." He was willing to accept the Senate provisions over the House language, as a compromise measure to "avoid expanding the scope of the OSH Act." He urged that OSHA be permitted to use its statutory rulemaking process to

> determine the need for, and scope of, regulations. . . . The House language is especially onerous. It not only prejudges the need for a standard, but prescribes detailed specifications. [It] is inconsistent with the OSH Act's requirements that final regulations be based solely on the evidence contained in the public record. (Brock, 1986)

Brock objected to "mandating coverage of state and local employees" and reminded Stafford that a decision required consideration by the authorizing committees in Congress. He opposed the inclusion of worker protection measures in the bill (Brock, 1986).

The administration's attempt to weaken worker protections must have carried some weight. A response was sent on March 5 from the chairs of the House

Committee on Education and Labor and the Health and Safety Subcommittee to Dingell, chair of the House Committee on Energy and Commerce and the conference committee chair (Hawkins & Gaydos, 1986). The letter was copied to Curtis Moore, Stafford's counsel, stating simply, "Curtis—House Demos to the rescue!!" (Maerki, 1986) Hawkins and Gaydos supported the full House language:

> Based upon our experience with the administration of the OSH Act, we know that without such a legislative directive, there may never be an administrative effort to protect employees engaged in toxic waste clean-up. . . . We supported . . . [the] provision . . . with the understanding that it would be accomplished by a free-standing amendment, outside the legislative ambit of the Superfund Act, thereby preserving the jurisdiction of the Committee on Education and Labor over the OSH Act. (Hawkins & Gaydos, 1986)

Hawkins and Gaydos supported the expansion of the standard's provisions to all state and local government employees, since OSHA coverage was already provided to employees in the 25 states and territories with state OSHA plans. They further strengthened their position that they maintained full jurisdiction over worker health and safety in general and specifically in the OSH Act (Hawkins & Gaydos, 1986).

Conference Committee Compromises

By March 18, the committee had agreed on the language for Section 126. Mallino protected most of the language in the House bill. Some compromises were made to satisfy the administration and some Republicans, but the primary ones were that the section would be free standing, not an amendment to CERCLA, and that the funding provision would be established as a use of the Superfund, rather than from the general fund.

The conference committee addressed four remaining issues: public worker protection, the specificity of the language, the requirement for 40 hours of training, and the phasing in of the regulations. The issues were raised by the chief counsel, Jack Clough, who reported a staff recommendation to "require EPA to promulgate a standard identical to the OSHA standard, to be applied to the roughly twenty-five states that have no state OSHA program" (U.S. Congress. Senate, 1986, pp. 00001021606–00001021613). The DOL had accepted the compromise.

Senator Lincoln Chafee (R-RI) assailed the "micro-managing" of the rulemaking process, and cited the requirement of a set number of training hours. Chafee acknowledged an earlier compromise, which required OSHA to address all the elements listed in the legislation but then be permitted to change the standard if doing so was substantiated by the hearing evidence. The compromise said that a challenge could be made. Chafee worried that it would produce a lawsuit against OSHA, tying up resources in a court battle. Clough and Dingell explained that challenges to the proposed rules would be made under the Administrative Procedures Act, as applied by OSHA. Chafee accepted this.

The conference committee's staff recommended that the committee clarify the stipulation for 40 hours of training. The training was to apply only to employees, supervisors, and managers who worked with hazardous substances. The committee agreed to either 40 hours of training or its equivalent. Dingell was receptive if the labor unions agreed, which they did. Discussion defined equivalent training as including what "existing employees might have already received from actual, on-site experience" (U.S. Congress. Senate, 1990, vol. 6, p. 5075).

The last issue was the time allowed for employers to comply with the final OSHA rule. The staff recommended that the interim rules should remain in effect for a full year after the promulgation of the final rule. All agreed.

In the final hours, one more change was made to Section 126. The House language, submitted by Mallino and written primarily by Seminario, had always stated that NIOSH would administer the $10-million training grant program. The language that eventually came out of the committee, however, said that NIEHS would run the program. Of all the compromises and substitutions agreed in the conference committee, this change had the greatest impact (see Appendix 1 for the language of Section 126).

THE SWITCH FROM NIOSH TO NIEHS

Millar, director of NIOSH under Reagan, had worked to block the passage of the High-Risk Occupational Disease Worker Notification and Prevention Bill, which subsequently was not passed by the Congress. Samuels and Mallino were the AFL-CIO staffers who had worked to secure its passage. The vote on the notification bill occurred shortly before the close of the conference committee on H.R. 2005. The effort made on both bills involved Seminario.

Samuels held strong views about NIOSH after experiences with the agency during the 1970s. He had coordinated the IUD's work with the OSHA Environment Network for the passage of the Toxic Substances Control Act (TOSCA) in 1976. He did not want to see NIOSH run programs established under that law. "TOSCA was considered to be an extension of the OSH Act, and the only reason it was not located in the Department of Labor and NIOSH is because we didn't trust NIOSH or OSHA," Samuels said. But this may not have been the only reason; Samuels has said that environmentalists preferred that the EPA administer the law.

Seminario was frustrated with NIOSH during the Reagan years, but saw OSHA and NIOSH as the two agencies that the unions had won with passage of the OSH Act. For her, the long-term strategy of her AFL-CIO department included assigning responsibilities to these agencies and holding them accountable for implementation. Seminario wanted both agencies to see the unions as their primary constituency. Placing a $10-million program at NIOSH might help strengthen NIOSH's relationship with organized labor. In addition, Seminario had worked on these issues with Melius, the HHE director at NIOSH. She knew that he had conducted HHEs in support of the IAFF's pursuit of protection for firefighters involved in HAZMAT ER.

Mallino was involved in both the high-risk worker notification bill and the Superfund effort. He respected Seminario's role. Politically, he needed her support to get the hazardous waste worker protection and training language. "We weren't going to go run a renegade operation, so we brought her in and essentially told her what we wanted to do," he said. Seminario was involved through the entire effort.

However, in the last days of the fight for the worker notification bill, Mallino and Samuels discovered that NIOSH's Millar had spoken at a briefing for corporate lobbyists about how to lobby against the bill. Both Mallino and Samuels were furious about this. They understood that the agency would have to testify in support of the administration's positions. Neither, however, could tolerate support for industry lobbying. NIOSH was "actively lobbying against the bill and we didn't trust or want anything to do with them. They had never given a grant to a union. We knew that all we would be doing was fighting for funding for the universities and for the employers" (Samuels, 1998). They decided to remove NIOSH from its potential position as the agency administering the Superfund training grant program.

Samuels had worked with Dr. David Rall, the director of NIEHS, on asbestos and other issues. Rall had been the chair of an interagency effort on environmental health science, from which he provided government support for Dr. Irving Selikoff and the unions on asbestos issues. Samuels suggested that Mallino write NIEHS into Section 126 and take NIOSH out. Mallino accomplished the change between 10 p.m. and 2 a.m. on the last night of the conferees' sessions. It involved agreement by Reps. Dingell and Roe, as well as Senators Stafford, Metzenbaum, and others. The primary support came from Rep. David Obey (D-WI), who was the ranking member of the House Appropriations Committee's Subcommittee on Labor and Health and Human Services. He was very close to Rall. Obey had helped to write the OSH Act in 1970 and had always, according to Mallino, been one of the major congressional supporters of OSHA and NIOSH. As Mallino saw it,

> David Obey was probably the biggest friend of NIOSH, that an institution ever had. But he was pissed off at NIOSH because of what NIOSH had become under the Reagan administration. He told me that I could tell members of Congress that if NIOSH gets this program, it will never be funded, because he would do everything that he could to de-fund it.

Rep. Roe submitted the change to the committee. The Republican committee members' staff did not oppose it. Mallino accomplished the change without consulting Rall. He informed Obey and asked that Rall be protected in the event of a political attack.

Moore called Rall the next morning to tell him that NIEHS would direct a $10-million-a-year worker training grant program. Rall had his legislative aide contact Melius at NIOSH. Melius then informed Millar, who was neither pleased nor upset. Millar then received a call from Rall, and Millar told him that he could accept what had happened (Melius, 1998; Rall, 1997).

Samuels also called Rall. Rall stated his interest in working with labor on the program. Samuels said that what he wanted for labor was "a fair shake and peer review" (Samuels, 1998). He explained to Rall that he wanted NIEHS to select proposal reviewers who were peers of the people who wrote the unions' proposals. He wanted reviewers who understood worker health education, such as university labor educators and occupational health professionals who were supportive of labor's goals. Dr. Rall agreed with the strategy (Mallino, 1997; Melius, 1998; Rall, 1997; Samuels, 1998; Seminario, 1997).

After Reagan signed the SARA bill, Lautenberg declared in the Senate, "We plan for the worst but insist on the best prevention. That legislation survived the conference. It's an enormous achievement" (U.S. Congress. Senate, 1990, vol. 7, p. 5631). And it had an enormous impact on the WETP.

CONCLUSION

This legislative victory required the resources of multiple social movements, skilled individuals, committed political allies, fiscal resources, an understanding of the politics and events of the moment, and, to some extent, the luck of misfortune. That is, often public fears stemming from industrial disasters could be used to move political action to avert, or appear to avert, similar disasters in the future. The Labor and Environment Coalition won strong community right-to-know and emergency preparedness provisions. Separately, labor won a health and safety training grant program and a mandate on OSHA and the EPA to issue worker health and safety regulations for industries that employed HAZWOPER workers.[14]

After the passage of SARA, labor successfully gained Congressional support to amend the legislation several times, affecting liability, certification, and funding issues. By 1989, it was obvious that $10 million a year was insufficient to support the WETP training program. A key amendment increased the program's funding to $20 million annually.

The successful passage of the worker protection provisions in SARA was coordinated by one of labor's skilled legislative strategists, demonstrating the importance of devoting social movement resources to such efforts. Dave Mallino, Sr., knew how to build a body of evidence to support the case for including worker protection measures in a reauthorized Superfund law. Working mostly with Democratic congressional allies, but also capable of addressing the concerns of Republicans, he maneuvered between the jurisdictional arenas within the House of Representatives and between the House and the Senate. The case was made that the Reagan administration's regulatory agencies had grossly failed to protect workers and that a legislative mandate was not only warranted but appropriate. Legal and ideological challenges had to be overcome, particularly regarding the scope of the OSH Act itself (whether it would apply to public sector workers) and the use of a Congressional mandate to move a regulatory agency.

We see the state being used as an arena for social conflict. Multiple social actors were represented. The lack of opposition from the hazardous waste management industry proved beneficial, and the lack of input from the manufacturing and processing industrial sectors was fortuitous. Mallino coordinated a multiunion effort. The building trades and the firefighters had different objectives, but collaborated to gain what was possible within the political environment. Professionals and scientists were brought in to strengthen labor's case, but interestingly, no testimony was sought from academic occupational health and safety training centers. Almost invisible in the efforts to secure worker protections were the environmentalists. Even though Peg Seminario and the Labor and Environment Coalition engaged in an extended effort to secure community right-to-know and emergency planning measures, the environmental organizations were not recruited to help pass the health and safety protection provisions.

Legislators and their aides took sides largely along party lines except in the Senate, where more liberal Republicans opposed a conservative Republican president in order to preserve environmental protection and demonstrate support of organized labor. Regulatory agency bureaucrats defended the administration's policies in the face of strong criticism. Lower-ranking bureaucrats staked out positions that were neither supportive of their agencies nor supportive of their constituencies, as seen in John Miles's argument that stronger enforcement of existing standards was all that was necessary, betraying both labor, which needed better protection, and employers who opposed enforcement efforts.

The SARA provisions that mandated the OSHA HAZWOPER standard and the WETP may have been the last major national health and safety victory in the mold of the old liberal era. In some ways, they mark the end of the reform era and the beginning of health and safety in the neoliberal era. The philosophical vestiges of the liberal era's (by then broken) social contract between capital and labor called for giving a little something to labor in exchange for dirty work and agreeing to let capital remain in charge of decisions about the means and modes of production and the investment and distribution of wealth. A mom and apple pie argument about protecting workers who put their lives on the line to respond to or remediate hazardous and toxic conditions was defensible. Ten million and then 20 million dollars a year for a training grant program was chump change. Worker protection regulations on an industrial sector whose pricing structures and credibility were based on regulatory compliance were not a particularly difficult pill to swallow.

The provisions, however, ushered in health and safety training in the neoliberal era. Unlike the New Directions training program, which funded activists to be the eyes and ears of OSHA and to mobilize health and safety activists throughout the industrial sectors, SARA would support training for a more limited set of workers and settings. It would frustrate some health and safety activists who didn't want to be pigeon-holed into training that was focused on a standard rather than on developing strategies for gaining the power to create healthy and safe workplaces. But labor was hemorrhaging steadily. Leadership support for health and safety activists and issues had always been inconsistent, depending on specific individuals and sectors, but now many in labor saw holding onto eroding membership and jobs as a much higher priority than any other issues in workers' lives.

APPENDIX 1:
Worker Protection Provisions of SARA

Public Law 99-499, 100 STAT. 1690
99th Congress
Superfund Amendments and Reauthorization Act of 1986 (SARA)
TITLE I
(29 USC 655)
Sec. 126. WORKER PROTECTION STANDARDS.

(a) PROMULGATION.—Within one year after the date of the enactment of this section, the Secretary of Labor shall, pursuant to section 6 of the Occupational Safety and Health Act of 1970, promulgate standards for the health and safety protection of employees engaged in hazardous waste operations.

(b) PROPOSED STANDARDS.—The Secretary of Labor shall issue proposed regulations on such standards which shall include, but need not be limited to, the following worker protection provisions:

(1) SITE ANALYSIS.—Requirements for a formal hazard analysis of the site and development of a site specific plan for worker protection.

(2) TRAINING.—Requirements for contractors to provide initial and routine training of workers before such workers are permitted to engage in hazardous waste operations which would expose them to toxic substances.

(3) MEDICAL SURVEILLANCE.—A program of regular medical examinations, monitoring, and surveillance of workers engaged in hazardous waste operations which would expose them to toxic substances.

(4) PROTECTIVE EQUIPMENT.—Requirements for appropriate personal protective equipment, clothing, and respirators for work in hazardous waste operations.

(5) ENGINEERING CONTROLS.—Requirements for engineering controls concerning the use of equipment and exposure of workers engaged in hazardous waste operations.

(6) MAXIMUM EXPOSURE LIMITS.—Requirements for maximum exposure limitations for workers engaged in hazardous waste operations, including necessary monitoring and assessment procedures.

(7) INFORMATIONAL PROGRAM.—A program to inform workers engaged in hazardous waste operations of the nature and degree of toxic exposure likely as a result of such hazardous waste operations.

(8) HANDLING.—Requirements for the handling, transporting, labeling, and disposing of hazardous wastes.

(9) NEW TECHNOLOGY PROGRAM.—A program for the introduction of new equipment or technologies that will maintain worker protections.

(10) DECONTAMINATION PROCEDURES.—Procedures for decontamination.

(11) EMERGENCY RESPONSE.—Requirements for emergency responses and protection of workers engaged in hazardous waste operations.

(c) FINAL REGULATIONS.—Final regulations under subsection (a) shall take effect one year after the date they are promulgated. In promulgating final regulations on standards under subsection (a), the Secretary of Labor shall include each of the provisions listed in paragraphs (1) through (11) of subsection (b) unless the Secretary determines that the evidence in the public record considered as a whole does not support inclusion of any such provisions.

(d) SPECIFIC TRAINING STANDARDS.—

(1) OFFSITE INSTRUCTION; FIELD EXPERIENCE.—Standards promulgated under subsection (a) shall include training standards requiring that general site workers (such as equipment operators, general laborers, and other supervised personnel) engaged in hazardous substance removal or other activities which

expose or potentially expose such workers to hazardous substances receive a minimum of 40 hours of initial instruction off the site, and a minimum of three days of actual field experience under the direct supervision of a trained, experienced supervisor at the time of assignment. The requirements of the preceding sentence shall not apply to any general site worker who has received the equivalent of such training. Workers who may be exposed to unique or special hazards shall be provided additional training.

(2) TRAINING OF SUPERVISORS.—Standards promulgated under subsection (a) shall include training standards requiring that onsite managers and supervisors directly responsible for the hazardous waste operations (such as foremen) receive the same training as general site workers set forth in paragraph (1) of this subsection and at least eight additional hours of specialized training on managing hazardous waste operations. The requirements of the preceding sentence shall not apply to any person who has received the equivalent of such training.

(3) CERTIFICATION; ENFORCEMENT.—Such training standards shall contain provisions for certifying that general site workers, onsite managers, and supervisors have received the specified training and shall prohibit any individual who has not received the specified training from engaging in hazardous waste operations covered by the standard. The certification procedures shall be no less comprehensive than those adopted by the Environmental Protection Agency in its Model Accreditation Plan for Asbestos Abatement Training as required under the Asbestos Hazard Emergency Response Act of 1986.

(4) TRAINING OF EMERGENCY RESPONSE PERSONNEL.—Such training standards shall set forth requirements for the training of workers who are responsible for responding to hazardous emergency situations who may be exposed to toxic substances in carrying out their responsibilities.

(e) INTERIM REGULATIONS—The Secretary of Labor shall issue interim final regulations under this section within 60 days after the enactment of this section which shall provide no less protection under this section for workers employed by contractors and emergency response workers than the protections contained in the Environmental Protection Agency Manual (1981) "Health and Safety Requirements for Employees Engaged in Field Activities" and existing standards under the Occupational Safety and Health Act of 1970 found in subpart C of part 1926 of title 29 of the Code of Federal Regulations. Such interim final regulations shall take effect upon issuance and shall apply until final regulations become effective under subsection (c).

(f) COVERAGE OF CERTAIN STATE AND LOCAL EMPLOYEES.—Not later than 90 days after the promulgation of final regulations under subsection (a), the Administrator shall promulgate standards identical to those promulgated by the Secretary of Labor under subsection (a). Standards promulgated under this subsection shall apply to employees of State and local governments in each State which does not have in effect an approved State plan under section 18 of the Occupational Safety and Health act of 1970 providing for standards for the health and safety protection of employees engaged in hazardous waste operations.

(g) GRANT PROGRAM.—

(1) GRANT PURPOSES.—Grants for the training and education of workers who are or may be engaged in activities related to hazardous waste removal or containment or emergency response may be made under this subsection.

(2) ADMINISTRATION.—Grants under this subsection shall be administered by the National Institute of Environmental Health Sciences.

(3) GRANT RECIPIENTS.—Grants shall be awarded to nonprofit organizations which demonstrate experience in implementing and operating worker health and safety training and education programs and demonstrate the ability to reach and involve in training programs target populations of workers who are or will be engaged in hazardous waste removal or containment or emergency response operations.

ENDNOTES

1. Sheldon Samuels explained to me what happens when representatives of the AFL-CIO Industrial Union Department (IUD) lobby Congress. "We'd go up on the Hill and they'd say, IUD, but who do you represent besides yourself? That was always the question to every department and to the AFL-CIO itself, because the people on the Hill understand the labor movement. They understand that very often the AFL-CIO and its departments do not speak for the unions because labor on almost every issue splits. That's the nature of the labor movement. And we were able to say we have the support and we'd name the unions and we'd always be able to say we've got support."
2. U.S. Congress. Senate, 1990. The history of SARA's passage is summarized from the preface, vol. 1., pp. v-vii.
3. The effort in the 99th Congress was initiated by the Senate Environment and Public Works Committee, which reported S. 51 on March 7, 1985. That bill was passed by the Senate on September 26, 1985. (It became H.R. 2005 due to a constitutional requirement that tax bills originate in the House [U.S. Congress. Senate, 1990, vol. 1, p. v].) In the House, the bill was H.R. 2817, approved by the Energy and Commerce Committee. This bill was amended by several other committees and the final language was set forth in a compromise bill, H.R. 3852, which was passed on December 10, 1985, and then inserted into the Senate-passed bill, H.R. 2005.
4. This occurred in late 1984 or early 1985. The information was collected through interviews. No interviewee could remember exact dates and no paper documentation was discovered.
5. These explanations were provided by key informants for this study: Seminario, Mallino, Samuels, and Elisburg.
6. It may be that at least some industrial unions assumed that an IUD effort would duly represent their efforts, and therefore, they didn't need to allocate resources to the effort. The possibility was suggested in a discussion with Rafael Moure, who was an industrial hygienist with OCAW when Mallino worked on these issues through the IUD.
7. Much of the information in this section was obtained in an interview with Weisberg.
8. The Council on Economic Priorities is a New York–based nonprofit organization established to research and disseminate unbiased information on the practices of U.S. corporations.
9. Other contractors supported strong health and safety measures but may have called for Superfund sites to be exempt from the requirement to pay prevailing wages, under the Davis-Bacon Act. William Wallace, representing the American Consulting Engineers Council (and was the director for hazardous and solid wastes, CH2M Hill), presented

six points the council wanted Congress to address in Superfund reauthorization. The council called for "the entire pool of qualified response contractors [to] be eligible to compete for contracts" (U.S. Congress. House of Representatives, 1985b, p. 1699).

10. Duffy cited a 1980 incident in Somerville, Massachusetts, in which firefighters followed guidelines for responses to releases of phosphorous trichloride. Because they had not received appropriate training, they did not know that when the guidelines called for the application of copious amounts of water, it meant much more water than for a normal fire. The result was the formation of a large acid cloud (U.S. Congress. House of Representatives, 1985a, pp. 86-87).
11. Ken Allen, in an interview with the author, said that hazardous waste management and hazardous waste remediation are two separate industries, at least they were in the late 1990s. Some other people I interviewed have agreed with him, while others have considered hazardous waste remediation as a segment of the hazardous waste management industry. Allen, in his role of working with construction contractors to bid on remediation work, understands the separation between the industries as existing because of the difference in the employers/companies conducting the remediation work.
12. Sen. Lautenberg (D-NJ) was on the committee. He supported the IAFF. Because Richard Duffy was from New Jersey, he gave the senator information about every HAZMAT incident to which NJ firefighters had responded. Lautenberg's staff gave strong support, largely due to their relationship with Duffy and the IAFF (interview with Richard Duffy).
13. Section 21 of the OSH Act established provisions for NIOSH and OSHA to support training activities of professionals, workers, employers, and agency staff. The act permits NIOSH to provide grants for training but is not clear as to whether NIOSH-funded training should be limited to professionals. (NIOSH policy is that it can support worker training programs.) The act does not state that OSHA can award training grants but does say that the agency can "provide" for the establishment of training programs. OSHA has used Section 21(c) as the authority for its training grants programs.
14. SARA, Section 126 (g) (2), required NIEHS to establish and administer a national training grants program. Its task was managing "grants for the training and education of workers who are or may be engaged in activities related to hazardous waste removal or containment or emergency response." The law also ordered OSHA to develop and promulgate a standard to protect workers in hazardous waste operations and ER. OSHA was obligated to address 11 worker protection provisions, including worker training. OSHA published interim regulations on December 19, 1986 (Hazardous Waste Operations and Emergency Response; Interim Final Rule, Fed. Reg. 51: 45654-45675), and a proposed final rule on August 10, 1987 (Hazardous Waste Operations and Emergency Response; Notice of Proposed Rulemaking and Public Hearings, Fed. Reg: 29620-29654). The rule's training requirements became the basis for the formulations on training that were later developed by NIEHS awardees.

REFERENCES

Barnett, H. C. (1994). *Toxic Debts and the Superfund Dilemma.* Chapel Hill: University of North Carolina Press.

Brock, W. E. S., U.S. DOL. (1986). Letter to Robert T. Stafford, chairman, Senate Committee on Environment and Public Works. Request for support on views regarding Superfund reauthorization provisions for worker protection (March 5). From files of Curtis Moore, former Republican counsel to the Senate Committee on Environment and Public Works.

Duffy, R. (1997). Interview by author, tape recording, Washington, DC (December 9).

Hawkins, A. F., & Gaydos, J. M. (1986). Letter to Rep. John D. Dingell (copied to J. J. Howard, J. J. Florio, & R. A. Roe). Response to administration criticisms of Section 128, H.R. 2817, and request for full support of the House language (March 5). From files of Curtis Moore, former Republican counsel to the Senate Committee on Environment and Public Works.

Iowa Laborers' Heavy Highway Training Fund. (1980). *Toxic and Hazardous Waste: Handling, Control, Removal and Disposal. A Resource and Information Manual.* Des Moines: Iowa Laborers' Heavy Highway Training Fund.

Jeffords, J. M., Goodling, W. F., Petri, T. E., Roukema, M., Chandler, R., Tauke, T. J., et al. (1986). Letter to Superfund conferees regarding Section 126, H.R. 2005 (February 10). From files of Curtis Moore, former Republican counsel to the Senate Committee on Environment and Public Works.

Maerki, V. (1986). Memo to Curtis Moore (March 7). From files of Curtis Moore, former Republican counsel to the Senate Committee on Environment and Public Works.

Mallino, D., Sr. (1997). Interview by author, tape recording, Washington, DC (December 10).

Melius, D. J. (1998). Melius, Dr. James, former director of the NIOSH Health Hazard Evaluation Division. Telephone interview by author, notes (February 18).

NIEHS. (1997). History Panel at Ten Year Anniversary WETP awardees meeting, author's audio recording (October 20). NIEHS Offices, Research Triangle Park (RTP), NC.

Rall, D. (1997). Interview by author, Washington, DC (December 10).

Samuels, S. (1998). Interview by author, tape recording, Solomon's Is., MD (January 16).

Seminario, M. (1997). Interview by author, tape recording, Washington, DC (December 10).

U.S. Congress. House of Representatives. (1985a). Committee on Government Operations. Subcommittee on Employment and Housing. *Hearings: OSHA and Hazardous Waste Sites.* 1st sess., 99th Congress. March 27. Washington, DC: GPO.

U.S. Congress. House of Representatives. (1985b). Committee on Education and Labor. Subcommittee on Health and Safety. *OSHA Oversight—Worker Protection at Superfund Sites.* 99th Congress, 1st sess. May. Washington, DC: GPO.

U.S. Congress. House of Representatives. (1985c). Committee on Public Works and Transportation, Subcommittee on Water Resources. *Reauthorization of Superfund.* 1st sess., 99th Congress. March 27. Washington, DC: GPO.

U.S. Congress. House of Representatives. (1985d). Committee on Education and Labor. Subcommittee on Health and Safety. *Worker Health and Safety in the Manufacture and Use of Toxic and Hazardous Substances.* 1st sess., 99th Congress. April 16. Washington, DC: GPO.

U.S. Congress. House of Representatives. (1985e). *OSHA's Failure to Protect the Health and Safety of Workers at Hazardous Waste Sites.* Ninth Report by the Committee on Government Operations (No. 99-140). 1st sess., 99th Congress. May 21. Washington, DC: GPO.

U.S. Congress. Senate. (1986). Committee on Environment and Public Works. Superfund Improvement Act, *Hearings Before the Committee on Environment and Public Works, House-Senate Conference on H.R. 2005.* March 1986. Alexandria, VA: Court Reporting Services, Inc.

U.S. Congress. Senate. (1990). *A Legislative History of the Superfund Amendments and Reauthorization Act of 1986, Public Law 99-499.* Vols. 1-7. Washington, DC: GPO.

Weisberg, S. (1998). Telephone interview by author (April 3).

CHAPTER 4

A Fair Shake and Peer Review

Placing the training program in NIEHS under the direction of David Rall created an opportunity to establish a program unencumbered by the historical efforts of industry and conservative politicians to minimize the capacity of OSHA and NIOSH to protect workers. Certainly the grant proposal review and administrative procedures of the National Institutes of Health (NIH) bureaucracy could be used to redirect the program from the goals and purposes intended by its labor authors. The program's appointed leaders, however, were scientists and professionals allied with and part of the workers' health and safety movement. They had already worked with labor and were familiar with its health and safety strategies and with both the successes and the demise of the OSHA New Directions program, the programmatic predecessor to the WETP. They sought to craft a program that could financially support the movement while advancing high-quality worker health education and training.

The breadth of activities supported by the OSHA New Directions program could not be replicated by a training grant program limited to hazardous waste operations and emergency response. Many in the movement were reluctant to submit a proposal to the new program, concerned by the likely limits of its scope. Yet, in an economy rooted in the production and use of synthetic chemicals, most industrial sectors employed workers with potential for exposure to hazardous waste materials. Only limited worker-oriented health and safety training was available for that substantial and diverse workforce. The NIEHS representatives met with health and safety movement leaders in unions and in academia to encourage them to apply for training grants. They were keenly aware that many health and safety movement organizations were struggling due to the loss of OSHA New Directions funds. They realized that this financial and political loss meant that at least for the moment the movement would need to accept a limited scope of activity. They believed, though, that the new program could be used to create a model form of training that would greatly advance all workplace health and safety training.

The NIEHS leadership saw that organized labor and the health and safety movement had been unprepared and unable to resist the Reagan administration's efforts to eliminate the OSHA New Directions program's funding for labor. They were determined to organize a program that created a national constituency that could resist future efforts to destroy the new program's capacity to support labor. They sought to set up a worker health education intervention that would create new standards of quality, content, and performance for worker health and safety training. Also, they sought to establish a programmatic foundation for an integrated and cohesive network within the U.S. health and safety movement, capable of defending the program against efforts to weaken or end it.

NIEHS STARTS A TRAINING PROGRAM[1]

NIEHS was founded in November 1966 as the Division of Environmental Health Sciences of the National Institutes of Health (NIH), which at that time was part of the federal Department of Health, Education, and Welfare (HEW). In January 1969, the division was elevated to the status of a national institute. NIEHS is a toxicology research agency that conducts biomedical research to promote an understanding of human disease mechanisms. The institute investigated environmental contaminants, including polychlorinated biphenyls (PCBs), polybrominated biphenyls (PBBs), heavy metals, and others. Its research included studies of target organs and the effects of contaminants on them. That work was part of an intramural research program. Simultaneously, the agency maintained an extramural research program, which supported work by scientists at U.S. colleges and universities, as well as environmental health centers, and training and career development programs (NIEHS, 1986b).

The National Toxicology Program (NTP) was based in NIEHS to coordinate toxicological studies within HEW. The executive council of the NTP consisted of administrators from regulatory agencies, including the EPA, OSHA, the Food and Drug Administration (FDA), and the Consumer Products Safety Commission. The executive council helped to ensure that all NTP activities related to the needs of the regulatory agencies. Thus, NIEHS began a limited involvement in occupational health issues.

Dr. David P. Rall, who had worked previously with the AFL-CIO, was appointed the agency's director in 1971, replacing Dr. Paul Kotin. Rall was the director of NIEHS when the WETP arrived there. He accepted responsibility for the training program, and viewed it as fitting with NIEHS's mission. NIEHS already gave grants to train scientists. Rall did not believe that training workers would be more difficult, only more costly (Rall, 1997).

Discussions With Representatives of Labor

For the most part, labor had not worked with NIEHS before, nor had many unions worked with Rall. Samuels and Rall had common experience, but not in such a way as to provide an experiential basis for understanding how the agency would manage the training program. Rall was contacted early by labor representatives to discuss how the program would be developed and run. Samuels indicated that he wanted the NIH peer review process applied to the application process, but that reviewers should represent the interests of labor. He urged that the peer review team be composed of people who were strong supporters of labor-based health and safety training programs, people who would understand what the unions would propose. In Samuels's words, they wanted, "a fair shake and peer review" (Samuels, 1998).[2] In addition, the agency was asked to establish the internal competence necessary to run the program, not as a research program, but as it was outlined in SARA (Seminario, 1997).

Most of the unions had never worked with NIEHS. The IAFF had a strong relationship with NIOSH through Dr. Melius on health and safety issues. The AFL-CIO Safety and Health Department also had a stronger relationship with NIOSH than with NIEHS. The AFL-CIO representatives sought assurances of support and cooperation from Rall, which he gave them. They also said that since they had coordinated the effort to pass Section 126 of SARA, they expected that a significant portion of the funding would go to unions.

Section 126 of SARA was written so that labor unions would be in a strong position as candidates for its funding. The section states that

> Grants shall be awarded to nonprofit organizations which demonstrate experience in implementing and operating worker health and safety training and education programs and demonstrate the ability to reach and involve in training programs target populations of workers who are or will be engaged in hazardous waste removal or containment or emergency response operations. (SARA, Section 126)

Both the unions and Congress expected rapid implementation; Rall had to find someone to run the program. Because of his public health beliefs and the imperative that the program should address the needs of those who had secured the legislation, he wanted someone with whom he could work closely and who was sympathetic to the needs of organized labor. He recruited Dr. John Dement, initially on a 90-day assignment. Dement directed NIEHS's internal health and safety programs. He was an officer in the Public Health Service and had worked at NIOSH before being assigned to NIEHS.

In addition to program management, NIEHS had to arrange grants, contracts, and financial management. Dr. Anne Sassaman had been recruited to NIEHS from the NIH Heart, Lung, and Blood Institute in Bethesda, Maryland, in July 1986 to direct the grant funding programs under SARA for which the agency would be responsible. Sassaman may have been recruited by Rall in anticipation of another program that was included in the Superfund reauthorization—the Superfund Basic Research Program. This was planned as a grant program that would fund research at universities, medical schools, and schools of public health on the human health impacts of uncontrolled hazardous waste sites. After SARA passed, Sassaman had only 10 months to solicit proposals and distribute funds to both the basic research and the worker training programs.

Carol Matheny was later recruited to the WETP from the National Institute for Arthritis (NIA), where she served as a biomedical research grants management specialist. With experience as an assistant administrative officer at the NIA, Matheny was "the only senior specialist with enough experience to handle the new program" (Matheny, 1998). She was instructed to outline budgetary and administrative guidelines. Her duties were to assess the financial management and evaluation systems for the grantees, as well as assist in planning, development, and implementation, both at NIEHS and for the grantees. She came into the program "cursing" (Matheny, 1998). Matheny's and Sassaman's support was invaluable in dealing with union awardees who had limited federal grant experience.

Review of Existing Worker Training Programs

Dr. Dement was familiar with OSHA's New Directions health and safety training and with the public health literature on this kind of training. He knew professionals, scientists, academics, and labor representatives in the health and safety movement. He knew how he wanted to organize a health and safety training grants program and he discussed ideas with experts in the field.

Dr. Eula Bingham had initiated New Directions during her tenure as director of OSHA. She, Rall, and Dement had talked about the organization of a national health and safety training program. An early concern of Dement's was that New Directions had not been organized in a way that fostered cohesiveness among its awardees. Dement and others believed that a lesson to be learned from New Directions was that it had failed to build an adequate constituency for both the agency and the program. New Directions grants were structured so that funding would end for most awardees after 3 years, by which time awardees were expected to have developed the internal competency to continue their health and safety programs without federal funding. As a result, in the view of the NIEHS strategists, when awardees completed their funding cycle, they did not necessarily perceive themselves as constituents of OSHA.

Aware of the changing power of labor in national politics and the impact of the deregulation efforts of the Reagan administration, Dement and others believed that a training grants program could and should be organized to promote greater support from and cohesiveness among its recipients. Dement and others also wanted to maintain closer links with other federal agencies.

Dement talked with health and safety educators in university-based labor education programs. Those programs had successfully used New Directions to establish health and safety education for workers and unions. Dement talked with them to determine whether a role for them in the WETP was appropriate. He and Rall worried about the ability of the unions to address many of the more technical health and safety issues related to hazardous waste and ER. They were concerned, too, about building NIH and NIEHS support for the program and believed that this support would be more likely if the awardees represented a mixture of unions and university programs, rather than only unions.

Dement communicated with health and safety directors and personnel at some unions that would likely be involved. He spoke with Margaret Seminario, for one. Seminario had decided that those unions eligible for the program would be able to represent their needs and interests without her continuing support. From that point on, her participation in the program was largely peripheral.

Another segment of the labor movement that was potentially eligible to participate was the network of occupational safety and health advocacy organizations that had been created around the country since the mid-1970s. These organizations were (and are) known as COSH groups—coalitions, committees, or councils on occupational safety and health. The leadership communicated with COSH representatives as well.

Dement and Rall conferred with those federal agencies that were involved in any way in worker health and safety training. NIOSH, the EPA, OSHA, FEMA, and the Agency for Toxic Substances and Disease Registry (ATSDR) participated.

Dement and Rall also met with some industry representatives (Dement, 1987; Dement & Vandermeer, 1987).

Establishing the Program

After doing this groundwork, Dement and Rall began to shape the program as they would present it in the request for applications (RFA). It would address the needs of the building trades and the IAFF. It would build on earlier federal support for health and safety training as established in OSHA's New Directions program. Also, it would use the successful practices and processes that NIH and NIEHS had developed to support successful grant programs, for example, the NIH process for peer review of proposals, and the NIEHS and NIH emphasis on building program cohesiveness (Lange, 1997).

Rall confronted two immediate obstacles. The Office of Management and Budget (OMB) stated that $10 million was an excessive amount for training workers who, OMB believed, should have already been trained by their employers. The OMB examiner finally accepted the need for training, with an assurance from Rall that all workers would be trained within 5 years (Rall, 1997). The second obstacle was the EPA, which opposed the requirement to "pass through" Superfund monies for distribution to NIEHS for the WETP. The EPA attempted to achieve a legislative change that would reestablish the program at the EPA. Rall's intervention helped to block this tactic. Representatives of the IUD and the Laborers Union talked with EPA officials about funding NIEHS for the training program and OSHA for the development of the interim standard as well as the proposed rule. They may also have discussed with EPA officials the issue of keeping the WETP at NIEHS. (Elisburg, 1998; Rall, 1997; Samuels, 1998).

Soliciting Comments

On December 15, 1986, Dement distributed a draft description of the NIEHS training grants program to potentially interested parties. The cover letter stressed the language of Section 126 of SARA about grant recipients: they had to be nonprofit organizations that could demonstrate the ability to access the target worker populations and that had experience running worker health and safety training programs. The cover letter also gave notice of a public meeting on January 12, 1987, to which interested parties could provide oral and written comments (NIEHS, 1986a).

The notice of the meeting was published in the U.S. Federal Register on December 19. It explained the meeting and the guidelines for oral presentations to NIEHS, and said that written documentation could be left with NIEHS staff. Written comments were accepted through January 18. The notice described the proposed NIEHS program and listed the targeted populations as workers doing the following types of work:

- Waste handling and processing at active and inactive hazardous substance treatment, storage and disposal facilities.
- Cleanup, removal, containment or remedial actions at waste sites.
- Hazardous substance ER.

- Hazardous substance disposal, site risk assessment and investigation, remedial actions or cleanup by state and local personnel.
- Transportation of hazardous wastes. (51 Federal Register, 1986a, p. 45556)

The notice stated that the training programs would satisfy the requirements to be established by OSHA in its rulemaking process. NIEHS encouraged single applications from multiple nonprofit organizations "to maximize worker group coverage, enhance the effectiveness of training, and bring together appropriate academic disciplines and talents." The notice said that NIEHS recognized the need "for close coordination between grantees, governmental agencies and other training providers in developing training curricula" (51 Federal Register, 1986a, p. 45558). NIEHS planned to hold a 3-day meeting soon after the awarding of grants. That meeting was viewed as critical by Dement, Rall, and others who viewed the demise of New Directions as due at least partially to its failure to build a constituency for the agency and the program. NIEHS intended to structure the WETP in such a way as to increase the potential for constituency building as a vehicle for protecting the program from future attacks.

The notice listed seven criteria under the heading, "Characteristics of Hazardous Waste Worker Training Programs." These were as follows:

- Demonstrated ability to identify, describe, access and train target populations . . .
- Past success in development and implementation of training . . .
- An experienced program director . . .
- Sufficient program staff with demonstrated training experience . . . Appropriate technical expertise including but not limited to toxicology and industrial hygiene.
- Facilities and equipment [for] . . . training activities, including hands-on instruction.
- A specific plan for preparing [a] course curriculum, distributing course materials, conducting direct worker training, and conducting program evaluations.
- A Board of Advisors . . . representing user populations, labor, industry, governmental agencies, academic institutions or professional associations with interest and expertise in worker training and hazardous waste operations. The board [was to] meet regularly to evaluate training activities and [would] provide advice to the Program Director. (51 Federal Register, 1986a, p. 45558)[3]

The criteria established the types of programs that would be supported under the NIEHS umbrella. They reflected the guidance that Dement and Rall had been given in their talks with individuals and organizations in labor, government, and worker health and safety education. The acknowledgment of the need for strong programmatic leadership and staffing recognized the difficulty that awardees would face in developing curricula and training for workers in an industry only just then emerging, an industry in which the specific hazards were not yet fully known. The criteria also acknowledged that the programs required sophisticated technical and scientific support, since the nature and health and safety impacts of many chemical components of hazardous wastes were far from known and not well understood. Matters were even more complicated because of the potential for diverse mixtures of chemicals at waste sites, which many in the field labeled "chemical soup."

Finally, the notice proposed the criteria for the review of submitted applications. At this point, all matters were open to comment and change. The criteria presented in the notice did, however, represent the program structure and process deemed most appropriate and workable by Rall and Dement after consultation with multiple parties. The detailed and specific nature of the proposal, despite the fact that it had been prepared in such a short time, revealed the expertise that Dement brought to the program.

The terms of the notice showed how the placement of the program at NIEHS influenced its development. Although the content of the notice reflected the series of discussions held by Dement and Rall, the programmatic processes set forth in the notice also directly reflected NIH operations and priorities. Because NIH did not have "standing regulations coverage for the new grants under section 126" (Peart, 1987), the WETP would be different from other NIEHS programs, and some adjustments to U.S. Public Health Service (PHS) procedures were required, as evidenced by specific program regulations.

The public meeting to discuss the WETP was held on January 12, 1987; its conveners described the background and the plans for moving forward and requested comments from interested parties. The agenda included presentations by Rall; Thomas Seymour, director of the Office of Fire Protection Engineering and Safety Standards at OSHA; and representatives from the EPA, FEMA, ATSDR, and NIOSH. Dement presented an overview of the program, with plans, priorities, and schedules. Public discussion took up the afternoon, after which Sassaman closed the meeting.[4]

Seymour discussed the interim rule for hazardous waste operations and ER, which OSHA had issued on December 19 and which was to become effective on March 16, 1987. OSHA wanted uniform national training developed, tied to the final rule that would be proposed in 12 months, and a procedure for certification of trained workers.

Tom Sell of the EPA described the training carried out by the EPA under RCRA, CERCLA, and SARA. He acknowledged that the EPA had given only limited worker training to date, but said it did offer hazardous materials (HAZMAT) incidents training with an extensive curriculum and course offerings. Representatives of other federal agencies discussed their involvement.

Dement reviewed the program description. Two types of grants would be offered: planning and program. Program grants would last for 5 years, with annual reapplication and renewal required. Proposals had to include hands-on and demonstration aspects of training. NIEHS would require and facilitate coordination and sharing among the grantees. Dement talked about the upcoming meeting in North Carolina, after the issuing of awards, for the purpose of reaching agreement on curriculum content, and said an annual grantees meeting would be required. He went over the grant application review process. A review for technical merit would be conducted by an ad hoc committee without government officials. A second review panel would include government and public representatives, who would look at relevance and program coordination. Applications were due on May 1 and awards would be made in late September 1987.

The discussion clarified certain issues. They included target populations, specifying that RCRA TSDF and private facility ER workers were covered; funding for capital equipment purchases; confirmation that the collection of fees would be permitted as long as the fees were used to support the awardees' training; the potential need for medical exams before training; insurance for trainers; and the payment of stipends for workers, travel, and related expenses.

TARGET POPULATIONS AND THE INITIAL AWARDS

The January 12 meeting made one thing very clear to the representatives of labor who had worked to gain the Congressional mandate for the program: university programs were going to present significant competition. As Richard Duffy of the IAFF said, "I, probably on more than one occasion during that meeting and afterwards, said 'Hey, this wasn't your gig. We pushed this through ourselves.' I think everybody thought, 'Why did we put it in NIEHS?'" This attitude became a point of conflict in the program.

OSHA had issued an interim final rule for Hazardous Waste Operations and Emergency Response (51 Federal Register, 1986b). In developing the regulation, OSHA used various materials as a basis, including the EPA's health and safety manual for its employees engaged in field activities (which is cited in Section 126 of SARA), existing OSHA standards, and the four-agency *Occupational Safety and Health Guidance Manual for Hazardous Waste Site Activities*. In the preamble to the interim rule, OSHA said that Congress intended a standard with "broad scope and application" (51 Federal Register, 1986b, p. 45655). The agency justified its action: "This interpretation is reinforced because SARA is a freestanding statutory provision and not an amendment to CERCLA. The clear Congressional intent then is to provide protection to employees whenever they deal with hazardous wastes" (51 Federal Register, 1986b, p. 45655). Nevertheless, OSHA decided to exclude workers employed at small-quantity generator facilities, that is, employers who had less than 90 days of hazardous waste accumulation.[5]

NIEHS chose to follow OSHA's lead in determining appropriate target populations. One health and safety professional with whom Dement and Rall had early discussions was Franklin Mirer, director of health and safety for the United Auto Workers (UAW). Mirer argued against NIEHS's exclusion of small-quantity generators. "I violently disagreed with them," he said (Mirer, 1998). OSHA had excluded hazardous waste materials from coverage under its hazard communication standard. With the exclusion from coverage of small-quantity generators, many workers regularly exposed to hazardous wastes would get no training at all. Mirer pointed to examples of industrial workers with significant hazardous waste exposures who would be excluded from the training. One example was workers who pumped sludge from the bottom of waste pits. Mirer did not prevail at this time and NIEHS did not broaden its proposed target populations.

Dement and Rall encountered opposition to any expansion of the target populations to include a broad range of industrial workers. The union representatives who had worked to achieve the OSHA standard and the NIEHS training program had intended their efforts to primarily address workers engaged in hazardous waste operations such as remediation, treatment, storage, disposal, transportation, and ER at hazardous waste sites and major HAZMAT incidents. They believed that $10 million would be adequate to support a training effort. By no means did the representatives discount the health and safety needs of workers in other industrial settings, but they had to safeguard the interests of the workers for whom they had won the protections. As Dement later said, "The construction trades didn't want to see the money used for generator sites. That is an astronomical expansion of the program, theoretically. Almost any industrial site generates hazardous waste" (Dement, 1997).

Labor representatives were alarmed by the number of university programs represented at the public meeting. Some feared that NIEHS would provide more funds to universities than labor thought appropriate to the building of what it viewed as its natural constituency (Dement, 1997; Duffy, 1997; Elisburg, 1997; Seminario, 1997). Section 126(g)(3) had been carefully worded by the labor representatives involved in securing worker protections in SARA so that labor unions would be the most qualified applicants. The term "nonprofit" and the phrase "demonstrate the ability to reach and involve . . . target populations of workers" were construed to define unions as the most appropriate grant recipients. "It wasn't necessarily viewed that it was going to be exclusively unions," Seminario said, "but there was a real sense that it had to be put in the hands of people who could actually reach folks."

Letters of Intent, Applications, and Peer Review

NIEHS published a program announcement on February 17, 1987, along with a request for applications. Approximately 145 letters of intent were received. Seventy-eight grant applications were submitted. Two review teams were organized, made up of representatives of labor, industry, academia, government, occupational medicine clinics, and ER organizations. Some independent professionals were included. The technical expertise of committee members included toxicology, industrial hygiene, labor education, and hazardous waste management. Professionals and scientists friendly to labor made up approximately half of the members of each committee. The committees were chaired by Dr. Frank Goldsmith, dean of the School for Labor Studies, Empire State College-SUNY, and Dr. James Melius, who by then had moved to New York State's Department of Health. The two vice chairmen were Dr. Knut Ringen of the National Cancer Institute and Basil Whiting, formerly with the Ford Foundation and OSHA's New Directions (NIEHS, 1987c). Dement and Melius worked to develop the final review criteria. Emphasis was placed on supporting the acceptability of the unions' proposals (Melius, 1998). Fifty applications were reviewed; 22 of them were recommended for approval and assigned priority scores based on established criteria for assessing technical merit.[6]

Reviewers paid attention to the ways in which each proposal related hazardous waste operations and ER activities to the criteria. Other important considerations included the extent of an organization's prior experience in training workers, and the organization's prior delivery and development of hands-on technical worker training. Reviewers also considered the appropriateness of the proposed ratio of staff to students.

The criteria, when considered by a team strongly supportive of labor-based worker health and safety training, enabled a fair assessment to be made of proposals submitted by unions. The criteria also gave NIEHS measures for program quality and excellence, in keeping with the NIH grant programs' well-established reputation for excellence (Dement, 1997; Dobbin, 1997).

The Awards

The second-level review of the 22 recommended applications resulted in the selection of 11 applications, which received awards on September 15, 1987. The secondary review criteria were as follows: (1) quality of the application, based on priority scores; (2) worker population coverage; and (3) geographic coverage, in an attempt to provide training for all target populations in all EPA regions (NIEHS, 1987a). Of the 11 funded applications, 5 were targeted to specific populations. Five university consortia, each consisting of multiple organizations, won awards. Consortia received awards and were encouraged for three primary reasons: (1) to minimize the duplication of curriculum development efforts; (2) to expand the geographic and worker population coverage; and (3) to reduce grant administrative costs (Dement & Vandermeer, 1987). All 11 awards were issued as program grants on the evidence that sufficient expertise and capacity existed for full programs across the nation addressing all target populations.

These organizations, representing more than 40 institutions, obtained grants:

1. The International Association of Fire Fighters. Target populations: ER personnel and first responders nationwide.
2. The International Chemical Workers Union. Target populations: industrial fire brigades and hazardous waste treatment, storage, and disposal facility workers. The awardee was a consortium that included the United Steel Workers of America, the University of Cincinnati, and the Greater Cincinnati Occupational Health Center.
3. The International Union of Operating Engineers. Target population: operating engineers in hazardous waste operations (heavy equipment operators in construction).
4. The Laborers-AGC Education and Training Fund. Target population: laborers engaged in hazardous waste cleanup. (This was the only joint labor-management trust fund that received an award.)
5. The Oil, Chemical and Atomic Workers Union. Target populations: hazardous waste treatment, storage, and disposal workers.
6. The Seattle Fire Department. Target populations: ER personnel and first responders. The Washington State Fire Training Service was a participant in this award.
7. The University of Alabama at Birmingham, Center for Labor Education and Research. Target populations: heavy equipment operators, laborers, waste transportation workers, and government personnel involved at hazardous waste sites. The Deep South Educational Resource Center was a participant in this award.

8. The University of California at Los Angeles (UCLA), Institute of Industrial Relations, Labor Occupational Safety and Health Program (the California Consortium).[7] Target populations: Superfund site workers; state and county ER personnel; waste transportation and waste site assessment personnel.
9. The University of Cincinnati, Department of Environmental Health (the Midwest Consortium).[8] Target populations: waste dump site workers and supervisors; treatment, storage, and disposal workers; ER personnel; and waste transporters.
10. The University of Lowell (now the University of Massachusetts Lowell), Department of Work Environment (the New England Consortium).[9] Target populations: waste site clean-up workers; ER personnel; treatment, storage, and disposal workers; and waste transporters.
11. The University of Medicine and Dentistry of New Jersey, Robert Wood Johnson Medical School (the New Jersey/New York Consortium).[10] Target populations: waste site clean-up workers and supervisors; site assessment personnel; waste, treatment, storage, and disposal facility workers; and waste transporters.

NIEHS justified funding the university consortia for specific reasons. First, they submitted strong applications. The reviewers understood that although the universities might not be able to access targeted workers as effectively as the unions could, those selected had developed strong track records for training workers in earlier efforts, especially under OSHA's New Directions program. The universities offered excellence in three key areas—curriculum development, evaluation, and (particularly when it came to medical, chemical, toxicological, and radiation issues) technical expertise. Rall and Dement, along with the review teams, believed these skills would be important for the WETP's success. Several university consortia, such as the UCLA grouping and the University of Lowell consortium (which included three New England COSH groups), had already demonstrated success in developing participatory methods for worker training, which was an emphasis of the program. Finally, the inclusion of the university programs was seen as a way to expand the program's political support, which was important when viewed in the context of a relatively weak labor movement that would need support should Congress decide to challenge the continuation of the program (Dement, 1997; Dobbin, 1997; Matheny, 1998).

Funding for the first awards ranged from $203,560 to $1,926,270. Six awards totaled between $650,000 and $800,000 each. The funding for LIUNA, the IUOE, and the IAFF was considerably less than the unions had anticipated from a program allocation of $10 million, which they had worked to achieve. At one point, the building trades unions considered a single application submitted by the Building and Construction Trades Department of the AFL-CIO, which would serve unions interested in hazardous waste work. The Operating Engineers opposed it because so much of the successful effort had resulted from their impetus. They wanted to develop a program that specifically met their needs. With the awards to university consortia, the building trades had to share resources with programs that might even be training nonunion workers.

The firefighters were in a similar situation, since they had fought to win the mandate to protect and train firefighter emergency responders. University consortia were funded to train other ER personnel, while the IAFF received less than the amount for which it had applied.

THE OSHA RULEMAKING PROCESS FOR 29 CFR 1910.120

At the same time that the WETP was getting underway, many of the awardees were weighing in on another aspect of SARA. The law required that OSHA promulgate a standard for the protection of workers in hazardous waste operations and ER work. Hearings during the rulemaking process for the proposed standard (which followed the issuance of an interim standard) coincided with the start-up of the WETP. The positions of various actors—unions, employers (in hazardous waste management and other industries), and government regulators, as stated in the hearings and written testimony—became the backdrop to the way in which NIEHS managers evaluated their flexibility in decision making to support the requests of awardees or awardee-aspirants.

When OSHA issued its interim rule for hazardous waste operations and ER in December 1986, it also issued a notice of proposed rulemaking and public hearings (NPRM) for a final HAZWOPER rule. In the notice, OSHA said that the proposed rule was the "first regulation since the passage of the OSH Act of 1970 to be mandated specifically by Congress" (52 Federal Register, 1987, p. 29636).[11] Several issues directly related to the success of the WETP were involved, including worker populations to be covered; mandatory hours of training; the cost of worker training; the certification of trained workers and instructors; and the accreditation of training programs. These issues were points of conflict between labor and management, and in some cases conflict with OSHA as well.

OSHA held hearings on the proposed rule in Washington, DC, and San Francisco on two dates in October 1987. Organizations that testified about the training requirements included WETP awardee organizations: the Laborers-AGC and LIUNA, the IAFF, the IUOE, the ICWU, and the USWA. In addition, Dement testified for NIEHS. NIOSH representatives also appeared. Employer representatives and associations from the following industries put their positions on the record: insurance; chemicals; hazardous waste management; construction; manufacturers of steel, paper, heavy machinery, and oil; and the fire service.

Worker Populations to Be Covered

OSHA had great difficulty in defining the scope of coverage for workers required to respond during HAZMAT emergencies. The agency clearly believed that Congress intended broad coverage of ER workers, and not coverage limited only to CERCLA-related hazardous waste sites. Then OSHA restricted the proposed rule's coverage to "only employers whose employees have the reasonable possibility of engaging in ER" (52 Federal Register, 1987, p. 29623). OSHA also said that employers who relied on outside ER teams would be excused from any requirement to provide ER training and protection to their own employees.

OSHA made clear that it did not intend to cover employees who might respond to "incidental spills" that could adequately be addressed in the immediate work area without assistance from ER personnel. The agency did not want to cover workers whose exposure would be below "established exposure levels," meaning not only OSHA permissible exposure levels (PELs), but also levels established by other national organizations, such as NIOSH and the American Conference of Government Industrial Hygienists (ACGIH).[12] OSHA said that not all ER organizations were required to respond to HAZMAT incidents. But any ER organization must provide enough awareness training to ensure that its members would "be sufficiently trained to recognize that an emergency situation exists which requires intervention" by a HAZMAT ER team, and know how to contact such a team (52 Federal Register, 1987, p. 29630). OSHA did not impose that provision for industrial workers whose employers would contract with an outside ER team rather than establish internal ER procedures.

The testimony of Seminario reflected the positions of the AFL-CIO and some, but not all, of its affiliated unions. Seminario maintained that the intent of the parties involved in the passage of SARA's Section 126 was for the mandate to be broad in terms of targeted worker populations, especially for ER activities. She reminded OSHA of its requirement under both the OSH Act and SARA to "issue regulations which cover all workers at significant risk of harm engaged in these operations" (Seminario, 1987). Testimony by the USWA and the ICWU supported Seminario's positions (ICWU, 1987).[13]

Mandatory Hours of Training

OSHA had proposed mandatory hours of training: 40 hours for hazardous waste site personnel, eight additional hours for hazardous waste site supervisors, eight hours of annual refresher training for all waste site personnel, and 24 hours annually for ER personnel, with more for specialist responders. Mention was made of awareness training for workers who would have to identify an emergency and contact trained responders, but no hours requirement was established for this.

The Laborers-AGC and LIUNA jointly called for at least 80 hours for laborers engaged in waste site operations. They argued that laborers at hazardous waste sites were subjected to higher exposure levels for longer periods of time than other personnel at remediation operations. Arguing that the 40-hour mandate from Congress was a minimum, they believed that:

> If 40 hours [of] training is adequate for the average waste site worker, it is unlikely to be adequate for those workers who require special precautions . . . and special training. . . . [In addition, laborers] . . . generally have an educational level that requires extensive repetitive educational techniques to achieve a level of understanding required for performance of their job duties. (L-AGC & LIUNA, 1987, p. 10)

The Laborers-AGC and LIUNA testified to their belief that 24 hours of training was inadequate preparation for ER workers. Testimony was submitted by the IAFF and the Seattle Fire Chiefs Association (both WETP awardees) that more hours of training were required for emergency responders (Soros, 1987).

By way of contrast, CDM Federal Programs Corporation, an environmental engineering consulting firm, opposed "across-the-board training requirements" (CDM Federal Programs Corporation, 1987), with special concern for a full 40 hours of training for most of its employees, who were generally college educated. The company wanted fewer hours for workers who would be on site for only a "couple of hours."

Certification and Accreditation Issues

The IUOE's testimony encouraged certification of both trainees and training programs. OSHA had suggested that workers who successfully completed training should be certified by their instructors and not be permitted to engage in hazardous waste operations without written certification. The union believed that the proposed rule would allow employers to make their own determinations about the extent and quality of training needed by employees, rather than to establish criteria for the mandatory training content and methods. Employers could issue certifications that would not reflect receipt of a uniform baseline amount of training.

In order to succeed in their businesses, the IUOE commented, employers had to minimize costs and maximize profits. In so doing, the IUOE testified, employers would minimize the costs of training. Since Section 119 of SARA indemnified contractors against liability for negligent acts committed during Superfund work, they "would appear to have no incentive whatsoever to expend funds for anything but the most superficial training and certification program" (IUOE, 1987, p. 5). To create an incentive for contractors to provide adequate and appropriate training, the IUOE urged OSHA to develop a mechanism for certifying programs based on course content and delivery. The IUOE also wanted OSHA to require the certification of all instructors, as well as all trained workers.[14]

Both the Laborers-AGC—LIUNA and Seminario maintained that certification of trained workers would protect the public as well as the workers. Certification was viewed as a way of keeping unscrupulous contractors out of the business (L-AGC & LIUNA, 1987; Seminario, 1987). Even OSHA in its notice about the rule said that the training "assures that site activities will be carried out by qualified personnel . . . [and where] there is a potential benefit to the environment" (52 Federal Register, 1987, p. 29637), especially in ER activities.

The USWA wanted OSHA to make any false certification by employers punishable under the OSH Act. The union reported that some employers coerced employees to sign statements that they had received full training when, in fact, the employer had not provided it (Barkman, 1987).

Arguing in opposition to the IUOE and USWA, Organization Resources Counselors, Inc., a management consulting group, declared that employer certification of employee training carried a liability that was legally binding and was taken seriously by employers. The firm opposed a national certification program and urged OSHA to forgo any procedures for more than employer certification of trained employees.

The criteria for certification would be ongoing on-site evaluation of workers (Organization Resources Counselors, 1987).

OSHA's review of the testimony provided the basis for a standard representing an industry influence that had been absent during the negotiations over Section 126 of SARA. Many of labor's arguments regarding emergency response workers, hours of training, and certification and program accreditation were not incorporated into the final rule.

WETP STARTS TO TRAIN

If the testimony on OSHA's rulemaking was gratifying, the WETP's leaders did not pause in designing the program's infrastructure to savor that moment; there was too much to do. One government worker with whom Dement and Rall had consulted over the organization of the program was Denny Dobbin, then labor liaison for the EPA. Dobbin was an industrial hygienist and occupational health policy specialist who had started with the PHS in the Division of Occupational Health in 1967. The division eventually became NIOSH. Shortly after OSHA's establishment, Dobbin was asked to serve as a liaison between OSHA and NIOSH. By the mid-1970s, he had been assigned as chief of the Environmental Investigations Branch of the Division of Field Studies and Clinical Investigations at NIOSH. This office conducted long-term studies on an industry-wide basis as mandated in the OSH Act.

When the National Cancer Institute (NCI) funded NIOSH to study the epidemiology of industrial carcinogens, Dobbin's division was recruited to assist. In 1978, Dobbin established the policy branch of the Office of Program Planning and Evaluation. In the early 1980s, Dobbin worked on a study on the prevention of work-related injuries and illnesses that, to some limited extent, addressed worker training issues. He left NIOSH in 1985 to become the EPA's labor liaison in the Office of Toxic Substances. At the EPA, Dobbin worked with unions and COSH groups to develop asbestos abatement worker training as part of an EPA-funded program under AHERA.[15]

At NIOSH, Dobbin had worked with Dement and Bingham, when Bingham was the director of OSHA. Rall, Dement, and Bingham discussed the need for additional staffing support in the WETP, and all agreed that Dobbin was the best candidate, given his history and his relations with labor. By the time of the public meeting in January 1987, Dobbin had been assigned part-time to help Dement and Rall develop the program. He traveled around the country to discuss how to organize the program. Dobbin knew health and safety activists in the international unions and at the IUD. He believed that labor was, and would be, the main "constituent to advance occupational health." After the first WETP awards were announced, Dobbin was hired to coordinate the program with Dement.

> We were trying to create something from scratch, and John [Dement], as an institute person, and then Denny [Dobbin], as he came in later, had expertise, had connections, knew a community that was not known to most other people on the staff. So, by virtue of that, there was a great reliance on their expertise and recommendations. (Sassaman, 1997)[15]

Inadequate Staffing Levels

The WETP required more grants management support than was needed for the usual NIEHS research grants, largely due to the labor awardees' lack of familiarity with the NIH system. Because the program was a worker health and safety education program rather than a research program, the NIEHS process of multiple-awardee program management required far more resources than was usual. NIEHS was accustomed to bringing together research grant principal investigators to share results and discuss common goals to support grant program cohesiveness. Using this same mechanism for a public health prevention program that encompassed 11 awardee organizations with multiple goals and interests demanded significantly more agency resources. Several of the WETP awards were larger than any of those made for basic research. The larger awards, often with multiple subcontracts, required additional effort in terms of tracking and management. The nature of the projects created difficulties for grant managers who had to assess matters such as requests for budget reallocations and the carryover of unexpended funds from one grant year to the next (Dobbin, 1997; Matheny, 1998; Sassaman, 1997).

Staffing levels in the Division of Extramural Research and Education have been determined by the federal budget allocation to the institute. During the period of the WETP, NIEHS, along with much of the federal government, had strict controls established with regard to the agency's full-time-equivalent employees. The WETP staff who worked solely on the WETP project were paid through the Superfund allocation that came through the EPA. NIEHS did not receive compensation for staff and managers who contributed less than a full-time effort to the WETP, such as Dr. Sassaman and some of the grants and contracts managers (Sassaman, 1997).

Another staffing difficulty stemmed from the differences in focus and content between the WETP and the basic research grants awarded by NIEHS. The differences created difficulties in sharing staffing resources, primarily because the basic research scientists and managers at NIEHS were not able to take a major interest in the worker training program and its issues. For these reasons, access to such people as Donald Elisburg, Knut Ringen, and Melius, who had experience managing government programs and also understood the needs of labor-based worker training programs, became invaluable to NIEHS as a means of supporting the management of the WETP.

This resource was particularly helpful for Carol Matheny, who faced the challenge of taking a grants management process that had been established for biomedical research and applying it to a worker training program. Unlike more open-ended biomedical research, which was funded to support scientific exploration and discovery, the worker training program had a set of targets and goals that Congress expected to be achieved. These included the development of a curriculum to address the targeted populations and the training of specific numbers of workers in each targeted area (Matheny, 1998).

Implementation Issues: Let 100 Flowers Bloom

As Dement, Rall, and Dobbin contemplated their work, they realized that the needs of the diverse target populations might require a range of curriculum approaches.

They established performance criteria and emphasized the importance of developing high-quality programs, but they left curriculum development to the creativity of the awardees in each sector.

Rall in particular, but also the team in general, wanted the awardees to understand that program evaluation would be an important component of any WETP efforts. After nearly a decade of worker health and safety training funded through New Directions at OSHA, only a small body of peer-reviewed literature existed on the effectiveness of worker health and safety training as an occupational health measure. The WETP awardees were urged to devise and incorporate evaluation plans. At the time, neither the awardees nor the agency had adequate funding, or innovative ideas, to support both adequate start-up efforts and a strong evaluation component. Nonetheless, this remained a high-profile issue, which received more funding and attention by the end of the WETP's second year of operations.

Some awardees believed that the funds would be better spent if a unified set of curricula was developed for use by all awardees, as multiple curriculum development efforts could result in redundancy of effort. Other awardees were adamant about developing their own curriculum. In fact, enough differences could be found in the training approaches, if not in the content, among the 11 awardees, that it can probably be said that most wanted to develop their own curricula. Some awardees, however, believed that curricula addressing common industry sectors could be commonly developed without compromising a sense of ownership in specific programs. The attitude did not prevail, though, and Dement took an approach that some individuals involved in the program have dubbed "letting 100 flowers bloom." Dement, however, felt confident about it: "I don't know what else we could have done. We were not in a position to specify a curricula [*sic*], nor . . . a mode of delivery."

Other Issues

Several union-based programs wanted to give stipends to participating workers; this was another problem requiring resolution. In the building trades, where workers were to be trained by the union before assignment to a contractor, a worker would have to be away from work for 1 or 2 weeks, depending on the program. Normally, in the trades, workers were not paid during periods of training. In this situation, however, the unions and NIEHS had to consider the fact that workers were being trained for an emerging industry. In order to promote the activities of a new set of contractors, a trained workforce was required. NIEHS and the unions grappled with the issue of balance involved in viewing the program as either a "jobs program" or a "public health program." For NIEHS, it was both, because the institute had a mandate to support the development of a new labor force. "We saw it as both," Dement said. "We saw it as an emerging industry. Whoever got that work was going to have to have the appropriate training."

Not all of the work in the hazardous waste management industry would be done by contractors who had negotiated contracts with unions. NIEHS was obligated to make the resources of the WETP available to all contractors and employers, union and nonunion. The WETP was a federal program supported by a national employer tax. The university programs were viewed as the mechanisms for the training. Thus, an immediate contradiction developed. NIEHS sought to build a cohesive network of organizations and immediately was faced with the problem that the obligation of university awardees to train non-union workers could potentially support the growth of a competing economic pressure on the union awardees. The boundaries for the negotiation of these issues in the WETP were the relative political strength of the unions, nationally and locally, and the sense of association and solidarity with the labor movement maintained by any university program.

BUILDING COHESIVENESS AND SUPPORT

When Rall and Dement talked with Bingham about OSHA's New Directions, Bingham gave them her opinions on the program's successes and limitations. One significant limitation that made a strong impression on Dement (and later Dobbin) was that OSHA had not emphasized collective meetings of the New Directions awardees to share their training experiences. In terms of the number of New Directions awardees, it might not have been feasible, but the fact remained that the New Directions awardees had not engaged in a process of building consensus on an approach to worker health and safety training and education. NIEHS's program managers decided that WETP awardees would meet regularly to discuss program experiences, the curriculum, and training delivery issues, as well as other issues concerning the regulatory and work site contexts of the effort.[16]

An initial meeting was held in November 1987 and a second 2 months later. The meetings focused on curriculum development and the sharing of resources to maximize the ability of all awardees to prepare for training. The meetings allowed the awardees to become familiar with each others' intentions in terms of program development, to share goals and objectives, and to make plans for curriculum development.

Marianne Brown, principal investigator for the University of California award and then director of the Labor Occupational Safety and Health Program at UCLA, helped Dement and Dobbin organize presentations on participatory education methods for one meeting. Brown and Daryl Alexander, than at the Labor Occupational Health Program (LOHP) at UC Berkeley, organized the agenda. They invited Les Leopold of the Labor Institute to introduce participatory adult education principles and methods. This institute is a nonprofit labor education organization that was at the time developing a worker-to-worker, small-group-activity method approach to worker health and safety training, and it was a subcontractor to OCAW on its training program. Leopold facilitated a training activity that led the awardees to discuss and analyze the elements of effective adult education. The emphasis on these topics at the early meetings established NIEHS's priority goal of incorporating participatory adult education methodologies in the awardees' programs (Brown, 1998; Dobbin, 1997).

The awardees would have relative autonomy to develop their programs as they found appropriate, but NIEHS established some priorities, which included employing participatory adult education methods, using hands-on training, and establishing the

NIEHS training programs as a benchmark for training quality in hazardous waste operations and hazardous materials ER (Dement, 1997; Dobbin, 1997).

Curriculum content was a major point of discussion, too. The book developed by the interagency task force on the occupational safety and health issues of hazardous waste work was regarded by Dobbin, Dement, and many awardees as a prime source of technical information. Although the groups developed their own curricula, NIEHS encouraged the development of a core set of topics. The NIOSH-OSHA-USCG-EPA book, *Occupational Safety and Health Guidance Manual for Hazardous Waste Site Activities,* and OSHA's proposed rule for hazardous waste operations and ER served as guides for the core topics. Most of the awardees developed their curricula to match the requirements of the OSHA rule, which was necessary since the rule mandated employer compliance with specific training requirements.[17]

Medical Issues

Certain medical issues related to training had to be settled. The awardees and the NIEHS administrators anticipated a strong need for appropriate procedures to "prevent individuals at high risk of heart attack or stroke from jeopardizing their health during exercises in which they wear self-contained breathing apparatus (SCBA), fully encapsulating suits, or both" (Gochfeld, Buckler, & Landsbergis, 1988). The gear was the respiratory and chemical protective equipment needed by hazardous waste operations and ER workers. During mock exercises, workers performed tasks such as moving 55-gallon drums while wearing the equipment. Considerable body heat builds up inside a fully encapsulated suit. An additional heat load results when workers wear the suits during outdoor activities under a strong sun. The strain of working in such equipment could endanger individuals who were at greater risk for acute cardiovascular events. Even for healthy individuals, working in the suits presented a significant risk for heat stress and heat stroke.

Individuals were assigned responsibility for medical clearance or medical surveillance in each awardee's program. Others who were interested were included on the program committees, which consisted of occupational physicians, occupational nurses, and industrial hygienists. This was one of the first collective efforts of the awardees, a working situation within which the awardees could collaborate. Questions were distributed for each committee member's comment. The comments were to be collated and used as a report of the committee's discussions "that can be circulated among the Training Centers and their lawyers" (Gochfeld et al., 1988) and as the basis for a training manual chapter on medical surveillance in hazardous waste operations and ER.

Administrative Procedures

In 1987, the PHS managed the largest number of grant programs in the federal government. The PHS had developed a grants administration manual to ensure consistent administration by its agencies (U.S. DHHS, 1991). Management of PHS grants is coordinated by program officials and grants management officers. The program official is responsible for assuring that adequate and appropriate staffing exists to support a program. The grants management officer complements the technical knowledge of the program official and supervises the business management aspects of the program. The two coordinate their work, but program officials have the freedom to "exercise their professional judgement with respect to their areas of responsibility without undue pressures or controls" (U.S. DHHS, 1991, p. I-3).

Rall made the WETP a component of the director's office, so that the program officer would answer to the director. In this way, he was better able to ensure that the program served the participating unions, as well as NIEHS's institutional needs. NIH maintained high standards for the avoidance of conflicts of interest, in accordance with DHHS rules (U.S. DHHS, 1981). Rall wanted to maintain close contact with the program to prevent fiscal or programmatic improprieties, as well as to control and correct them should they occur. He was particularly concerned about the unions' lack of familiarity with the NIH grant funding mechanisms and rules (Dobbin, 1998b; Lange, 1997; Matheny, 1998; Rall, 1997; Sassaman, 1997).

Matheny was the WETP grants management officer. As defined in the PHS rules, she worked closely with the program managers (Dement and Dobbin under Rall). She assessed the available levels of flexibility, either permitting or restraining some planned strategies. Matheny came to appreciate the goals of the WETP awardees, strongly believed in the need for the universities and unions to work closely, and supported what the unions developed. On the rare occasions when fiscal management was not conducted in accordance with NIH rules, Matheny and the program managers worked diligently with an awardee to correct the problem and prevent new problems (Dobbin, 1998b; Matheny, 1998; Rall, 1997; Sassaman, 1997).

Program Regulations

By mid-1988, the WETP had drafted program regulations, which were required due to the ways in which the program differed from most at NIEHS. NIEHS published an NPRM in the Federal Register on June 15, 1989, and the *Final Rule for the Hazardous Waste Worker Training Program* was published in the register on October 22, 1990. The supplemental information section of the final rule included comments on the NPRM and an explanation of the agency's action with regard to the comments. One comment was that hands-on training should be required as a component of the detailed training plan submitted in any proposal for funding under the WETP. NIEHS agreed, noting that "agency evaluation of existing grants has shown that hands-on training is key to successful hazardous waste worker training" (55 Federal Register, 1990, p. 42566).

OSHA and the EPA had each promulgated their final rules for hazardous waste operations and ER, as 29 CFR 1910.120 and 40 CFR Part 311, respectively. (Section 126 of SARA mandated the coverage of state and local government employees by EPA regulations, which would be identical to those promulgated by OSHA. The EPA final rule was promulgated on June 23, 1989, as 54 FR 26658.) NIEHS justified the scope of its training program as including a range of workers with actual and potential exposure to hazardous waste materials by noting that both OSHA and the EPA agreed on this interpretation of the intent of Congress in SARA. In 1989, NIEHS expanded the targeted populations eligible for training under the WETP.

Contact With Other Government Agencies

Dement and Dobbin were particularly concerned that the WETP should receive broad support from other federal agencies addressing occupational health and safety, environmental protection, and hazardous materials ER. All of the labor unions in the WETP stressed the importance of such agencies supporting and interacting with the program. Initially, particular emphasis was placed on increasing OSHA's backing for strong regulations that protected a range of workers. Support from the EPA was important early on, due to the interagency agreement for the provision of funding to NIEHS by the EPA. The EPA was also the central coordinating agency for Superfund and HAZMAT ER.[18] NIEHS worked with OSHA and NIOSH to assure that attention was given to the health and safety needs of workers involved in hazardous waste operations and ER.

NIEHS sought to ease tensions in its relationship with NIOSH that may have resulted from the reassignment of the program from NIOSH to NIEHS. NIEHS believed that Congress never intended that the institute should link the Superfund training with the Superfund Basic Research Program. The basic research entity at NIEHS had been an early component of Superfund reauthorization, whereas worker training was not given to NIEHS until the end of the legislative process. NIEHS entered into a contract with NIOSH whereby funding was provided to NIOSH for awards to its existing network of educational resource centers (ERCs) for graduate education and professional training to promote the work of a range of occupational health professionals. The ERCs used the NIEHS funding for professional training on hazardous waste operations and ER. Nonetheless, relations between the two agencies remained slightly strained, mostly due to the impression at NIOSH that the WETP would have been more appropriately placed at an occupational health research institute than at a biomedical research facility.

NIEHS also attempted to coordinate with FEMA. That agency was assigned responsibility for some oversight and coordination of the network of state emergency response commissions and local emergency planning committees that were mandated in the Emergency Planning and Community Right to Know Act, or Title III of SARA. Provisions were to be made to train public-sector HAZMAT ER personnel. NIEHS worked with FEMA in activities coordinated by the EPA. The firefighters' union helped in communication between NIEHS and the National Fire Academy (then a branch of FEMA), which had trained such ER teams.

NIEHS coordinated, to the extent that it was feasible, with other federal agencies and departments with regard to its worker training. One such agency was ATSDR, which developed toxicological profiles and conducted health effects research on chemicals at hazardous waste sites. By the late 1980s, environmentalists were calling for the investigation and cleanup of federal facilities that had potential for becoming, or were known to be, hazardous waste sites. In addition, the impending end of the Cold War evoked national discussions about the closure and use of military bases and nuclear weapons research and production facilities managed by the Department of Defense (DOD) and the Department of Energy (DOE). NIEHS took part in early talks about the training needs of workers who might engage in those cleanups. Within a few years, the DOE entered into an agreement with NIEHS for worker training.

Difficulties at NIEHS—Primary Prevention Program in a Biomedical Research Bureaucracy

Another difficult issue for the WETP's managers was integration within NIEHS. It was a rather "touchy" matter, showing only slow and limited progress. Many at NIEHS could not appreciate the validity of running a worker training program, especially one that bolstered labor unions. Former and existing NIEHS training had aimed to develop a national biomedical research infrastructure. According to some, but not all, of the WETP staff, many scientists at NIEHS viewed themselves as medical researchers, but not as public health researchers. They worked to understand biological mechanisms in order to develop cures or organ-system-specific mechanisms to prevent adverse effects from chemical exposures. At best, some division directors tried to offer minimal support or at least cooperation to the WETP. At worst, agency personnel and scientists were openly hostile to the program. They were much more interested in the other Superfund program, Basic Research, at NIEHS (Dement, 1997; Dobbin, 1997; Lange, 1997; Rall, 1997; Sassaman, 1997).

WETP TECHNICAL AND PROGRAMMATIC SUPPORT

Dement and Dobbin crafted various mechanisms to give technical and programmatic support to WETP awardees. Meetings evolved into at least semiannual business gatherings. They helped to create the sense of a national program among the awardees. They were organized to build and disseminate the goals, efforts, and progress of each organization, as well as to understand the organizations' challenges and obstacles. The intention was to facilitate an exchange of ideas, collaboration in efforts to avoid duplication, the conservation and extension of resources, and the gradual development of a sense of cohesiveness, so that awardees felt they were part of a national program and also part of a national health and safety movement. Again, the instructive experience that moved NIEHS to create this mechanism was New Directions, which had had limited success in similar efforts (Dement, 1997; Dobbin, 1997).

NIEHS invited personnel from other agencies to attend meetings so that they would develop an increased awareness of the WETP and its work. Their participation helped the awardees "know" other agencies with which relations could be developed or strengthened. Usually, one meeting each year was held at NIEHS's offices in North Carolina, but at least one was held at or near the home site of an awardee. In this way, NIEHS created greater knowledge among awardees of each other's programs, almost as if they had provided hands-on training. Adherence to this plan also built in greater equity for travel expenses, which were substantial for West Coast awardees who were obligated to travel east for North Carolina NIEHS meetings (Dobbin, 1997).

In the earlier years, more often than not, conflicts between the awardees would become apparent at the meetings. The agenda usually included an opportunity for each awardee to present an update on its program's efforts. The awardees did not meet with a common set of political objectives, because they represented different institutions and industrial sectors, and their meeting was tantamount to an obligation under the funding agency's requirements. The organizations, for the most part, had not applied to the program in order to strengthen their roles in a national health and safety movement. Rather, each intended to build a program for its own specific needs and those of the workers they served in each geographical area or industrial sector. Often, awardees discussed aspects of local work that might clearly oppose the aims of a fellow awardee.

> I think we certainly haven't ironed out all of those issues, but I think at least they've been aired—a lot of them have been aired to a point that you understand where they are. I think each grantee has benefited at least from the perspective that the other ones have, and the appreciation of why they [have it]. In some cases making the programs more alike, but sometimes just frankly understanding why they are different and [that it's] for a reason. (Dement, 1997)

Awardee Meetings

The meetings, of course, had multiple uses. Examples come from three sessions held during the 16 months starting in March 1989.[19] The March 6-7 meeting was held jointly with FEMA representatives and focused on ER issues. FEMA was moving forward to address emergency planning and response mandates established under SARA Title III. One element of this was the training of ER teams at FEMA's National Emergency Training Center, which incorporated work by its National Fire Academy and Emergency Management Institute. The FEMA presentation raised awardees' awareness of that work, and identified possibilities for programmatic linkages between awardees and regional and local FEMA-supported efforts.

A presentation was made by Thomas Seymour, who was in charge of OSHA's development and promulgation of the final rule for the Hazardous Waste Operations and Emergency Response standard. He explained the role of the EPA in protecting workers employed by local and state government organizations in the 26 states that had not established a state OSHA plan.[20] A key issue was the number of hours of awareness-level training that OSHA intended employers to deliver. The standard was not going to mandate a specific number of hours, but would establish a set of employee competencies as training objectives. OSHA anticipated that 4-6 hours of training would be required to develop worker competence.

Finally, Richard Duffy of the IAFF explained the requirements of the national emergency responder training standards established by the National Fire Protection Association (NFPA). NFPA establishes consensus standards to guide and direct fire-fighters' work. OSHA based its emergency responder training on NFPA standards.

The next awardee meeting was held in Monterey, California, on June 11-14. Midway through the program's second year, the awardees had developed significant curricula and were delivering courses and expanding. As examples of their progress in developing training staff, the IUOE had 149 instructors, OCAW had 26 worker-trainers, and the Midwest Consortium had a 56-hour course for training trainers. The IAFF, which was not delivering training, was distributing training curricula and materials to fire departments nationally to develop internal training capacity and had produced seven high-quality training videos and 600 slides. The California Consortium had also developed a course for training trainers, which incorporated participatory training theory and methods. Gail Bateson, from UC Berkeley, had written a manual to address literacy issues. It was an initial effort that would grow to be a major contribution of the California Consortium to the national program. In addition to the standard menu of courses, the New England Consortium had developed one for media workers who reported on hazardous waste site issues and HAZMAT emergencies. It was both a method of health and safety training and an outreach tool.

The awardees spent considerable time addressing marketing and outreach efforts. Whether the programs had to sell their courses or just promote them in order to reach targeted workers, every program was faced with the challenges involved in creating public and employer awareness of their efforts. The awardees had published newsletters and printed brochures. Some received responses to their press releases, while others had greater luck with ads placed in professional journals.[21]

The certification of workers, trainers, and training programs was addressed. Certification issues overlapped with concerns about evaluation and testing. These were important and sensitive issues that became long-running conflicts not only between awardees but also between awardees and NIEHS administrators. However, most of the awardees were interested in program certification as a way to strengthen their ability to reach and draw in workers in need of training. Dobbin and John Moran, a technical expert with the Laborers-AGC, decided to have the program sponsor a "technical workshop" at which awardees, government staffers, and private industry personnel would establish minimum criteria for the training. The workshop was booked for Spring 1990. A planning committee was selected from among the awardees.

A third example is an awardees' meeting in Des Plaines, Illinois, on June 6-7, 1990. Des Plaines is the home of the OSHA Training Institute, and NIEHS shaped the meeting to increase OSHA's exposure to the program. NIEHS invited staff from the Training Resources and Data Exchange, which had a 5-year contract with the DOE for training. The agenda included substantive discussions about training needs for clean-up efforts at the DOE and DOD sites. Also getting attention was the continuing lack of will by OSHA and the EPA to enforce the HAZWOPER standard. When awardees learned that EPA officials had spoken disparagingly about the WETP, they focused on ways to demonstrate the strengths and achievements of the program.

Dement and Dobbin designed meetings to build a sense of cohesiveness among the awardees and to integrate the WETP with related federal efforts. Each awardee program was a component of much larger, often bureaucratic, organizations, such as universities and international labor unions. At the start, the awardees unsurprisingly were much more interested in their own organization's goals, but NIEHS appears nevertheless to have successfully promoted a sense of shared political interest and purpose.

A Clearinghouse

Dobbin believed that a national clearinghouse would be a useful support to the program. It could serve as a repository for curricula developed by the WETP and also as a distribution center dealing with requests for these public domain materials. A clearinghouse could help promote the training at national and regional conferences and be a vehicle through which employers and government personnel could learn about the training.

The Laborers-AGC (L-AGC) accepted a supplement to their training award in September 1989 to run the clearinghouse. The L-AGC negotiated with Sheldon Samuels to run it from the Workplace Health Fund (WHF) under the name of the National Clearinghouse on Occupational and Environmental Health. Four purposes were established for it:

> 1. [to] provide a resource center for grantee training materials, curricula, etc.; 2. arrange meetings, seminars and workshops on technical issues of interest to the grantees; 3. publish newsletters, brochures and a catalog of materials available at the Clearinghouse; 4. provide a communications network and traveling exhibit promoting the training activities of the grantees and the NIEHS program. (NIEHS, 1990)

The clearinghouse was directed by Samuels with support from Elisburg, legal counsel from the WHF, and Neil Thursby, director of the L-AGC's training. The clearinghouse's staff consisted of a project manager, an associate director and information specialist, administrative assistants (part-time), and other WHF staff as needed. The clearinghouse also had an advisory committee made up of awardee representatives.

The clearinghouse's work in its first year included the setting up of a trainer network among the awardees. NIEHS saw the network as a way of better integrating trainers' work into the national program. The network was also viewed as a way to promote sharing among the trainers across programs. "There have been difficulties in establishing the trainer network," a July 1990 site review of the clearinghouse reported, "primarily because of lack of cooperation by the grantees, who are reluctant to share information about their trainers with others, and do not consider this a high priority" (NIEHS, 1990). It took until 1994, when awardees sent their trainers to a national trainers' exchange conference, before the awardees were secure enough in their programs to place a higher priority on supporting a deeper involvement of their trainers in the national program.

Since September 1989, the clearinghouse has organized two technical workshops annually to address topical issues and has provided technical support for training programs. The clearinghouse maintains sets of curricula developed by NIEHS grantees and publishes weekly on-line information about the training program and issues related to HAZWOPER work and training. Its resources are not used only by the grantees; 40–60% of requests come to it from private industry and the rest from unions, academics, and public officials.

A 1995 review noted that the WETP had "made a substantial contribution to a more systematic, analytical and scientific approach to training program development, delivery and evaluation in terms of advancing the state of the art." It pointed to seven published program-related studies from 1988 to 1995. Said the panel: "This is no small accomplishment given the generally weak emphasis on training evaluation [nationally] in the past" (NIEHS, 1995, p. 25).

The expectations for the clearinghouse were fulfilled; a review panel has called its archive "the most extensive, accessible collection of its kind in the country." It can now be searched by computer at http://tools.niehs.nih.gov/wetp/.

Evaluation of Training

Rall insisted on evaluation of the training, looking at the "product." He wanted to know whether it was effective in helping to prevent workers from being injured on the job and from developing adverse health outcomes from toxic workplace exposures (Rall, 1997). Sassaman believed that to justify the program's placement at a research institute, NIEHS needed to undertake evaluation (Sassaman, 1997). Dement viewed evaluation as an important component of quality assurance measures. He believed the awardees could develop approaches for evaluation, but as an initial step, he included the naming of a program advisory board as one criterion in a request for applications. Dement saw the boards as functioning to review each program (Dement, 1997; Dobbin, 1997). Dobbin wanted to see evaluation because he believed that worker health and safety training had to be raised to a higher status among health and safety professionals and regulators. Part of his aim in sponsoring a technical workshop to develop minimum criteria for training was to lay the basis for evaluation. Dobbin understood that criteria had to be formulated on which evaluation could be based (Dobbin, 1997).

In 1989, the WETP used administrative funds to give the Midwest and the New Jersey/New York consortia supplemental funding for evaluation projects. A group led by Dr. Thomas Robins at the University of Michigan's School of Public Health was funded to conduct a mail survey and telephone interviews of trainees from four awardee organizations: the Midwest and California consortia, OCAW, and the ICWU. Dr. Audrey Gotsch, principal investigator of the New Jersey/New York Consortium, coordinated the development of uniform tests that could be used in both pre- and-post-training, and solely in post-training.[22]

The group sought information from trained workers about any changes in their work practices, to find out whether the trained workers talked with coworkers about the training or attempted to make health and safety improvements in their workplaces, and if the latter was attempted, to ascertain the degree of success. As an initial evaluation of NIEHS training, the group established some criteria that were used for much of the evaluation that followed. Although the Michigan group continued to perform evaluation for the Midwest Consortium, other organizations afterward conducted their own efforts.

The work of Gotsch's group was carried out in response to a request by Dement and Dobbin to develop a scientific basis for the questions that would be used in post-training tests. OSHA considered proposing a set of questions to set a standard that would require and define the accreditation of HAZWOPER training programs. Dobbin wanted to demonstrate that it was possible to employ statistically valid questions.

Gotsch's group proposed to collect the questions used by awardee organizations in their 40-hour site worker courses. Participation by awardees was voluntary. Six of seven awardees who offered such courses attended a May 1990 meeting on evaluation. They voiced concerns due to the newness of the programs. Collaboration "should not include evaluating program effectiveness . . . [but should] focus on improving and validating [evaluation and testing] methods currently in use" (Gotsch, 1991). In March 1991, Dobbin wrote to Gotsch to underscore NIEHS's support for the work and express concern that it was more than a year behind schedule.

Dobbin later said that NIEHS did not realize how difficult it would be to get the awardees to agree to do the work and to decide how to do it. Conflicts arose over study design, data collection and sharing, and fears by some union programs that their performance would be compared unfavorably to that of university-based awardees. Dobbin later came to believe that the effort might have been more successful had NIEHS led it rather than contracting it to an awardee.

LEGISLATIVE CHANGES

Congress had amended the worker training portion of SARA twice by 1989. First, the WETP's annual funding was doubled to $20 million. The first awards under the new funding were made in September 1990. The other amendment was a change in the language of Section 126(d)(3), on certification and enforcement. OSHA had to promulgate certification procedures that were "no less comprehensive" than the EPA's in its accreditation plan for asbestos training under AHERA.

Both changes had profound impacts on the WETP. The former funded five additional awardees and an expansion of the program to new target populations. The latter led to the issuance by OSHA of an NPRM for a hazardous waste worker and ER training accreditation plan. Dobbin and Moran, as has been mentioned, planned a technical workshop at which the WETP was to develop minimum criteria for HAZWOPER training, which it hoped OSHA would use in its standard. The workshop moved the WETP to new levels of cooperation, excellence, and conflict. The WETP moved from its 2-year start-up phase into another, more mature phase of full implementation.

CONCLUSION

Sheldon Samuels's hunch that Dr. David Rall would support labor was right. The appointment of John Dement and Denny Dobbin to run the program, and Dement's decision to let 100 flowers bloom, set the program on the path to becoming a new foundation for the U.S. health and safety movement, which by the early 1990s had been weakened by the neoliberal assaults on labor and the state. The original lobbying support that secured the SARA provisions was sustained, providing the WETP with an external link to Congress that could balance any reluctance or incapacity on the part of NIEHS to advocate for the program. Donald Elisburg, based in the program's clearinghouse, was able to assist with management and organize a network of labor and public health professionals who could provide guidance to the WETP leadership on how to maneuver through the federal bureaucracy. These necessary supports aside, though, the WETP's start-up success benefited from the NIEHS program leadership's initial efforts to recruit organizations engaged in the health and safety movement. Having succeeded in doing this, they carefully worked within the NIH structures to organize cohesion within the awardee network and establish alliances with other federal agencies such as the EPA, OSHA, NIOSH, FEMA, the DOD, and the DOE . Awardees were strongly encouraged to use advisory boards to build alliances that would enhance and defend both their own program and the national program. All of these strategies were quickly proved to be necessary.

Reagan administration officials in the Office of Management and Budget, the EPA, and OSHA all worked to reduce the funding for and/or the scope of the training program and the protections that would be mandated in a standard. Although industry representatives were barely aware of the effort to get the training grant and OSHA standard language into SARA, they used the OSHA rulemaking process to limit the training and other measures labor wanted for enhanced HAZWOPER worker protection. The WETP leadership worked with its awardees, the trade unions, and university programs, providing strong arguments for a strong OSHA standard. Labor and management, with their respective government supports, argued over hours of training, evaluation, and curriculum content—contested areas of work environment protection that would be codified and made enforceable by OSHA. Seemingly of limited significance, these arguments reflect bitterly contested views about employers' responsibility for protecting the health and safety of workers.

With that effort in the background, the WETP leaders began to shape a unified effort among the awardees, emphasizing the incorporation of participatory and hands-on training and discussions regarding a range of technical issues. Dement and Dobbin wanted the program to generate a body of evaluation research literature to provide evidence of what worked and did not work in health and safety training. They believed that the future struggles against efforts to limit the program would be well served by a body of scientific literature. They learned early on from these efforts that the diversity of deep beliefs and political perspectives on health and safety strategies were areas for conflict.

We will see that despite philosophical differences about worker health and safety approaches, the neoliberal restructuring of the U.S. economy and politics created conditions that forced divergent labor and health and safety strategies to converge with astounding similarity. Nonetheless, within the WETP as in most other areas of labor, ideological frameworks not only lag behind the pace of change in experience but perhaps even help to protect the believers in those frameworks from facing a harsh contradictory reality.

ENDNOTES

1. Historical information about NIEHS is derived from an unpublished agency brochure, *A History of Progress: NIEHS, The First 20 Years (1966 to 1986)* (NIEHS, 1986b). Its accuracy was confirmed by former NIEHS staff.

2. Dr. Anne Sassaman, a former director of the NIEHS Division of Extramural Research and Training, remembers representatives from labor asking for "what they thought was their fair share."
3. Rall and Dement required a board of advisors, primarily as a mechanism for quality assurance and a way to support the evaluation of awardee programs (Dement, 1997; Dobbin, 1997; Dobbin, 1998b; Lange, 1997; Rall, 1997). Its success has varied among awardees.
4. The meeting agenda was located in the files of the New England Consortium, University of Massachusetts Lowell. In the same file were typed notes from the meeting.
5. OSHA raised concerns that small-quantity generators included dry cleaners and gas stations, and said that workers in such facilities are not hazardous waste operators "in the normal meaning of the term" (51 Federal Register, 1986b).
6. The applications were judged on how they addressed these criteria: (1) identification of the target hazardous waste worker populations to be served by the training program; (2) training plan for curriculum development, instructor training, and course delivery; (3) qualifications of the program director, staff, and consultants; (4) training facilities and resources; (5) quality control and evaluation plan, including qualifications of the proposed board of advisors, mechanisms for project coordination, and plans for evaluating courses and instructors; (6) students: mechanisms for gaining access to students from each proposed target population, and information on whether the students would already be employed; (7) current and past training record; (8) institutional environment and administrative support; and (9) budget: appropriateness of spending plans for specific program areas, especially reviewing curriculum development spending in the first two years, in anticipation that it would be completed by the third year (NIEHS, 1987a, 1987b).
7. This consortium included UC Berkeley, Labor Occupational Health Program; UCLA, University Extension Service; UC Davis Extension Program; UC Irvine Extension Program; University of Southern California, Continuing Education Program; and the Los Angeles Committee on Occupational Safety and Health (LACOSH).
8. The university-led consortium included the Greater Cincinnati Occupational Health Center; the University of Illinois; the University of Kentucky; the University of Michigan; the University of Wisconsin; Murray State University; Michigan State University; Purdue University; and the Southeast Michigan Coalition on Occupational Safety and Health (SEMCOSH).
9. This consortium included Boston University School of Public Health; Harvard Educational Resource Center; Tufts University, Center for Environmental Management; Yale University, Occupational Medicine Program; the Massachusetts Coalition for Occupational Safety and Health (MASSCOSH); the Connecticut Committee for Occupational Safety and Health (ConnectiCOSH); the Rhode Island Committee for Occupational Safety and Health (RICOSH); and the Maine Labor Group for Health.
10. This consortium included the New Jersey Department of Labor; Hunter College, School of Health Sciences; Empire State College; the State University of New York; the American Red Cross; OCAW Local 8-149; and the New York Committee for Occupational Safety and Health (NYCOSH).
11. Denny Dobbin remarked in an interview that the interim standard represented "one of the fastest standard-making [processes] we ever did because they were told to do it and just did it. It was great. I mean they put it together and it was defensible." In the NPRM for the final rule, OSHA said it used materials developed by the EPA and the interagency task force that was mandated in CERCLA.
12. See Slatin and Siqueira (1998) and Van Gelder (1996) for a situation in which a worker died from acute exposure to a hazardous waste material that did not exceed a PEL.

Hazardous waste materials present inherent health and safety dangers that cannot necessarily be controlled through normal industrial hygiene practices, such as reliance on accepted exposure levels.

13. Although most representatives of labor could support the broadest possible coverage by an OSHA standard, with provisions for maximum protection, tying the standard to the training program made this kind of support difficult for some. Broader coverage by OSHA would support the inclusion of more WETP applicants. Without substantial additional funding, this would mean smaller awards for successful applicants than desired, often too small to support full operations.
14. The IUOE had supported Congressional passage of language that would establish contractor indemnification under SARA. This was viewed as a necessary incentive for contractor entrance into the new waste remediation industry. For the IUOE, it was an essential element in the union's jobs and organizing strategy. Having won the language, they required strong provisions to create an equal incentive for contractors to protect workers.
15. The Asbestos Hazard Emergency Response Act of 1986 (AHERA), Section 2656, authorized a training grants program for "nonprofit organizations that demonstrate experience in implementing and operating health and safety asbestos training and educational programs for workers who are or will be engaged in asbestos-related activities" (The Asbestos Hazard Emergency Response Act of 1986 [AHERA], 1986).
16. Tobey, Revitte, and others have said that New Directions developed participant cohesiveness, training evaluation, and other areas. The discrepancy with regard to the views of professionals like Dement and Dobbin, from their discussions with Dr. Bingham as well as their own experiences, is likely related to the time of observation. Tobey and Revitte (1981) wrote about the program at its peak in 1981, while Dement and Dobbin were aware of its collapse.
17. Curriculum development in several programs (LOHP and the Labor Occupational Safety and Health program at UCLA (LOSH) in the California Consortium, the New England Consortium, OCAW, and the ICWU) was led by individuals who were strongly rooted in Freirian pedagogy and practiced a range of participatory training methods. The educators distinguished between participatory training and courses developed to empower workers to take protective action in a workplace. Empowerment-oriented training aimed to be learner-centered, but the OSHA rule tended to force a more curriculum-centered approach.
18. In 1978, Section 311 of the Clean Water Act mandated the establishment of the Environmental Response Team (ERT). CERCLA, RCRA, and SARA activities are coordinated through the EPA's Office of Solid Waste and Emergency Response (OSWER). ERT evolved into a branch in OSWER. Its purview is oil spills, HAZMAT emergencies, and long-term remedial activities. For more information see http://www.ert.org/.
19. The notes that provided this information were taken by John Morawetz of the ICWU Hazardous Waste Worker Training Program. The selected meetings were not the only WETP grantee meetings held between January 1988 and June 1990. The author searched NIEHS files and asked directors of several awardee organizations for records of early meetings and activities. Most had not maintained files from the early period. NIEHS's files were largely lost during multiple relocations of its offices between 1989 and 1996. Other organizations lost or disposed of files as well.
20. Section 18 of the OSH Act required states to establish a state-based occupational safety and health regulatory and enforcement agency. As described by Mintz (1984), the elements of such programs include the following: state standards and enforcement must be "at least as effective" as federal efforts; the states must employ qualified personnel; and, under Section 18(c)(6), all this applies to public workers in the state.

21. The university programs trained a spectrum of professional workers: engineers, geologists, chemists, and other environmental scientists employed by government and private consulting firms.
22. NIEHS had hoped that a cross-tabulation and comparison of the limited evaluation efforts conducted by awardees could strengthen the validity of each set of results. Dr. Gotsch was originally asked to review all of the evaluation efforts, and to compare and contrast their designs and methods to determine what research was conducted and how it could be strengthened. The task proved too difficult due to inter-awardee proprietary issues and it was later reduced (Dobbin, 1998a).

REFERENCES

51 Federal Register. (1986a). National Institute of Environmental Health Sciences, Superfund Hazardous Waste Worker Health and Safety Training Program, Notice of Meeting. Vol. 51, pp. 45556-45559. Washington, DC: GPO.

51 Federal Register. (1986b). U.S. DOL, 29 CFR 1910, Hazardous Waste Operations and Emergency Response, Interim Final Rule. December 19, Vol. 51, pp. 45654-45675. Washington, DC: GPO.

52 Federal Register. (1987). U.S. DOL, 29 CFR 1910. Hazardous Waste Operations and Emergency Response, Notice of Proposed Rulemaking and Public Hearings. August 10, Vol. 52, pp. 29620-29654. Washington, DC: GPO.

55 Federal Register. (1990). U.S. DHHS. NIH. NIEHS, Hazardous Waste Worker Training, Final Rule for the Hazardous Waste Worker Training Program. Vol. 55, 204, pp. 42566-42569. Washington, DC: GPO.

The Asbestos Hazard Emergency Response Act of 1986 (AHERA), P.L. 99-519. Section 2656. (1986).

Barkman, M. R. (1987). OSHA HAZWOPER Rulemaking Hearings: Post-hearing Testimony of the United Steelworkers of America, by Melena R. Barkman (October 30). OSHA Docket S-760 A, Exhibit 61/61 A. U.S. DOL.

Brown, M. P. (1998). E-mail correspondence with author (October 29).

CDM Federal Programs Corporation. (1987). OSHA HAZWOPER Rulemaking Hearings: Testimony. October 5. OSHA Docket S-760 A, Exhibit 34. U.S. DOL.

Dement, J. (1987, November/December). NIEHS Awards 11 grants for Hazmat Training Programs. Environmental Management News, 2(6), 17-20.

Dement, J. (1997). Interview by author, tape recording (October 20).

Dement, J., & Vandermeer, D. (1987). Overview of the NIEHS Hazardous Waste Worker Health and Safety Training Grants Program. October 14. RTP, NC. NIEHS.

Dobbin, D. (1997). Interviews by author, tape recording, Los Angeles (April 10).

Dobbin, D. (1998a). E-mail correspondence with author (December 1).

Dobbin, D. (1998b). Interviews by author, tape recording, RTP, NC (May 5).

Duffy, R. (1997). Interview by author, tape recording, Washington, DC (December 9).

Elisburg, D. (1997). Interview by author, tape recording, RTP, NC (October 21).

Elisburg, D. (1998). E-mail correspondence with author (February 9).

Gochfeld, M., Buckler, G., & Landsbergis, P. (1988). Memo to Members of the Superfund Training Grantees Medical Committee (January 27).

Gotsch, A. R. (1991). Letter to principal investigators of NIEHS awardee organizations participating in an evaluation effort being conducted by UMDNJ, with attachment, A Plan for Collaboration Among NIEHS Grantees Performing 40/80-Hour Hazardous Waste Site Training (April 19, 1991). From files of the New England Consortium, Department of Work Environment, University of Massachusetts Lowell.

ICWU. (1987). OSHA HAZWOPER Rulemaking Hearings: Comments of the International Chemical Workers Union, AFL-CIO (October 5). OSHA Docket S-760 A, Exhibit 46, U.S. DOL.

IUOE. (1987). OSHA HAZWOPER Rulemaking Hearings: Comments of the International Union of Operating Engineers (October 5). OSHA Docket S-760-A, Exhibit 43, U.S. DOL.

L-AGC & LIUNA. (1987). OSHA HAZWOPER Rulemaking Hearings: Testimony and Exhibits of the Laborers-AGC Education and Training Fund and the Laborers' International Union of North America, AFL-CIO (October 5). OSHA Docket S-760 A, Exhibit 31, U.S. DOL

Lange, S. (1997). Interview by author, tape recording, RTP, NC (October 15).

Matheny, C. (1998). Interview by author, typed responses by interviewee, and notes from interview, Durham, NC (July 29).

Melius, D. J. (1998). Melius, Dr. James, former director of the NIOSH Health Hazard Evaluation Division, telephone interview by author, notes (February 18).

Mintz, B. (1984). OSHA: History, Law, and Policy. Washington D.C.: BNA Books.

Mirer, F. (1998). Telephone conversation with director of health and safety, United Auto Workers Union (July 14).

NIEHS. (1986a). Cover letter from John M. Dement, PhD, with program announcement, to parties with appropriate capabilities, and a potential interest in applying for the worker training program grants (December 15). University of Massachusetts Lowell. From files of the New England Consortium, Department of Work Environment.

NIEHS. (1986b). A History of Progress: NIEHS, The First 20 Years (1966 to 1986). Unpublished brochure. Durham, NC. From files of Carol Matheny.

NIEHS. (1987a). Letter of award notice to successful applicants, from John Dement, acting SWT program manager, review team summary statement attached to letter (September 4). The New England Consortium, Department of Work Environment, University of Massachusetts Lowell.

NIEHS. (1987b). Response letter to those who submitted letters of intent to apply to the SWTP, package, including a response to issues raised at the public meeting and a summary of factors that would be considered during proposal review (March 27). The New England Consortium, Department of Work Environment, University of Massachusetts Lowell.

NIEHS. (1987c). Rosters of the Special Review Committees for the Superfund Hazardous Waste Worker Health and Safety Training Program, for review meetings on July 7-9 and July 14-16, 1987 (July 7). From NIEHS SWTP files, RTP, NC.

NIEHS. (1990). Site Visit Report for NIEHS: National Clearinghouse on Occupational and Environmental Health, July 16-17. From NIEHS WETP, RTP, NC.

NIEHS. (1995). An Evaluation of the NIEHS Superfund Worker Training Grant Program: External Panel Report. December 28, 1995. Final copy release, April 16, 1996.

Organization Resources Counselors. (1987). Testimony of Organization Resources Counselors, Inc. (November 23). OSHA Docket S-760 A: Exhibit 39, U.S. DOL.

Peart, L. D. (1987). Memo for the record, NIH/PHS (January 6). Management Operations Branch, NIEHS WETP

Rall, D. (1997). Interview by author, Washington, DC (December 10).

Samuels, S. (1998). Interview by author, tape recording, Solomon's Is., MD (January 16).

Sassaman, A. (1997). Interview by author, tape recording, RTP, NC (October 16).

Seminario, M. (1987). Testimony of Margaret Seminario, Associate Director, Department of Safety, Health and Social Security, AFL-CIO (October 15). OSHA Docket S-760 A, Exhibit 32, U.S. DOL.

Seminario, M. (1997). Interview by author, tape recording. Washington, DC (December 10).

Slatin, C., & Siqueira, E. (1998). Does a Collateral Duty Require Less Protection: Workers, Hazardous Materials Emergency Response, and OSHA's Failure to Protect. *New Solutions, A Journal of Environmental and Occupational Health Policy, 8*(2), 205-219.

Soros, C. C. (1987). Exhibit 52. Letter dated October 6, 1987, to OSHA from president Local 2898 IAFF, Seattle Fire Chiefs Association. OSHA Docket S-760 A, U.S. DOL.

Superfund Amendments and Reauthorization Act of 1986 (SARA), U.S. Public Law 99-499. 42 USC 9601. (1986).

Tobey, S., & Revitte, J. (1981). Building Worker Competence. *Labor Studies Journal, 6*(1), 41-52.

U.S. DHHS. (1981). Standards of Conduct: Regulations Which Apply to All HHS Officers and Employees. In Department of Health and Human Services (Ed.), Personnel Pamphlet Series (January 23, No. 6).

U.S. DHHS. (1991, March). PHS Program Officials Handbook. Office of the Assistant Secretary for Health, Office of Management, Public Health Service.

Van Gelder, L. (1996, November 13). Trash Collector Dies After Inhaling Discarded Acid. *The New York Times,* p. B1.

CHAPTER 5

Cohesion, Conflicts, and Excellence: The WETP Grows

NIEHS directed its worker training program with the intention of fusing the awardees into a cohesive group addressing hazardous waste operations and emergency response workers' health and safety issues and training needs. In this process, they confronted conflicts that often reflected differences in strategies and institutional needs between the different union awardees who represented workers in various industrial sectors, as well as between the unions and the university-based awardees.[1] Examining the conflicts will help to relate their significance to broader issues of worker health and safety. The evidence repeatedly reveals one path to success: Both NIEHS and the awardees prioritized excellence as a central value with which to achieve their goals.

EXPANDING THE PROGRAM

By the end of its second year, out of recognition of the WETP's successful start-up and the need for additional resources, Congress doubled its funding to $20 million a year. More funding meant the expansion of the programs of some awardees and the drawing in of a new set of grant winners, bringing the total to 16, involving 58 institutions.

On October 17, 1989, WETP personnel met to formulate an expansion plan in accordance with the increase in funding. Attending were Drs. Anne Sassaman and John Dement, as well as Denny Dobbin, Carol Matheny, and several others from NIEHS.[2] They first addressed the drafting of a request for applications in a solicitation for competitive supplements to existing awardees' grants and new applications. Next, they had to increase staffing to deal with growth. They agreed to press for more staff and office space (Dobbin, 1989).

The participants assumed that many new proposals would address the needs of public emergency responders, especially in local government. They also assumed that most of the best-qualified applicants would be existing awardees (Dobbin, 1989). Strong interest was anticipated, and they decided to write the request for applications (RFA) in such a way as to limit them to organizations that could best deliver training efficiently and provide the strongest coverage of target populations. The RFA set the coverage of large and well-identified audiences as a review criterion. Access to workers and the ability and intention to deliver hands-on training were emphasized.

The team decided that the program could be expanded appropriately to include training for workers at businesses and operations that generated hazardous waste. The RFA said that successful applicants should (1) target nationwide and regional coverage; (2) cover no less than statewide political jurisdictions (thereby limiting proposals addressing municipalities); (3) maximize the use of existing curricula; (4) multiply the training impact through "train-the-trainer" programs; and (5) represent a collaboration or consortium of two or more nonprofit organizations (Dobbin, 1989). The last point marked the continuance of the desire of NIEHS managers to maximize the number of organizations and institutions included in the WETP while minimizing the number of awardees with whom NIEHS would have to directly interact (Dobbin, 1997).

On December 28, 1989, an RFA was announced in the Federal Register (U.S. DHHS-NIEHS, 1989). In addition to the delineated criteria, the program was enlarged to cover workers engaged in transporting hazardous materials. The expansions later multiplied the conflicts among the awardees.

PROGRAM STAFFING—JOSEPH (CHIP) HUGHES

Early in 1990, NIEHS hired Joseph (Chip) Hughes as a public health educator to help manage and coordinate the administrative and technical aspects of the WETP. Hughes had a wealth of background and experience in labor and community development education, organizing, and research; occupational and environmental health education and policy research and analysis; social and industrial development research; and program administration. During the 1970s, he was the research director at the Institute for Southern Studies, a fellow with the John Hay Whitney Foundation, and director of education and training at the Carolina Brown Lung Association. In these positions, he had developed and published reports on energy development, land ownership, agriculture, military spending, and industrial development; he had researched and evaluated the effectiveness of state-operated OSHA enforcement programs and workers' compensation systems in the Carolinas; and he had activated training programs and educational materials for textile workers. He had also implemented and evaluated an OSHA New Directions grant program in collaboration with the Amalgamated Clothing and Textile Workers Union.

During the 1980s, Hughes worked as a researcher for the U.S. Department of Labor, the National Institute of Mental Health, the North Carolina Safety and Health Project, and the Clean Water Fund of North Carolina. He worked on community and worker education and organizing projects for the Farmworkers Legal Services Corporation, the Workers Defense League (AFL-CIO), the East Coast Farmworker Support Network, and North Carolina Fair Share's Utilities Campaign.

Hughes's skills, background, and activist orientation strengthened the WETP's administration. He interacted comfortably with both the labor and university programs and helped coordinate activities at NIEHS and with other federal agencies.

QUALITY ASSURANCE: SITE REVIEWS

Both the WETP administrators and many awardees wanted to develop training programs that would be highly regarded for their excellence and viewed as models for training in the industrial sectors covered by the OSHA and EPA HAZWOPER regulations.[3] NIEHS personnel, past and current, repeatedly said that the primary reasons for an emphasis on excellence were commitments to public health practice and the prevention of workplace injuries and illnesses. Other reasons included accountability to Congress and the EPA; a desire to demonstrate to employers the level of quality expected of efforts to comply with OSHA worker health and safety training requirements; and the need to determine a basis from which a scientific evaluation of training effectiveness could be made. These were noted in the summary report of the 1990 site visit reviews (NIEHS, 1991e).

NIEHS maintained—and still maintains—two primary tools for quality control and assurance in awardee programs. These were in addition to the requirement for awardees to establish an independent board of advisors and create mechanisms for ongoing evaluation of training quality, effectiveness, and appropriateness. The WETP required each awardee to submit an annual progress report along with its yearly reapplication. Before any award of funding for each consecutive project year in a multiyear award, NIEHS required that awardees submit a noncompetitive reapplication. This became an opportunity for NIEHS to review annually each awardee's financial expenditures and program accomplishments. Program and financial management staff successfully used the reapplications to identify the strengths and weaknesses of each participating program. They also used the process to confer with the principal investigators about concerns or about directions that NIEHS wanted to encourage (Dement, 1997; Dobbin, 1997; Matheny, 1998; National Clearinghouse for Worker Safety and Health Training, 1995).

The second tool for quality assurance and control was peer-reviewed site visits under the supervision of NIEHS staff. NIEHS conducted some site visits to awardee programs during the first 2 years. Rall wanted to continue these reviews and received additional administrative funding for two temporary staff assignments for this purpose. Hughes was given one of the positions, as a program and policy analyst; this was the way he was brought into the program. The other position was given to Cheryl Shultz, PhD, who had been a deputy director of the North Carolina state OSHA office.[4] Individual consulting contractors, accompanied by Shultz, Dement, Dobbin, and Matheny, and on occasion Rall, visited several awardees for progress reviews assessing a range of activities, including curriculum development, trainer preparation and competency, training delivery, and fiscal management. In addition, limited numbers of visits by a peer review team were made in 1989. Afterward, NIEHS planned for formal peer-reviewed site visits in 1990. NIEHS wanted to make sure that each of the awardees would receive "a minimum of one on-site review that would be representative of their overall training program" (NIEHS, 1991e). The NIH peer review system ensured that funds expended for the WETP had "high program relevance and [were] solidly grounded in technically sound institutions and organizations" (NIEHS, 1991e, p. 3).

Review visit protocols and goals were established. Each awardee faced a 2-3 day "inspection" by a team of five outside reviewers accompanied by NIEHS administration and grants management staff. The teams observed real-time training, both classroom and hands-on. The process was designed so that reviewers could assess "[t]he balance between didactic classroom training and hands-on field exercises" (NIEHS, 1991e) with an emphasis on reviewing technical accuracy and the competent use of training and education methods. The criteria for rating were based on those stated in the original program announcement. Each awardee evaluation assessed progress in achieving the goals set forth in the awardee's own proposal to NIEHS. Like the grant application review teams, the site reviewers represented labor, universities, employers, government, ER organizations, and independent professionals.

The reviews had four key objectives: (1) program quality assurance and control, reviewing awardee compliance with the program's terms as established in each award notice; (2) providing a "state-of-the-art analysis" that would help awardees improve their efforts; (3) setting up an "intermediary review"; and (4) assessing the quality and impact of each program so as to reflect the status of each awardee and the total program (NIEHS, 1991d).

To achieve uniform reviews, NIEHS developed guidelines and a checklist. Review teams received instructions for preparing reports, which were to include a program description; a critique of a program's strengths and weaknesses, as per the review criteria; a budget discussion, assessing the appropriateness of the budget and its utilization in the training program; and a summary and recommendations. The guidelines were based on long-established NIH rules.

The reviews were completed in 6 months and a summary was presented to NIEHS in August 1990. At a meeting, Hughes gave a progress report to help the reviewers understand the overall status of the program. He noted that, from September 1, 1989, to August 1990, most awardees had dramatically increased the number of courses delivered as compared with the previous two years—to approximately 2,900 courses for 71,480 workers. The increase in training activities resulted in significant reductions in the costs per course and per workers trained, Hughes noted (1990b).

Alan Stevens assisted NIEHS with the site reviews through an interagency agreement with NIOSH. Stevens had formerly been a director of extramural programs at NIOSH. The contract with Stevens was a conscious act by NIEHS designed to strengthen its ties with NIOSH, which held Stevens in high regard.[5] At the August meeting, Stevens commented on some of the barriers the program faced. He particularly pointed to the fact that "little actual site clean-up is going on in the country" (Deutsch, 1990), but said that a significant national hazardous waste site analysis and assessment was underway. This analysis was being conducted by professionals who had received health and safety training from the WETP. Stevens believed that the awardees' training of these professionals was necessary and appropriate as the nation prepared for clean-up work.

The discussion then focused on general comments made by site visit reviewers and on developments in hazardous waste worker training (Deutsch, 1990). Steven Deutsch, a labor educator from the University of Oregon who chaired the review committee, summarized its findings in 18 recommendations. Many of them became guidelines for the future direction of the NIEHS program, based on the evidence of their inclusion in RFAs that were issued in 1991 and 1994 (50 Federal Register, 1991; NIH Guide, 1994). The committee recommended the following:

- working to reach HAZMAT ER workers and hazardous waste transportation workers;
- emphasizing evaluation and quality control of the training; it was suggested that NIEHS stress outcome-oriented evaluation objectives;
- emphasizing awardee efforts to facilitate program self-sufficiency;[6]
- interacting and communicating better with federal regulatory agencies addressing hazardous waste operations and ER worker protection, particularly addressing certification;
- communicating better with hazardous waste clean-up employers about their perceived needs for training, especially in clean-up efforts coordinated by the DOE and DOD;
- addressing underrepresented workers, such as those in remote geographical areas, nonunion workers, those with significant literacy barriers, and those for whom English is not their primary language (particularly Spanish-speaking workers);
- organizing greater outreach to employers who have to provide this kind of training for employees;
- conducting periodic NIEHS assessments to determine the "learned lessons" of the program;
- ensuring that materials are appropriate for the widespread mixed training audiences of blue-collar and professional workers, in light of specified hazardous waste operations trends; and
- stressing the importance of "solid industrial hygiene and toxicology content in all training." (Deutsch, 1990)

Many of the recommendations were accepted and acted on by the WETP. NIEHS set the direction for such activities either through RFAs or through awards for supplemental funding. Awardees focused their efforts anew on these goals.

FORMING CONSENSUS: THE WETP STRENGTHENS COLLECTIVE ACTIVITIES

The WETP was well established by its third program year (September 1989–August 1990). The awardees, each with specific interests and intentions, worked collectively as a component of the national health and safety movement that addressed worker training and education issues and related those issues to hazardous waste operations and ER workers. On January 28, 1990, OSHA issued an NPRM for the accreditation of training programs for hazardous waste operations (U.S. DOL, 1990). The agency issued the notice in response to a Congressional mandate in amendments to SARA that became law with the passage of an omnibus budget reconciliation bill in December 1987.[7] (The amendment to Section 126 of SARA was inserted by Sen. Edward P. Boland [D-MA] and was referred to as the "Boland insertion" in future discussions of the amendment in the WETP and by other interested parties.)

Through multiple channels, it became increasingly evident that the awardees were developing worker-oriented training of a high level of quality and excellence.

Dement and Dobbin worried about the training that was provided in accordance with the OSHA HAZWOPER standard by nongrantees, such as employers, consulting groups, and universities and colleges. Programs that they observed or that were reported to them, Dement said, sometimes assembled "25 or 30 or 50 people in a conference room on a weekend and you hammer away, and you make a lot of money, and they come over with a certificate, and they are 'trained.'" With OSHA's issuance of the NPRM for accreditation, NIEHS began to consider how best to use the experience and expertise of its awardees to encourage OSHA to establish "reasonably high benchmarks" (Dement, 1997). Dobbin and John Moran, who served as a technical expert with the Laborers-AGC program, wanted the WETP to sponsor a technical workshop for its awardees and invited guests to establish minimum criteria for HAZWOPER training. Its purpose would be to develop a document on minimum criteria for hazardous waste worker and emergency responder health and safety training that OSHA would endorse in its process of promulgating a training program accreditation rule. They also hoped that, in Moran's words, the document "might serve as a specification for employers who were purchasing training programs or developing [their own training programs]." They understood that NIEHS could produce only a set of guidelines as program models, but they wanted to see OSHA, other federal agencies, and employers base their training specifications on NIEHS guidelines.[8] They intended to produce a consensus document developed by technical representatives from a network of national programs, and they invited experts from industry, labor, government, and academia.

THE EFFORT TO ACHIEVE A MINIMUM CRITERIA DOCUMENT

Moran and Dobbin have described the way in which the spring 1990 technical workshop to develop minimum criteria for training was developed by NIEHS, as well as its outcomes (Moran & Dobbin, 1991). Moran had Superfund site experience and knew the wide variations in the training programs that were offered. He had found that "the principal emphasis among many of the training providers was just to get in the number of hours required" (Moran, 1998).

The process for a technical workshop that Moran and Dobbin established was used repeatedly by the WETP and therefore warrants some review. At the spring 1989 awardees' meeting, an ad hoc committee was established to steer and plan the workshop. A draft, or "straw-man" document, primarily written by Moran and Dobbin, was submitted later to the committee for review.

CONFLICT OVER TESTING

A meeting of the planning committee was scheduled for January 4 and 5, 1990. In the meantime, Sylvia Krekel and Michael Merrill, both of OCAW, sent a letter about trainee testing issues to the committee members (OCAW, 1989). The first working draft of the "straw-man" document that was distributed by Dement and Moran established a requirement for training organizations to administer a closed-book, multiple-choice exam. OCAW strongly objected to making the test one of the minimum criteria. The union stressed the importance of an "appropriate evaluation process" for all of the NIEHS awardees but believed that a multiple-choice exam would not be appropriate for all of them. OCAW offered revisions in an effort to "ensure that our minimum criteria are both flexible enough to be relevant to every situation and rigorous enough to guarantee that only programs of the highest quality offer training courses" (OCAW, 1989). The statement showed that NIEHS had facilitated a process that afforded opportunities for voicing opposition yet at the same time maintained its commitment to building cohesiveness.

OCAW representatives stated that a closed-book multiple-choice test would not be "an adequate measure of a person's ability to do a particular job" (OCAW, 1989). They challenged the assumption in the draft document that such a test was an adequate method for the training programs to certify workers as being adequately skilled to satisfactorily perform hazardous waste operations and ER activities.

Merrill had previously written an article in response to OSHA's draft proposals for the accreditation rule (Merrill, 1989). In this article, he strongly opposed OSHA's proposal to use the EPA's Model Accreditation Plan for Asbestos Abatement Training as the format for its rule. Although Section 126 of SARA had been amended to require a program "no less comprehensive" than the EPA model, Merrill argued that OSHA's adoption of that model would be inappropriate. OSHA suggested that generic training like that provided off-site by the NIEHS awardees was not adequate for such high-risk employees as those engaged in hazardous waste operations. Merrill argued that, combined with the testing requirement, the proposed standard would "encourage the proliferation of superficial, exam-driven cram courses masquerading as safety and health training programs . . . [and] the fact that the proposed standard allows training programs to develop their own tests guarantees that this will happen" (Merrill, 1989, p. 9). Merrill also contended that prohibiting generic courses by duly accredited programs would encourage employers' avoidance of health and safety training that would help workers to challenge their employers' practices. He argued that

> Instead of certifying employees as "safe," the standard should aim instead at certifying employers as "responsible." Employers should be required to demonstrate that they have provided their employees with training from a nationally-recognized, fully-accredited safety and health training program. And before they are accredited, training programs should be required to submit to a full-scale peer review by an independent panel of health professionals and training experts no less comprehensive and rigorous than that called for in the competition for federal grants. (Merrill, 1991, p. 50)

OCAW maintained its opposition to the use of closed-book multiple-choice testing to evaluate the program's effectiveness in training workers. According to Moran, the most difficult issue facing the workshop was the position taken by OCAW on testing. It was not the only issue, though. A range of others came up at the meeting (NIEHS, 1990a). Representatives of 8 of the 11 awardees were present. Most of the members of the committee were concerned that OSHA was not realistic in its listing of the course material that training providers would be required to present. OSHA had agreed to employer demands for the establishment of a limited training course

(24 hours instead of 40 hours) for those personnel who would be only occasional site visitors and thus free of significant health and safety risks. The committee decided that rather than set criteria for the training, it would write to OSHA explaining its objections to the limited occasional site visitors' training. Another major concern was the appropriateness of using a written test to assess instructor competence.

The testing issue arose again during an "intense debate" (NIEHS, 1990a) over the evaluation of trainees after their initial training ended. The issue was whether individuals or groups of trainees should be evaluated. Representatives of the Laborers, the Operating Engineers, and the Midwest Consortium contended that "an individual trainee should attain a minimum level of knowledge and skill before he or she could be considered to have 'successfully completed' a hazardous material course" (NIEHS, 1990a). The representatives believed that a minimum level of trainee proficiency should be shown by the use of written examinations and/or skill demonstrations. Here again, OCAW argued for group learning, which would be evaluated through instructor observation and anonymous pre- and post-course surveys. Language that permitted both modes of evaluation was accepted.

THE CONSENSUS DOCUMENT

One last issue was whether to invite technical experts to the workshop. Moran believed that technical authorities would provide external expert peer review and thus increase the credibility of the final document. No one objected. Dobbin strongly believed that representatives of the various federal agencies dealing with hazardous waste and ER issues should be invited and asked to address the opening plenary session. It was a prime example of the way that Dobbin and NIEHS integrated the WETP with other federal efforts.

At the end of the planning meeting, several work groups were formed to craft sections of the document. With the involvement of awardees and other key participants, a level of consensus was established even before the workshop took place. This provided sufficient support to enable the draft to be substantially completed at the 3-day workshop. The revised "straw-man" document was widely distributed to awardees and to "a broad range of external experts for review and comment" (Moran & Dobbin, 1991, p. 108).

The workshop that was held on March 22–24, 1990, in Washington, DC, produced a consensus document (Moran & Dobbin, 1991) that represented the successful implementation of NIEHS's strategies to build a national constituency for health and safety training. NIEHS obtained strong participation from its awardees. The WETP organized a challenge to OSHA's and the EPA's weak support for worker health and safety training. Despite this, OSHA continued to waver in response to its Congressional mandate to implement HAZWOPER training certification procedures. To date, its effort has resulted only in a nonmandatory appendix that details criteria for the training programs. The appendix is based on the NIEHS's minimum criteria, but omits significant portions of them.[9]

The Minimum Criteria Workshop and Document produced a consensus on some important training issues for HAZMAT ER workers. Central among them was a consensus statement that "Emergency responders' training programs should be included" for coverage under the OSHA accreditation rule, 29 CFR 1910.121

(NIEHS, 1991b, p. 21). But OSHA subsequently chose to exclude these training programs from its rule. Another area of consensus concerned the minimum set of topics and categories that were defined as needing to be included in ER training, which exceeded those established by OSHA. In addition, OSHA largely failed to set a standard for training course duration that would provide adequate time to address the topics necessary for the various levels of ER training. The ER subgroup agreed that "The number of hours of training as prescribed by OSHA for training of emergency responders is inadequate to appropriately teach them the health and safety material required for their protection" (NIEHS, 1991b, p. 22).

The subgroup listed 10 categories of ER personnel for whom training programs would include a means of assuring professional qualification in performing ER duties. The list did not include "industrial personnel whose full-time job is not chemical ER" (NIEHS, 1991b, p. 22). The section noted that other chemical emergency responders might be covered by 29 CFR 1910.120, but the training programs did not need to include "a means of assuring professional qualification" as emergency responders. This demonstrated that the NIEHS program and its awardees addressed the differences between defined ER workers and those "whose full-time job is not chemical ER." The tacit agreement that the standard's section (q)(6) applied to all workers with emergency response duties reflected the awardees maturing respect for the unique worker training needs met by each program. It also, however, expressed an underlying tension resulting from insufficient program resources to address the large number of workers who were actually and potentially at risk of exposure to hazardous materials in emergency incidents.

SUPPLEMENTAL AND NEW AWARDS

At the same time that NIEHS was coordinating the process of developing the minimum criteria, it was also preparing to expand the WETP. NIEHS issued an RFA on December 28, 1989, to which it received 41 responses. Nine came from existing awardees seeking supplemental funding, and 11 were new applications. The existing awardees, of course, had the advantages of "already developed curriculum, established target populations and delivered training that can be evaluated" (NIEHS, 1990b). Most of the new awards were directed toward training for industrial and public-sector ER. NIEHS justified its decision based on OSHA's identification of those responders as the largest worker populations in need of health and safety training (NIEHS, 1991f, p. 22). However, NIEHS also acknowledged a "shortage of available training for both site workers involved in Superfund clean-ups and at hazardous waste treatment and disposal facilities" (NIEHS, 1991f, p. 22). Consequently, supplemental funding was provided to the L-AGC, the ICWU, and OCAW to cover more workers in more geographic areas. The ICWU, the L-AGC, and the OCAW, all received supplemental funding to train workers at DOE nuclear facilities undergoing environmental restoration. The ICWU consortium expanded to include several new unions—the International Association of Machinists, the Flint and Glass Workers Union, and the Aluminum, Brick, and Glass Workers Union.

One of the new awards was made to the Alice Hamilton Consortium, which was directed by a Washington, DC, area COSH group, the Alice Hamilton Occupational Health Center, and included several other COSH organizations, AFSCME, and two universities. One member of this consortium was the Alaska Health Project (a COSH group), which proposed to develop training for oil spill clean-up workers. The Exxon Valdez oil spill disaster had devastated the Alaskan shoreline the previous year. Many untrained workers had been brought in to participate in the cleanup. As part of OSHA's final HAZWOPER rulemaking, OSHA determined that oil products would be included in the definition of hazardous waste materials, despite oil industry objections and criticism that OSHA was disregarding the Congressional decision not to call oil products hazardous materials. NIEHS used the OSHA determination to support its belief that oil spill clean-up workers required health and safety training.

Other new awards were made to the UAW for auto workers at waste-generating facilities; to the IBT for transporters of hazardous materials; to the George Meany Center for Labor Studies, directing a consortium that would address the training needs of railroad workers; and to the Service Employees International Union (SEIU) for training highway workers, sewage and water plant operators, and gas utility workers.

Several university consortia received supplemental funding as well. The California Consortium was funded to include the University of Arizona, which was to develop Spanish curricula. The Midwest Consortium received funding to include the United Brotherhood of Carpenters (UBC) Health and Safety Fund of North America, AFSCME, the University of Minnesota, and Roane State Community College in Tennessee.

THREE YEARS OF PROGRESS

By September 1990, the original 11 awardees had established their programs, developed curricula and approaches, trained instructors, and delivered a sizable number of training courses for thousands of workers. An NIEHS report of the WETP's progress outlined its accomplishments through August 1990 (NIEHS, 1991f).

The L-AGC and IUOE programs had developed the capacity for training at local and regional training centers that were equipped to provide mock hazardous waste site hands-on training for clean-up workers. OCAW and the ICWU had developed course curricula for workers involved in the treatment, storage, and/or disposal of hazardous wastes, and for workers responding to HAZMAT emergency incidents in their workplaces. The ICWU had established a national training center, while OCAW had developed a network of locally based trainers. The Seattle Fire Department and the IAFF had both developed training materials for public-sector emergency responders. The curriculum addressed the levels of response activities established in NFPA and OSHA standards. The various university-based consortia had devised and were delivering a range of courses for a spectrum of targeted worker populations engaged in hazardous waste operations and HAZMAT ER. The awardees had a network of training centers and instructors that covered the West Coast, the South, the Midwest, the mid-Atlantic, and the New England states. The WETP awardees were meeting the training needs of hazardous waste site workers at Superfund sites and state and private hazardous waste site clean-up operations; they were also meeting the training needs of workers at RCRA TSD facilities and workers with responsibility for in-plant HAZMAT ER actions; and "[a]pproximately sixty percent of the NIEHS-supported training was focused on reaching public-sector emergency responders, such as police and firefighters" (NIEHS, 1991f, p. 7), covering populations targeted in Section 126 of SARA and in SARA's Title III.

In the first 3 years of the WETP, the awardees delivered 7,151 courses, in which 165,504 workers were trained. Workers had been trained in all 10 federal regions, with the majority of those trained being located in New Jersey and New York, on the West Coast, and in the Midwest (NIEHS, 1991f; 1995, p. 13).[10]

Between September 1, 1989, and August 31, 1990, the NIEHS staff coordinated the planning and implementation of the Minimum Criteria Technical Workshop, conducted visits to all awardee sites, reviewed the site visit reports, processed and coordinated reviews of 41 applications either for supplemental funding or for new awards, and oversaw the national training grant program, including the processing of continuing reapplication proposals and progress reports.

In that period, the awardees nearly tripled the number of courses delivered in comparison with the previous year and doubled the number of workers trained. They also committed staff resources to plan a national workshop to establish a consensus document detailing the minimum criteria for hazardous waste operations and ER training. They all prepared for site visits—a significant effort, since each awardee developed its programs thorough progress reports and presentations made to the reviewers. At least half of the organizations prepared proposals for supplemental funding to support expansion, even while they prepared for the on-site reviews.

OSHA HEARINGS

In another important effort, nearly all of the awardees reviewed drafts of the hazardous waste training program accreditation rule that OSHA had proposed on January 26, 1990. In July, OSHA announced a schedule for hearings on the rule, which would be held in the week of October 2, 1990. The hearings were rescheduled twice, with final dates in January 1991 in Washington, DC, and February 1991 in Cincinnati. Most of the initial awardees gave written comments and oral testimony to OSHA, as did NIEHS.

A review of efforts by NIEHS and the awardees to change OSHA's proposed training program accreditation rule demonstrated the importance of training to the national health and safety movement. In anticipation of OSHA's hearings, NIEHS scheduled two meetings for awardees. The first was a mini-technical workshop on quality of training issues for emergency responders, held in Washington, DC, on December 11, 1990. Hughes told awardees that NIEHS wanted to develop a proposal "for inclusion of ER training with the OSHA 1910.121 regulations" (Hughes, 1990a). Hughes presented questions about emergency responder health and safety training and asked awardees to fax their answers to NIEHS so they could be summarized as a basis for discussion.

The meeting helped the awardees shape their comments for OSHA. One unresolved issue, which was at least put on paper, was the need to define HAZMAT

ER workers. Included in the definition, but missing from the Minimum Criteria Document, were workers with ER as a collateral duty; such a worker was later defined as "[a]n individual who, as a function of his employment, is expected to react or respond to a hazardous material incident as an individual or a member of a team at a single work site or system" (National Clearinghouse on Occupational and Environmental Health, 1990). Workers with this kind of duty added to their job responsibilities did become a greater focus of the WETP with regard to new awardee organizations, such as the two service-sector unions and the rail unions. As the WETP's scope expanded to address more ER workers, the needs of workers with a collateral duty to respond to HAZMAT incidents became a greater focus for the ICWU and OCAW. Both unions had originally dealt more with workers at RCRA treatment, storage, and disposal facilities.

The second meeting, also a technical workshop, was held in Cincinnati, Ohio, on February 10-11, 1991. NIEHS had contracted with the Association of Occupational and Environmental Clinics (AOEC), a national network of occupational medicine clinics, to develop health effects training modules for use by the awardees. Although excellent materials had been developed by the awardees, most saw the value of having a set of case-based modules developed by clinicians. The goal was to help AOEC develop general criteria for health effects curriculum modules for hazardous waste and ER worker training.

At the end of a memo on the meeting, Dobbin added a note telling awardees that OSHA's hearings on the proposed rule would be held in Cincinnati on the 3 days after the workshop. NIEHS planned this so that awardee representatives who intended to testify at the hearings could attend the workshop and the hearings without any conflict. This exemplified the effort by NIEHS staff to build cohesiveness in the program so as to strengthen the national health and safety movement. The workshop itself demonstrated the ways in which NIEHS integrated the efforts of occupational health professionals with those of labor in developing worker-oriented health and safety training.

Dement, Dobbin, and Hughes all submitted testimony on behalf of NIEHS at the OSHA hearings. They carefully described the mechanisms for peer review of proposals and program site visits. NIEHS submitted 34 pages of testimony with three appendices, including sections from the Minimum Criteria Document and a thorough review of the literature evaluating the effectiveness of worker safety and health training. NIEHS urged the coverage of all 1910.120 training programs in the accreditation rule (including emergency responder training); the accreditation of annual refresher training; the establishment of 40 hours of training as a minimum for all hazardous waste site personnel; the incorporation of specific quantitative and qualitative measures of effectiveness, as detailed in the Minimum Criteria Document; the incorporation of a peer review process; and the use of NIEHS's Characteristics of Hazardous Waste Worker Training Programs, stated in the original NIEHS program announcement "as minimum criteria for evaluating worker training programs which seek OSHA accreditation" (NIEHS, 1991g, p. 14). Remarks from the awardees generally addressed the issues covered by NIEHS, as well as some others related to each industry sector or type of program offered.

ISSUES, CONFLICTS, AND GROUP DYNAMICS

The success of the NIEHS staff in establishing consensus and cohesiveness did not eliminate conflicts. In fact, serious conflict arose during the WETP's fourth year. The key areas of contention involved definitions of target populations, the division of resources to serve those populations' needs, and the determination of the appropriate amount of training for each group. The conflicts resulted primarily from individual awardees' interest in addressing the largely unmet needs of specific workers while not understanding the extent of the unmet needs of other workers. The NIEHS staff were positioned to facilitate processes through which the awardees could raise and address conflicts. The staff then would make administrative judgments about the degrees of support for each competing interest.

Particularly problematic was the requirement to provide training that addressed criteria set in a regulation. The legislative language related the training program directly to the OSHA standard. This fact caused concerns about appropriate target populations for training. Throughout the program's development, this matter produced conflicts between the program administrators and the awardees. The willingness and skill of the administrators in negotiating conflict resolutions demonstrated their commitment, as activists, to supporting the awardees' constituents.

Training course duration (in hours) was problematic particularly for awardees who gave ER training. Although the WETP and its awardees vigorously urged OSHA to expand the number of hours it required for ER training, OSHA maintained its initial concessions to employer demands as against extensive training requirements for workers who would be engaged in ER actions.[11] Many awardees planned to give more training to ER workers than was required by a strict interpretation of the standard. In this matter, NIEHS supported the development and delivery of more extensive training and had included an increase in the allotted training time in recommendations to OSHA for its accreditation rule. WETP awardees faced the problem of not being able to sell the extended training to employers who questioned whether they had to provide that much time away from work for ER training. Some awardees bowed to employers and delivered shorter courses. They did this quite successfully, training a large number of public ER workers; still, the issue developed into a significant conflict and even threatened the stability of the WETP.

Hughes presented comprehensive training statistics at the October 22, 1990, awardees' meeting. In one chart, he broke down the training statistics by federal region and program year. The statistics for Region 2, primarily New Jersey and New York, were astounding. In the third year, 30,835 workers had been trained, which was double the number in each of the next two highest regions and approximately 10 times greater than the numbers in most other regions. On closer examination, it became obvious that the New Jersey/New York Consortium had trained a vast number of public-sector ER workers. Hughes's figures also described the sizes of the targeted populations, which demonstrated that, by far, the emergency responder workforce exceeded all other HAZWOPER categories (NIEHS, 1991f).[12]

The IAFF was worried about the statistics on the training of ER workers. The firefighters' union argued that the statistics were an indication of some awardees' efforts to satisfy administrative "bean counters," and actually did an injustice to the needs of firefighters. The conflict in the program reflected a long-standing dispute in the ER sector between the direction of resources to firefighters and the direction of resources to police. The New Jersey/New York Consortium worked closely with the New Jersey State Police to train them for transportation-related HAZMAT ER.

The conflict was further broadened by the IAFF's contention that firefighters were the primary HAZMAT emergency responders. The IAFF argued, based on its experience, that many employers in the manufacturing, distribution, and other industrial sectors, particularly smaller employers, relied on public fire departments for HAZMAT ER, rather than establishing their own teams. Consequently, the IAFF argued that firefighters should be the priority target for ER training resources. This stance set the IAFF and the two industrial unions in the WETP against some of the university programs that trained industrial ER workers. The ICWU and OCAW argued that, more often than not, the employers of their members did not call on fire departments to respond to HAZMAT incidents. Their employers maintained ER teams or fire brigades, or contracted out such services, or expected line workers to assume ER as a collateral duty. They noted that employers were generally opposed to local fire departments gaining knowledge of employers' operations. The conflict centered on which ER workers should be the priority population for the expenditure of training resources.

Other ER worker training issues were more easily resolved, at least among the awardees. For example, by the time of the OSHA accreditation rule hearings, the WETP and its awardees had achieved a reasonable consensus and were able to recommend that OSHA should establish 24 hours of training as a minimum for awareness- and operations-level emergency responder training. OSHA set 8 hours as the minimum number for operations-level training and set no minimum number of hours for awareness-level training.[13] Since many employers were unwilling or unable to release workers for 8 hours of training, much training did not last that long.

Throughout the winter of 1991, discussions continued, in the effort to carve out a definition of ER workers and the appropriate length of their training courses, particularly awareness- and operations-level training. The IAFF raised the issue again at the May 1991 awardees' meeting at the Mine Safety and Health Administration (MSHA) training academy in Beckley, West Virginia.[14] By this time, the awardees had informally agreed on certain related issues. First, they decided that the length of operations-level ER training by WETP awardees would be set at 24 hours, as recommended to OSHA. This decision placed the awardees at a competitive disadvantage against other training vendors who offered operations-level training of 8-16 hours duration. (OSHA required at least 8 hours of this type of training.) All agreed, though, that 24 hours was the minimum length of time in which workers could achieve the level of competence mandated in the OSHA 1910.120 standard. The awardees also informally agreed, at NIEHS's urging, that awareness-level training conducted in less than 8 hours would not be submitted for reporting by NIEHS to the EPA, other than to demonstrate the amount of training provided in addition to reportable courses.[15] Despite these agreements, the IAFF remained convinced that inadequate resources were being allocated to meet the overwhelming needs of firefighters.

At a "Lessons Learned" workshop held by NIEHS in August 1991, NIEHS presented the awardees' responses to a survey on, among other things, the appropriate target populations for training. The IAFF gave a comparatively limited reply, suggesting that the target populations were only clean-up workers at uncontrolled waste sites, and

> hazardous materials emergency response personnel charged with providing emergency services through the community. Every effort should be made to focus the NIEHS grant program to provide adequate resources to assure that emergency response personnel, specifically firefighters, receive *professional operational level* hazardous materials training on a nationwide basis. Though many worker groups have a need for First Responder Awareness level training, firefighters in most communities have primary responsibility for initial response to hazardous materials incidents. They are also most likely to encounter unidentified hazardous materials in the course of their work. (NIEHS, 1991d, IAFF response)

NIEHS received a range of responses that revealed continuing conflict over the issue. The awardees' responses addressed: industrial ER workers; industrial workers who might be responsible for cleaning up HAZMAT spills; transportation workers; and employees of small businesses who might be responsible for cleaning up HAZMAT spills (NIEHS, 1991d).

The matter remained unresolved for the IAFF as late as the October 1991 awardees' meeting, at which the union announced that it intended to push for more stringent training requirements for emergency responders. The IAFF noted that such requirements might not be needed by industrial fire brigade personnel, but said that the union could not compromise the training needs of its members. The IAFF was willing to support different standards for workers in different industrial sectors if a practical solution could be established. The Teamsters opposed a split standard; they preferred that their members meet the more stringent one. Other awardees did not address the IAFF proposal at this time.[16]

A SENATOR REQUESTS INFORMATION

During this time when discussions and debates were taking place among the awardees, NIEHS unexpectedly received a request for program information in April 1991 from Senator Barbara Mikulski (D-MD), chair of the Veterans Administration, Housing and Urban Development, and Independent Agencies Subcommittee, which held jurisdiction over appropriations for Superfund activities. Mikulski wanted to "ensure that NIEHS worker training grant funds are distributed prudently and according to the intent of the law" (Mikulski, 1991). She asked NIEHS to answer 11 questions about plans for the WETP training, concluding with this one:

> Given the increasing demand to clean up hazardous waste sites including DOD and DOE nuclear waste sites, and given the limited training grant resources

> available, can you provide the Committee with a list of priorities for the allocation of NIEHS training funds over the next three years[?] (Mikulski, 1991)

Senator Mikulski's letter was apparently written at the behest of some labor union representatives who, according to David Mallino, believed that too much Superfund money was being used by the universities to provide awareness-level ER training. These union representatives hoped that the letter would force a shift in priorities, with a greater share of the funds going to advanced training for a smaller group of targeted workers. Mallino explained, however, that the NIEHS had taken into account a separate part of SARA, which seemed to require coverage of in-plant workers as well as clean-up specialists. A number of chemical plants had recently exploded, and it was obvious that workers in these facilities needed training. Consideration of who could potentially be exposed to hazardous waste in other sectors of industry made it obvious to health and safety staff and educators in other unions and academic programs that a range of workers could legitimately come under the provisions of Section 126 of SARA.

The NIEHS staff drafted answers to the senator's questions. In response to the final question about NIEHS's priorities for funding over the next 3 years, NIEHS said that the priorities had recently been publicly stated in the agency's promulgated Hazardous Waste Worker Training Program regulations.[17] Labor market data supported the priorities for training in each targeted population, including waste site clean-up workers, in-plant hazardous waste and ER workers, and HAZMAT transportation workers.

Some of the universities complained vehemently to Mikulski. Mallino said that Mikulski "felt kind of blind-sided . . . and you don't do that to a member of Congress. . . . even though she believed that it was a legitimate thing to do, she felt that she had not been made fully aware of what the politics were" (Mallino, 1997).

The matter was successfully resolved, from many perspectives. NIEHS demonstrated that appropriate judgments had been made with regard to both training awards and program oversight. The university programs and the unions representing worker populations who were not originally considered targets in need of protection and training continued their efforts. The unions that believed funds were not being appropriately distributed accepted the current arrangement, but they had provided NIEHS with a justification for maintaining these unions as high-priority targets for funding.

Conflicts over the distribution of funding persist, as might be expected in a competitive arrangement with funding levels that are inadequate to address extensive needs. Several labor representatives, however, made clear in interviews their satisfaction with having a basically supportive government agency make the funding distribution decisions rather than having a situation where an AFL-CIO or union staff person or committee was responsible for facilitating a collective decision among the eligible unions.

ACCOMPLISHMENTS AFTER 5 YEARS

The 1986 Superfund Reauthorization was passed for a 5-year period. In November 1990, Congress unexpectedly reauthorized the Superfund law for 3 years and extended the Superfund tax for 4 years (Barnett, 1994, p. 260). NIEHS issued a competitive RFA to fund worker training for the federal fiscal years 1992 through 1994,[18] years that saw some key program accomplishments.

By August 1991, the WETP had established best-practice guidelines through collective program experiences and the development of the Minimum Criteria Document. It had also made initial advances toward putting training evaluation measures in place to capture the outcomes of training. It confidently asserted that "Worker Training is Primary Prevention" (NIEHS, 1991d). The program had grown from 11 to 16 participant nonprofit organizations. By August 1992, 12,647 courses had been delivered, ranging from fewer than 8 hours up to 80 hours in length, to more than 285,000 workers across the country.

In its 1995 compendium, NIEHS profiled its awardees (National Clearinghouse for Worker Safety and Health Training, 1995). The two original building trades union programs had trained nearly 650 instructors (IUOE 500, L-AGC 142). The ICWU, IUOE, and L-AGC programs had all established state-of-the-art union training centers. The ICWU, OCAW, and UAW had trained workers as course instructors. All awardees were offering multiple-day training courses, each with at least 30% of course time devoted to hands-on activities. A number of excellent train-the-trainer programs had been established. The California Consortium had developed a day-long training session on participatory training methods for hazardous waste trainers that built on materials from a number of awardees and the curriculum was distributed to all awardees. One aspect of the curriculum that became a mainstay of many NIEHS training programs was the learning game called Toxic Jeopardy (California Consortium, 1990).

Innovative and participatory curricula had been developed. The IAFF's curricula included manuals and videotapes that were distributed widely to local fire departments for training volunteer and career firefighters. The materials were designed to build on each other to meet the needs of firefighter HAZMAT ER competence. The California and New England consortia both developed innovative participatory activities. The two consortia, along with OCAW, the ICWU, and others, devised materials that were "worker-centered or -oriented." OCAW originated various curricula that employed an innovative small group activity method coupled with a worker-to-worker training approach.

By the end of the fifth year, nearly all of the awardees were engaged in comprehensive evaluation of their programs and courses. Some of the more experimental and comprehensive approaches were developed by the ICWU, the University of Kentucky as part of the Midwest Consortium, the New Jersey/New York Consortium, the New England Consortium, and OCAW. In addition, NIEHS had implemented a well-developed program of peer review of its grantees.

In addition to hazardous waste clean-up and RCRA treatment, storage, and disposal facility workers, the WETP had successfully addressed the needs of workers with responsibilities for HAZMAT incident ER. The New Jersey/New York Consortium and the other university programs were training a range of public-sector ER workers. The IAFF was training firefighters. The George Meany Center for Labor Studies trained rail workers. OCAW, the ICWU, and the UAW trained workers with in-plant ER duties. SEIU and AFSCME targeted workers in public works departments and waste water and water treatment facilities, as well as other public facilities and institutions where HAZMAT incident ER might be required.

Several awardees had begun to focus on identified underserved worker populations. The California Consortium produced materials in Spanish, and with the expansion in the third year to include the University of Alabama, began planning to train workers along the U.S. border with Mexico. It had also developed limited-literacy manuals for blue-collar workers who had not had a traditionally complete educational background (that is, through the 12th grade). The Laborers-AGC had also sponsored literacy programs. The Alice Hamilton Consortium presented courses for rural Native American communities in Alaska and for African American and Spanish-speaking workers in small companies. The UAW had also targeted employees in small- to medium-sized workplaces outside the Big Three auto companies because these were "generally workplaces that have few if any resources to devote to health and safety training" (National Clearinghouse for Worker Safety and Health Training, 1995, p. 58).

DIRECTIONS AND PROBLEMS IN YEARS 6 THROUGH 10

The Federal Grant and Cooperative Agreement Act of 1977 established three forms of federal assistance relationships: contracts, grants, and cooperative agreements. Grants and cooperative agreements both gave support to the stimulation of specific activities that benefited the public, as opposed to the government, and were authorized by federal statute. The difference between the two is that, whereas grants are provided without substantial involvement by the awarding agency and the recipient, a cooperative agreement is awarded in the anticipation of substantial involvement by the awarding agency.

The WETP's administrators believed that since the program was conducted with their substantial involvement, therefore, the mode of assistance should be changed from the provision of grants to cooperative agreements. The 1990 site visit peer review process coupled with the overall effort of the first 4 years led the program administrators to this decision. Dobbin presented the rationale for the nature and extent of NIEHS involvement in a memo to Sassaman. The nature of NIEHS involvement was through "coordination, communication, technical assistance, and quality assurance . . . [accomplished through] . . . frequent contact, clearinghouse activities, technical workshops, site visits and meetings [and in addition] . . . continual involvement with other agencies" (NIEHS, 1991a). This document, too, revealed the emphasis on program excellence:

> A high level of quality in this program is essential. NIEHS will coordinate overall program evaluations to show the impact of the training on reducing worker-related injury and illness. The literature in this area is meager. . . . NIEHS will strive to assess the overall effectiveness of the training in terms of the nation's needs. (NIEHS, 1991a)

The issue defining the grants as cooperative agreements was raised with the NIEHS National Advisory Environmental Health Sciences Council and received council approval (NIEHS, 1991c).

The awards issued in September 1992 expanded the WETP to include 18 awardees. Two more joint labor-management trust funds were included—the Carpenters Health and Safety Fund and the National Ironworker and Employer Apprenticeship Training and Journeyman Upgrading Fund. An award was made to a national consortium of community colleges, under the direction of the Kirkland Community College Environmental Training Center in Iowa. Participation by the Seattle Fire Department was phased out.

On September 24, 1992, the DOE and NIEHS entered into an interagency agreement to develop worker training for hazardous waste workers at nuclear weapons facilities. The program was established by Congress in Section 3131 of the National Defense Authorization Act for fiscal years 1992 and 1993. In fiscal years 1993 and 1994, NIEHS made seven grants to existing awardees through this mechanism. The NIEHS's DOE training program awardees were the Carpenters, the ICWU, the Operating Engineers, the L-AGC, the New Jersey/New York Consortium, OCAW, and the IAFF. On August 12-13, 1993, NIEHS sponsored a technical workshop on curriculum for DOE training in support of the awardees' need to address nuclear industry worker health and safety.

Dr. Rall retired in 1990, and in 1991 Dr. Kenneth Olden was appointed as director of NIEHS, becoming the first African American to head an institute within the National Institutes of Health. Dr. Olden had been a cancer researcher for much of his career. Earlier, he had worked at the National Cancer Institute and then he had assumed leadership at Howard University's Cancer Center, prior to his appointment at NIEHS. Dr. Olden also had been the cochair of the American Cancer Society's Mid-Atlantic Region National Black Leadership on Cancer and its National Advisory Committee on Socio-economic Disadvantage. Olden strongly believed that the work of NIEHS was basic science research in the interests of public health, and it took him a while to come to appreciate the WETP. But steadily, Dr. Olden came to value the program and support its initiatives and awardees, which fitted well with his own goal of establishing an illness prevention orientation for the agency. A new WETP direction that came to receive his support was a program expansion into minority worker and environmental justice issues.

In 1994, NIEHS issued an RFA for another 5-year round of awards (NIH Guide, 1994). NIEHS said that $37 million was authorized. It included $20 million from the EPA for the WETP, $3 million from the EPA for the new Minority Worker Training Program (MWTP), $11 million from the DOE for nuclear clean-up workers, and $3 million from the DOT for HAZMAT transportation workers. (The DOT funds were not fully appropriated. The Teamsters and the George Meany Center for Labor Studies each received $125,000 for one year only.) Because of the increase in funding and scope, NIEHS allowed applicants to propose participation in multiple programs.

On September 1, 1995, the third award period of the program began, with 20 awardee organizations representing more than 90 institutions. The new awardees in the WETP included AFSCME (becoming an independent awardee); and in the

Minority Worker Training Program, DePaul University (Chicago), Clark Atlanta University Environmental Justice Center (in consortium with the Xavier University Deep South Environmental Justice Center and the L-AGC), and Jackson (Mississippi) State University. The Ironworkers became a subawardee of the Carpenters and the Teamsters became a subawardee of the L-AGC.

PROJECTS AND EXPANDED DIRECTIONS

Under Hughes's direction, Ruth Ruttenberg and Associates, Inc., were commissioned to conduct a labor market study of hazardous waste operations and ER. Ruttenberg, an economist, had presented testimony in pre-SARA hearings about the need for hazardous waste worker health and safety protection and training. The study's objective was to "describe and project the number and types of jobs needed to clean up the nation's hazardous waste sites" (Ruttenberg, Weinstock, & Santamaria, 1996, p. 5). The study made projections through the year 2010. It identified the trades most associated with hazardous waste remediation work and estimated the demand for remedial action workers over a 15-year period. The study gave strong support particularly to building trades unions in their efforts to demonstrate the importance of their health and safety training programs and the number of workers they were preparing for the work. The national political gridlock over hazardous waste site remediation issues, however, blocked any positive impact the study might have had.[19]

ENVIRONMENTAL JUSTICE

In 1994, planning to extend its training efforts to address environmental justice issues, NIEHS collected information from its awardees about their activities in support of underserved populations of workers. Several awardees, for example, were training in Spanish, most extensively the California Consortium, but also the L-AGC and the Teamsters. Several awardees were training Native American workers, especially the L-AGC and the Alice Hamilton Consortium through the Alaska Health Project. Other awardees had recruited environmental justice advocates to their advisory boards and some had become involved in training urban minority youths for jobs in the environmental industry (NIEHS, 1994).

The NIEHS training for minorities—the MWTP—established with the 1995 awards, resulted from $3 million of additional funding authorized and allocated by Congress to train young people from urban minority communities for work in the environmental industry.[20] NIEHS was ordered to fund and coordinate several pilot programs in this area. The awardees for this program included the three programs already identified and a consortium of the L-AGC with Cuyahoga Community College (Cleveland) and San Francisco State University; the Carpenters Health and Safety Fund; a New York City-based subconsortium within the New Jersey/New York Consortium, consisting of Hunter College, the Magnolia Tree Earth Center, West Harlem Community Action, El Puente de Williamsburg, and the South Bronx Clean Air Coalition.

These programs broadly expanded the activities supported by the WETP. The minorities program awardees provided preemployment job training that included literacy, life skills, and other training, in addition to a range of HAZMAT and waste remediation health and safety training. These have proven to be resource-intensive programs that face many challenges, not the least of which are helping participants stay enrolled and placing them in jobs when their training is done. NIEHS has urged its WETP and MWTP awardees to deal with worker training needs related to the redevelopment of former industrial and commercial urban sites that have become inactive due to environmental contamination—best known now as brownfield sites. NIEHS sponsored a technical workshop on environmental job training for urban inner-city youth in January 1995. NIEHS awarded OCAW additional funds for workshops that brought workers and community environmental activists together to discuss hazardous waste and ER issues. NIEHS believed that the workshops would enhance worker training through a better understanding of community issues.

Sharon Beard, an industrial hygienist, was hired to manage the MWTP. Beard had worked with the WETP for the previous year to build agency competence to run programs for minority worker populations. She coordinated a January 1995 technical workshop and guided the MWTP. Beard came to the agency with a wealth of environmental health science laboratory and field experience. She holds a master's degree in environmental science and health policy. Her graduate research focused on technical and policy issues at urban hazardous waste sites in a community of color, the Roxbury area of Boston. Beard had worked closely with the Dudley Street Neighborhood Initiative, a key community-based environmental justice organization. In addition to conducting a partial human health assessment of 17 of the 54 contaminated sites in the Dudley neighborhood, she developed *A Citizens' Guide to Contaminated Site Issues in Urban Communities* (Adams, 1995). Beard's technical and policy experience enabled NIEHS to extend its WETP approach so as to effectively work with minority awardees.

TECHNICAL WORKSHOPS AND CONSENSUS DOCUMENTS

NIEHS continued to sponsor semiannual technical workshops. The model established for the Minimum Criteria Workshop was used for a second one on the same issue, but this time developing interpretive guidance on the original document. The goal was to create a consensus document that OSHA could use either as a basis for promulgating its proposed accreditation rule or as an appendix to 29 CFR 1910.120.

OSHA used this consensus document as a basis for a nonmandatory appendix—Appendix E—to the Section 1910.120 standard training curriculum guidelines. After the publication of the appendix, OSHA told NIEHS that it had been created to help private-sector employers establish high-quality training programs, which, in the future, would be accredited by OSHA (after the promulgation of 1910.121). OSHA also informed NIEHS that the Hazardous Waste Management Association had written to OSHA Director Joseph Dear expressing concerns about the appendix. In response, Dear convened a meeting in September 1994, to which industry associations were invited to comment on the revision of Appendix E. By March 1995, OSHA had not received a single comment from employers or their associations.

NIEHS and DOE cosponsored two technical workshops to deal with the health and safety needs of hazardous waste operations and ER workers related to the introduction of new remediation technologies, again using the process established for the Minimum Criteria Workshop. The workshops were extremely demanding because of the complexity of the technical issues. However, they did result in a report and a proposal for the development and implementation of technology safety data sheets that would provide health and safety information for remediation process technologies similar to the information that is provided on material safety data sheets for chemical substances.

Other WETP projects included "Measuring and Evaluating the Outcomes of Training," the title of a two-day technical workshop that produced a comprehensive report about methods and approaches that can be applied to evaluating worker health and safety training. Two national trainers' exchange conferences had been held, one in Maryland in September 1994 and the other in California in April 1997. The conferences were organized to bring together the awardees' trainers, as opposed to the technical experts and administrators who usually attended such workshops. The trainers presented their best modules and activities, shared views, and developed relationships for further communication. The California-Arizona Consortium's Labor Occupational Health Program at UC Berkeley was supported by NIEHS to develop a manual that would help worker health educators understand and address literacy issues among workers. The manual was completed in 1994, and assistance in using it was proffered (Szudy & González Arroyo, 1994).

THE SECOND DECADE— NEW CHALLENGES AND CHANGING PRIORITIES

In 1995 the U.S. Congress, under new Republican leadership, let the Superfund tax expire. The fund had a surplus of $3.8 billion in 1996, but was steadily drained and in 2003 it went bankrupt. Letting the fund fees expire signaled a withdrawal from the "polluter pays" principle upon which the Superfund had been based. It also signaled a steady decline in the remediation of hazardous waste sites by both federal and state programs. This created a new set of challenges for the WETP and its awardees, who needed to demonstrate that HAZWOPER worker training was needed and being delivered. Some of the emphasis upon the needs of building trades workers was shifted to meet the needs of workers in a broader range of industrial sectors, including health care. Some increased attention was given to pollution prevention training rather than simply pollution remediation. The debates among the awardees about these changing emphases, though, were short-lived, as a new set of priorities took center stage.

In 2001, the WETP engaged with its awardees in a strategic planning process to address the program's future directions and priorities. The fall awardees' meeting was going to include a technical workshop for the collective completion of the strategic plan. On September 11, however, two commercial aircraft that were deliberately flown into the World Trade Center (WTC) in New York City, resulting in their total destruction, not only delayed the WETP strategic planning process but moved the WETP into new directions.

Buildings, such as the World Trade Center towers, constructed in the latter part of the 20th century contain large quantities of toxic materials and materials that will release toxic chemicals when burned. The towers contained asbestos for insulation, mercury and other heavy metals in lighting fixtures, various forms of plastics, and the many toxic chemicals that are used in machinery and electrical and office equipment. When concrete is pulverized, as it was in this case, the dust becomes highly caustic and capable of destroying respiratory tissues. Turning two huge urban skyscrapers into dust can result in nothing less than a massive hazardous waste site.

The many courageous first responders who went to search for and rescue people trapped in the building were entering what very shortly would become a toxic waste site hot zone. No prior evidence suggested that the buildings would collapse, and time was of the essence in order to save the lives of the thousands of people in the buildings. The sudden and massive collapse of the buildings precluded any consideration of the measures needed to protect the response crews. What was obvious to worker health and safety professionals and activists, though, was that far too many workers, both emergency responders and the construction workers who came in to help move the rubble and find victims (workers who were newly classified as "skilled support personnel"), lacked the prior appropriate health and safety training and protective equipment for this horrific work environment.

This was obvious to the WETP's leaders and awardees as well. Along with OSHA and NIOSH, they went to the scene and rapidly helped raise attention to the health and safety protection measures needed by the search and rescue and waste removal workers. John Moran and Don Elisburg were tasked to conduct an assessment of the working conditions and the protective measures needed. Multiple awardees brought resources and provided training as needed. The IAFF and the IUOE set up quick training for their members and others on the site. The IUOE and the Carpenters, along with OSHA, provided respirators and conducted tests to assure their proper fit. Moran and Elisburg's report concludes that

> What has emerged in this massive disaster and the protracted and complex response is the fact that rescue, recovery, and other activities have occurred in a scenario never anticipated by the safety and health legislation or the subsequent standards/regulations. The injury and illness reports for the initial weeks of the search and rescue activity were at unacceptable levels. Moreover, the exposure data, as well as the potential for serious exposure to toxic materials (including asbestos) among the construction response workers, raises significant concerns. Accordingly, how to respond to such situations demands serious attention in the context of worker protection and training needs. (Moran & Elisburg, 2001, p. 3)

New York City and the nation mourned the loss of many of the city's firefighters. Few recognized, however, that these were not only firefighters but hazmat emergency responders. Twenty-one years after the Chemical Control fire in Elizabeth, NJ, where the *New York Times* captured in a photograph the firefighter without chemical protective gear working side by side with EPA workers in full protective gear, the photos from Ground Zero looked all too similar.

The WETP moved direction with the rest of the federal government in the aftermath of the events on September 11, 2001. Concerns about weapons of mass destruction (WMDs) became a new priority. The WETP began to address ways to best protect the health and safety of workers who had to respond to disasters resulting from the use of WMDs. Following the discovery of pipe bombs in postal boxes and anthrax delivery via the postal service, there was a national recognition that WMDs could come in several forms—chemical, biological, radioactive, nuclear, and explosive—just like the substances that could be found at hazardous waste sites. The WETP and its awardees were already well prepared to develop worker health and safety training that would address these issues. Given the concerns about "homeland security," some attention was also given to the lack of security at chemical and other industrial facilities and the ease with which "terrorists" could destroy production facilities and cause economic and public health damage.

Worker health and safety protection and training were low priorities for most federal agencies addressing homeland security. In fact, the Bush administration and the chemical industry used the new events and concerns as an excuse to withhold from the public Toxics Release Inventory information that had formerly been available through the community right-to-know measures achieved in SARA. WETP leaders worked with OSHA and other agencies in the development of a worker safety and health support annex to the National Response Plan. The WETP was responsible within this for developing a training support annex—the Emergency Support Activation Plan. It was able to support extensive efforts to build the capacity of its awardees to prepare workers for future events similar to those that had recently occurred, although discussions within the program mirrored the concerns raised by many in public health that these efforts were a distraction from more pressing and ongoing health needs.

Nonetheless, WETP capacity was being built, and the effort to assure integration with a broader federal infrastructure was merely a continuation of what had been done before. The key difference at this point was that the Department of Homeland Security had been established with the authority to direct all national security and response efforts. WETP leaders worked hard to be included but not to lose their control of the program and keep their autonomy so that they could stay on mission. These efforts proved valuable but were frustrated when Hurricanes Katrina and Rita devastated the U.S. Gulf Coast region.

The flooded and destroyed areas of Louisiana—especially New Orleans—Mississippi, Texas, and Alabama were covered with hazardous wastes disturbed from identified and regulated waste sites as well as those resulting from the destruction of buildings and facilities where they had been used or stored, and those coming from motor vehicles that had been destroyed or covered by the flood waters. In addition to these hazards, the soaked debris and remains in the southern heat supported the extensive growth of toxic molds. Other biological and safety hazards abounded for clean-up workers in a disaster that remained hazardous and contaminated in many areas for more than 2 years.

The WETP's efforts to provide disaster-specific health and safety training to the many workers cleaning up and restoring the area were frustrated and curtailed by the bureaucratic and political stranglehold that shaped the response to the devastated area. Hurricane Katrina triggered the National Response Plan, which had been revised in the post 9-11 period and included the WETP's safety and health training support annex. Within a few weeks after the hurricanes, the WETP's clearinghouse issued just-in-time training materials, including a booklet in Web-downloadable and print formats and available in English, Spanish, and Vietnamese: *Protecting Yourself While Helping Others* (NIEHS, 2005).[21]

WETP awardees began deploying training assistance almost immediately after the disaster: the IAFF covered various emergency response topics; SEIU deployed trained nurses along the Texas Gulf Coast; and the American Federation of Teachers (part of the ICWU consortium) provided mold remediation training for teachers brought in to repair school buildings). The University of Alabama provided training to members of the Communications Workers of America who were engaged in the massive effort to repair communications lines. The Center for the Protection of Workers Rights, an awardee consortium composed of building trades unions, and the Hazardous Materials Training and Research Institute, part of a community college consortium, provided training to FEMA and U.S. Army Corps of Engineers contractors and personnel. Dillard University's Deep South Center for Environmental Justice and the United Steelworkers (which had merged with the former Oil, Chemical, and Atomic Workers Union) provided training and support to help residents remediate and return to their homes. The UCLA Labor Occupational Safety and Health Program, the directing organization of what had started as the California Consortium, working with the National Day Laborer Organizing Network, investigated and reported on the occupational safety and health issues facing the many Latino day laborers doing much of the clean-up and recovery work in the affected areas. In 2006, some WETP awardees received supplemental funding to provide more comprehensive courses to address the specific hazardous conditions at these work sites and better prepare workers engaged in the work.

The WETP reviewed the lessons learned from the experience and was highly critical of the failure to responsibly address occupational health and safety issues in the Katrina response and remediation effort. Stating that the Katrina response, like the WTC response, demonstrated a "'systems failure' that underpins the generally ineffective response to worker safety and health related training" (National Clearinghouse for Worker Safety and Health Training, 2006, p. 11), it offered a commitment to future response efforts and some self-criticism. It then provided a stern reprimand to the federal response system:

> At least as evidenced by the first six months of the Katrina response, worker safety and health and related training are simply not a priority and are, it appears, only an annoyance that hinders the "production operation" mentality that was also characteristic of the WTC response and cleanup. (National Clearinghouse for Worker Safety and Health Training, 2006, p. 11)

SUMMARY OF ACCOMPLISHMENTS

In 2007, the WETP supported 18 primary worker training grantees, in conjunction with over 100 collaborating institutions. It awarded funding to 10 labor unions, some of which are union consortia that include an additional 18 unions. The WETP's annual funding was more than $37 million. It supported training in all 50 U.S. states. In addition to its core hazardous waste worker training program and the program for nuclear workers, supported with funds from the Department of Energy, the WETP had two program areas addressing minority worker training (the original program and another for brownfield development projects). It has provided several supplemental funding programs for awardees that have addressed issues related to hazardous materials disaster preparedness. The WETP has also supported six grants to encourage the development and application of training materials and presentation formats based on computer and electronic communication and media technologies.

By October 2007, the WETP awardees had collectively provided extensive training over 20 years. In the hazardous waste worker training program, 1,645,924 workers had been trained in 91,529 courses, with 21,637,720 contact hours. Through the 14 years of the nuclear workers' training program, 290,769 workers had been trained in 21,303 courses (3,957,863 contact hours). In a period of 12 years, the two minority worker training programs had trained more than 6,750 workers and succeeded in placing about 67% of them in jobs. These latter programs have helped to infuse the community-based environmental health program with worker health and safety awareness and advocacy, potentially developing new leaders of the environmental justice movement. The program received $603 million from 1987 to 2007.

Many of the unions participating in the WETP have extensive networks of workers who have been trained and work as trainers (worker-trainers). For example, the training programs of the Service Employees International Union (SEIU) and the United Auto Workers both support worker-trainers who are health and safety leaders in their facilities and regions. The SEIU program alone has more than 100 trainers across the United States.

Since the successful 1997 National Trainers' Exchange Conference, three more have been held (2000, 2004, 2007), continuing to build an awareness among worker-trainers that they are part of a national effort, and that there is a health and safety movement in which they can participate. At the 2007 conference, Chip Hughes asserted to participants that the WETP and its awardee organizations have the potential to build a national infrastructure for occupational health and safety. Don Elisburg, speaking about the future of the program, said, "Nothing could be more important than maintaining the high standard of the training we provide." Sharon Beard complimented the trainers, noting, "You are the ones who define excellence every day with the work you do." The conference was a powerful success, integrating technical information with training to support popular education approaches and many workshops designed to share successful training from across the spectrum of industrial sectors. It was a wonderful way to celebrate the accomplishments of the WETP's 20 years.

CONCLUSION

The WETP has achieved robustness in size, activity, and achievement. It has achieved a measure of cohesion and excellence that was its initial aim, and a high level of satisfaction for those who have made it happen. The overall, and still evolving, initiative has become the single most significant worker health and safety training effort in the history of the U.S. health and safety movement, at least in terms of years of operation, in terms of allocated monies, and certainly in terms of the numbers of workers trained and programmatic complexity. Collaboratively, the program participants have established a comprehensive set of benchmarks for worker health and safety training.

Individuals and organizations don't usually have opportunities to apply for government grant funding to build a movement—and even when they do, organizational goals will often take priority over movement goals. The WETP leadership sought to strengthen a movement by supporting the development of strong individual programs. These dual goals established the basis for both conflicts and collaboration between awardee organizations and with broader social movements.

The WETP's boundaries have been established by multiple forces and by its leadership's efforts to sustain its strength. Because it is part of the national Superfund program, any WETP expansion has been framed within the context of hazardous waste work and emergency response to hazardous materials incidents. Certainly, though, boundaries were set by the past three decades of attacks on the state's capacity to promote the interests of the working class through progressive tax policies, regulation and enforcement, and the legal protections won by labor and the left/liberal alliance during the New Deal and the post-World War II liberal era. These attacks were coupled with a conservative political consensus in Washington, DC. The greatly weakened labor movement largely withdrew from its never-too-strong platform on worker health and safety. The weakened environmental movement had largely abandoned hazardous waste issues to pursue sexier issues that would better attract members, donations, and foundation dollars—often looking toward a sustainable future without sufficiently addressing the past-to-present environmental destruction and its ever-mounting legacy of degradation and disease that disproportionately burdens people of color and the working class. It is no wonder that the program's goal has so often been stated as that of developing excellence in worker health and safety training.

The stated emphasis on excellence is evidence of pride among the WETP leadership and participants, as well as a program goal. Striving for training program excellence, however, was a protective strategy. The program needed to be defended against those in the federal government who would seek to reduce its funding or control its emphasis. Awardees who had to sell the training would have had trouble marketing training to employers who were required to provide training but not worker-centered training that would include information about workers' legal rights and the ways to use OSHA. Union awardees would meet resistance from employers with whom they had labor contracts but who would prefer to purchase training from a commercial vendor to avoid providing the union with a forum to train and mobilize workers. Within some unions, training to build rank-and-file activism would raise leadership fears of a challenge to their control and management, as well as creating difficulties in dealing with company owners.

The emphasis on excellence was a tacit recognition of and a strategy to counter these weaknesses of the labor and the health and safety movements. Certainly workers deserve high quality health and safety training that provides them with the information and practice they need to develop strategies to prevent workplace injuries, illnesses, and fatalities. Training should be excellent, but during a period of political strength for labor, this point would not need to be emphasized in such a way.

Yet the WETP has steadfastly organized itself to support the goals of health and safety activists from a broad swath of industrial sectors. The right to a safe and healthy work environment has been promoted in training delivered to hundreds of thousands of workers across the country for 20 years. Still, the WETP leadership has consistently limited the program's scope in order to sustain its strength. As an element of the national Superfund program, any WETP expansion has been framed within the context of hazardous waste work and emergency response to hazardous materials incidents.

The weakening of both the labor and environmental movements in the 1990s limited the potential scope of any government program to protect workers' health and safety. In that context, the WETP leadership established a foundation for a sustained successful strategy to build the strength of the national health and safety movement, with the resources to recruit new members and develop new leaders.

The next two chapters explore two WETP awardees and the programs they developed: those of the Oil, Chemical, and Atomic Workers International Union and the Laborers–Associated General Contractors. Both are union programs, the latter in cooperation with industrial management and the former struggling all the while for acceptance by industrial employers. Studying these programs helps us understand the health and safety needs and political orientation of two critical sets of workers—those employed to produce hazardous materials, which generates substantial hazardous waste, and those who will clean up hazardous waste. Both sets of workers face potential exposures and conditions that can cause injuries, illnesses, and even death, all as part of their jobs. In these settings, having a health and safety training program that can help workers understand these threats and also how to prevent them or at least prevent the exposures is a valuable step toward changing these conditions of work. More importantly, having these programs controlled and developed by the unions increases the likelihood that the training will strive to achieve the above-mentioned goals and the likelihood that the workers will have opportunities to make sure that the training addresses their concerns and needs.

The chapters briefly discuss the political and economic context of each industry, the unions' historical relations within the industrial sectors, and the history of the unions' health and safety leaders. The directions each union chose for its training program and the curriculum and training program organization it chose to develop are reviewed. We will see that the constraints of the WETP, as well as those imposed by the politics of the unions themselves, set the boundaries for the training programs. The OSHA standard mandated more training than most employers would have provided on their own, but it also established another set of boundaries for the training. Each union found creative ways to push the sets of boundaries (see Appendix 2 for Similarities and Differences between the OCAW and L-AGC Programs). But employers' collective influence on the government, the modes of production, and labor-management relations forces the unions to a strong reliance on their allies in the WETP leadership, even though, as we have seen in the last two chapters, they push to move the WETP to provide stronger support for their own goals and directions. The unions, however, had to accept that although they were able to win government mandates and funding for training programs, they could not successfully demand these things from employers in their industries. Examining the history and details of these training programs is important because they demonstrate the creative potential and success of a government program, the WETP, that is oriented to support autonomous action on behalf of workers' health and safety. The WETP-supported training programs provide a vibrant alternative to the empty results of the current corporate drive for deregulation and market-based incentives supporting voluntary industrial measures to protect workers' health and the environment.

APPENDIX 2:
Similarities and Differences between the OCAW and L-AGC Programs

Characteristic	L-AGC	OCAW
Type of work	Environmental construction—cleanup of hazardous waste	Oil, chemical, nuclear production that creates hazardous waste
Worker education level	Usually high school graduation is highest level attained	Often at least some post-secondary education
Labor-management relations	Joint labor-management training programs, but open shop sector enabled concessionary demands from management in1980s	Strongly unionized sector, but industry restructuring in 1980s enabled concessionary demands from management
Collaboration with professionals	Professionals help develop and implement. Maintain a broad network throughout duration of program	Professionals help develop and implement. Move to rely more on worker-trainers for program development in later stages
Training certification	Training certification sought: credential for union jobs	Training certification opposed: members already employed
Program certification to demonstrate excellence	Certification of program sought for employer buy-in	Certification of program sought for employer buy-in
Worker-to-worker training	Laborers train Laborers—at training centers	OCAW worker-trainers operate nationally and at locals

APPENDIX 2 (Cont'd.)

Characteristic	L-AGC	OCAW
Hands-on training emphasis	Develops H&S understanding and work skills	Small group activities to build H&S and advocacy skills
Worker skill development goal	Skilled workers to support union contractor competitiveness	Skilled H&S systems analysts-activists to push improvements
Core strategy	H&S training as safe jobs and organizing strategy	H&S training as safe jobs and mobilizing strategy

ENDNOTES

1. The Seattle Fire Department was one of the original 11 awardees. It has little place in this research because: (1). the department's participation in the NIEHS program ended after the sixth year; and (2) the primary focus of this research was the union programs and the way that NIEHS managed the overall program.
2. Information about the meeting and the decisions made with regard to the request for applications and staffing changes was obtained from a memorandum for the record, submitted by Dobbin, dated October 23, 1989 (Dobbin, 1989). The memorandum was found in the NIEHS WETP files, RTP, NC.
3. The emphasis on excellence was a common theme expressed in interviews and communications with key NIEHS personnel, staff of the two awardee organizations in the case studies in this project, and individuals from other awardee organizations. It is also reflected in the promotional materials of the National Clearinghouse and the various awardee organizations.
4. Unlike Hughes, who stayed on with the program, Shultz left at the end of her assignment. She made significant contributions while affiliated with the program (Dobbin, 1998).
5. See Dobbin (1998).
6. The summary report does not define program self-sufficiency. NIEHS and the reviewers have steadily emphasized it over the years. Several awardees have noted that in general employers remain unwilling to assume the cost of high-quality training, particularly when it is worker oriented. In the face of such resistance, awardees have argued, government funding for worker health and safety training is necessary for the provision of training. Self-sufficiency has been emphasized out of concern that the government might not always be willing to fund worker health and safety training, and out of a belief that it is the responsibility of employers and the unions representing their employees to establish joint labor-management mechanisms to support the provision of appropriate training. Proponents of self-sufficiency have also argued that universities should assume greater responsibility for supporting worker health and safety training programs, which are an essential aspect of social and industrial development. This information is taken from the author's notes on NIEHS WETP program meetings between 1990 and 1998.
7. A draft of the OSHA rule for Accreditation of Training Programs for Hazardous Waste Operations (U.S. DOL, 1988) was informally circulated among the NIEHS awardees in the late fall and early winter of 1988–1989. The draft is dated October 28, 1988, and listed as Docket No. S-760-B. A copy, with a cover letter from Carol Rice, director of the

Midwest Consortium, was obtained from the files of the New England Consortium, University of Massachusetts Lowell.

8. NIEHS believed that Congress intended the agency to support "model programs." It was NIEHS's justification for an emphasis on quality, as well as on program expansion. The goal was not simply to train a certain number of workers but also to develop models of excellence for worker health education and training. NIEHS hoped that the minimum criteria for training would be applied to all OSHA-required health and safety training (Dobbin, 1998).
9. The ability of NIEHS and WETP awardees to move OSHA to adopt the nonmandatory appendix to its 1910.120 standard is definitely a WETP success. OSHA's reluctance and inability to fully incorporate the Minimum Criteria Document as a basis for a training program accreditation standard remains a source of frustration for the WETP and its awardees. These events were not explored in this study because they occurred after the program's fifth year.
10. The figures released in 1991 were revised upward in the 1995 report. In 1991, the figures were 4,467 courses and 120,747 workers.
11. See Slatin and Siqueira (1998) for a discussion of the inadequacy of OSHA's definition of the scope of ER activities, as well as its training requirements for workers with hazardous materials ER as a collateral duty.
12. Some information used in this section was obtained from a review of the author's notes on this meeting.
13. For further discussion of the number of hours established for emergency responder training, see Slatin and Siqueira (1998).
14. NIEHS arranged for the meeting to be held at the MSHA training academy as a way to introduce MSHA personnel to the WETP and its awardees (Dobbin, 1998).
15. The awardee organizations may have continued to offer courses shorter than 8 hours as a way of introducing their training and soliciting agreements for full training courses.
16. This information was taken from the author's notes on the meeting, which were typed and distributed to members of the New England Consortium. Although the Teamsters supported the IAFF position, they met strong resistance from employers to accepting any training from the union. For example, United Parcel Service (UPS) repeatedly chose to pay a vendor for training rather than receive free training controlled and provided by the Teamsters. In May 1992, the issue remained unresolved. OSHA had contracted with the Eastern Research Group to conduct a survey of ER training. During this process, the IAFF reported that it had talked with general industry representatives who were willing to have OSHA remove municipal and volunteer firefighters from the ER requirements. This plan disturbed the representative of the rail workers training program, who believed that rail workers would lose protection. The ICWU also strongly disagreed with the IAFF on this approach.
17. A final rule was posted in the Federal Register on Monday, October 22, 1990 (FR, Vol. 55, No. 204, pp. 42566–42569).
18. The U.S. federal fiscal year runs from October 1 through September 30 of the following year. The federal fiscal year is identified by the calendar year starting in January following the October start date. For example, the federal fiscal year beginning on October 1, 1990, is fiscal year (FY) 1991. Since the first awards for the NIEHS WETP were issued in late September 1987, they were funded by the federal FY 1987 budget, even though the program year ran for most of FY 1988. The NIEHS WETP awards have always been made near the end of the federal fiscal year.
19. For discussions of the political economy of the Superfund program, see Barnett (1994) and Hird (1994).

20. It was an appropriations initiative established by Congressman Stokes (D-OH).
21. *Learning From Disasters; Katrina Response Safety and Health Training,* a full report of the WETP's participation in the response and recovery efforts on the Gulf Coast is available for download at the Clearinghouse Web site, www.wetp.org. See National Clearinghouse for Worker Safety and Health Training (2006).

REFERENCES

50 Federal Register. (1991). Availability of Request for Applications, NIH-NIEHS-ES-92-01, RFA Title: Hazardous Materials and Waste Worker Health and Safety Training, Vol. 56, 207, pp. 55330-55331. Washington, DC: GPO.

Barnett, H. C. (1994). *Toxic Debts and the Superfund Dilemma.* Chapel Hill: University of North Carolina Press.

Adams, L., Beard, S., Bloomfield, L., Connelly, D., Davidson, S., & Tawa, T. (1995). *A Citizens' Guide to Contaminated Site Issues in Urban Communities.* Thesis for Masters in Science, Tufts University, for the Dudley Street Initiative, Medford, MA.

California Consortium. (1990, July). *Training of Trainers Session: A Day-Long Session on Participatory Training Methods for Hazardous Waste Trainers.* Labor Occupational Health Program UC Berkeley and Hazardous Substances Program, UC Davis. Berkeley, CA.

Dement, J. (1997). Interview by author, tape recording (October 20).

Deutsch, S. (1990). Year 3 Site Visit Review Meeting, Summary (August 27). From NIEHS WETP files, RTP, NC.

Dobbin, D. (1989). Superfund Worker Training Program—Plan for Supplemental Funding: Meeting October 17, Memorandum for the Record (October 23). From NIEHS WETP files, RTP, NC.

Dobbin, D. (1997). Interviews by author, tape recording, Los Angeles (April 10).

Dobbin, D. (1998). Telephone correspondence with author (December 3).

Hird, J. A. (1994). *Superfund: The Political Economy of Environmental Risk.* Baltimore: Johns Hopkins University Press.

Hughes, J. (1990a). Memo from Chip Hughes to NIEHS Hazardous Waste Worker Training Grantees. Re: Concerns for the Technical Workshop on Accreditation of Emergency Responder Training (November 30). From NIEHS WETP files, RTP, NC.

Hughes, J. (1990b). Memo from Chip Hughes to the Site Review Committee. Subject: Indicators of Progress by NIEHS Worker Training Program Grantees (August 27). From NIEHS WETP files, RTP, NC.

Mallino, D., Sr. (1997). Interview by author, tape recording, Washington, DC (December 10).

Matheny, C. (1998). Interview by author, typed responses by the interviewee, and notes from interview, Durham, NC (July 29).

Merrill, M. (1989). *Deficiencies of the Proposed OSHA Standard on the Accreditation of Training Programs for Hazardous Waste Operations.* May. New Brunswick, NJ: Institute for Management and Labor Relations, Cook College, Rutgers University.

Merrill, M. (1991). No Test Know-How: Deficiencies of the Proposed OSHA Standard on the Accreditation of Training Programs for Hazardous Waste Operations. *New Solutions, A Journal of Environmental and Occupational Health Policy, 2*(2), 47-58.

Mikulski, B. (1991). Request for information regarding the distribution of training grant funds (April 19). U.S. Senate, Committee on Appropriations, Washington, DC.

Moran, J. (1998). Telephone interview by author, tape recording (July 27).

Moran, J. B., & Dobbin, D. (1991). Quality Assurance for Worker Health and Safety Training Programs: Hazardous Waste Operations and Emergency Response. *Applied Occupational and Environmental Hygiene, 6*(2), 107-113.

Moran, J. B., & Elisburg, D. (2001). *Response to the World Trade Center (WTC) Disaster: Initial WETP Grantee Response and Preliminary Assessment of Training Needs*. October 6. Washington, DC: National Institute of Environmental Health Sciences, Worker Education and Training Program, National Clearinghouse for Worker Safety and Health Training.

National Clearinghouse for Worker Safety and Health Training. (1995). Compendium on the National Institute of Environmental Health Sciences Superfund Worker Health and Safety Training Program: in Hazardous Materials, Hazardous Waste Operations, Emergency Response. NIEHS Worker Education and Training Program, RTP, NC.

National Clearinghouse for Worker Safety and Health Training. (2006, April). Learning from Disasters: Katrina Response Safety and Health Training—Report of a National Technical Workshop, March 8-9, 2006, Birmingham, AL. Washington, DC: Worker Education and Training Program, National Institute of Environmental Health Sciences.

National Clearinghouse on Occupational and Environmental Health. (1990). *Notes From the NIEHS Technical Workshop on Quality of Training Issues for Emergency Responders*. December 11. Washington, DC.

NIEHS. (1990a). Minutes of the Draft Document and Technical Workshop Sessions. Ad Hoc Planning Committee Meeting (January 45): From files of Department of Work Environment, University of Massachusetts Lowell.

NIEHS. (1990b). Superfund Worker Training Program NIEHS Staff Triage Summary. April 2. From NIEHS WETP files, RTP, NC.

NIEHS. (1991a). Memo from Denny Dobbin to Dr. Sassaman. Justification of Cooperative Agreements for Hazardous Materials and Waste Worker Health and Safety Training. (August 19). From NIEHS WETP files, RTP, NC.

NIEHS. (1991b). Minimum Criteria for Worker Health and Safety Training for Hazardous Waste Operations and Emergency Response: NIEHS Training Grant Technical Workshop on Training Quality. Second Printing. December. Washington, DC: National Clearinghouse on Occupational and Environmental Health, Workplace Health Fund.

NIEHS. (1991c). Minutes of the National Advisory Environmental Health Sciences Council Meeting (May 20-21). Bethesda, MD.

NIEHS. (1991d). NIEHS SWTP Lessons Learned Workshop, Summary Characteristics of Effective Programs, and handout of responses to Participant Questionnaire (August 27). From files of the New England Consortium, Department of Work Environment, University of Massachusetts Lowell.

NIEHS. (1991e). Summary Report of the 1990 Site Visit Reviews of NIEHS Worker Training Grantees. April. NIEHS Hazardous Waste Workers Training Program.

NIEHS. (1991f). Superfund Worker Training Program For Hazardous Materials, Waste Operations and Emergency Response: Three Year Progress Report (Fiscal Years 1987-1989). February. U.S. Department of Health and Human Services, NIH.

NIEHS. (1991g). Testimony of the National Institute of Environmental Health Sciences on the Occupational Safety and Health Administration's Proposed Standard for Accreditation of Hazardous Waste Operations and Emergency Response Training: 29 CFR 1910.121. January 29, Docket No. S-760-B. Washington, DC. Submitted to the U.S. Department of Labor.

NIEHS. (1994). Worker Education and Training Program Environmental Justice Accomplishments. NIEHS WETP. July.

NIEHS. (1995). Compendium on the National Institute of Environmental Health Sciences Superfund Worker Health and Safety Training Program, in Hazardous Materials, Hazardous Waste Operations, Emergency Response. June. NIEHS, RTP, NC.

NIEHS. (2005). *Protecting Yourself While Helping Others. Version 11.* Worker Education and Training Program, Hurricane Response Initiative. 48 pages. November. Washington, DC. http://tools.niehs.nih.gov/wetp/index.cfm?id=391

NIH Guide. (1994). Hazardous Materials Worker Health and Safety Training: RFA ES-95-001. October 28, Vol. 23, 38, p. 19.

OCAW. (1989). Letter from Sylvia Krekel, Hazardous Waste Worker Training Project director, and Michael Merrill, Rutgers University, to members of the NIEHS Ad Hoc Committee, with attached fax copy of a memo from Merrill to Krekel, Proposed Revision in John Moran's Minimum Training Program Certification Criteria for Training Providers. Dec. 21. Craig Slatin's files, Cambridge, MA.

Ruttenberg, R., Weinstock, D., & Santamaria, L. (1996). *Labor Market Study of Hazardous Waste Workers and Associated Emergency Responders: Prepared for NIEHS and U.S. EPA.* September. Bethesda, MD: Ruth Ruttenberg & Associates, Inc.

Slatin, C., & Siqueira, E. (1998). Does a Collateral Duty Require Less Protection: Workers, Hazardous Materials Emergency Response, and OSHA's Failure to Protect. *New Solutions, A Journal of Environmental and Occupational Health Policy, 8*(2), 205-219.

Szudy, E., & González Arroyo, M. (1994). *The Right to Understand: Linking Literacy to Health and Safety Training.* Berkeley: University of California Berkeley.

U.S. DOL. (1988). *Draft #7. Accreditation of Training Programs for Hazardous Waste Operations.* Occupational Safety and Health Administration. 29 CFR 1910 [Docket No. S-760-B]. Oct. 28. Washington, D.C.

U.S. DHHS-NIEHS. (1989). Availability of Request for Grant Application; Hazardous Materials and Waste Worker Health and Safety Training, NIEHS. December 28, Vol. 54, 248. U.S. DHHS (NIEHS).

U.S. DOL. (1990). Notice of Proposed Rulemaking; Accreditation of Training Programs for Hazardous Waste Operations. January 28, Vol. 55, 18, pp. 2776-2794. Federal Register.

CHAPTER 6

OCAW Worker-to-Worker Training

The Oil, Chemical, and Atomic Workers International Union (OCAW) assumed a leadership role as a WETP awardee, motivated perhaps by the fact that it lost a worker every month in an on-the-job fatality. A relatively small union, OCAW represented workers in key industrial sectors that produced hazardous materials and waste. Long before the WETP came into existence, the union was a national leader in the occupational health and safety movement that developed in the late 1960s. It helped erect the health and safety apparatus that exists both in the federal government and in many AFL-CIO-affiliated unions.

OCAW's training program devised a curriculum and an approach that encouraged its members to act to improve health and safety in their workplaces. Through training, OCAW tried to turn workers into health and safety systems analysts who could collectively address faults in an employer's systems of safety. Its training program built on an earlier concept incorporated in its health and safety work. It involved creating a network of occupational safety and health education coordinators (OSHECS), that is, production line workers who had received training and, in turn, then conducted training and gave outreach and support to workers over their health and safety issues.

The OCAW program aimed to establish a model of excellence for worker health and safety training in the petrochemical, oil, chemical, and nuclear industries. The union sought excellence in multiple program components: curriculum, trainer training, worker-trainers, and training and program evaluation. This emphasis on excellence was believed necessary to "disarm company critics" (Merrill, 1991a, p. 342). After all, the union was limited in its political and economic power to gain access to its members without employer consent. So, excellent health and safety training that met the employers' regulatory mandate became a vehicle for the union's efforts to mobilize its members.

OCAW AND ITS INDUSTRIES

OCAW represented workers in three industrial sectors: oil, petrochemical and chemical, and nuclear (primarily weapons and research facilities).[1] During the first 5 years of the WETP, however, OCAW's training focus was primarily on workers in the oil and petrochemical and chemical industries. A brief description of the industries as they existed in the mid-1980s is necessary to understand OCAW's program.

In the 1970s, two shocks hit the international oil industry. The first was an Arab nations' embargo against the industrialized Western nations in response to the Egypt-Israel war in October 1973. The second was sharp oil price increases after the fall of the shah of Iran in 1979. By the mid-1980s, U.S. oil companies were responding to changed international and national conditions (deregulation of U.S. oil prices, environmental regulation, economic recession). The industry saw the shutdown of some major facilities and a wave of mergers. Smaller companies struggled for survival as the industry faced a crisis of "too much product and no place to put it" (Mazzocchi, 1982). Major companies began to diversify into other energy fuels (such as uranium and coal). Some companies were purchased by corporations based in other industries.

The chemical industry consists of a group of industrial sectors, several of which are closely linked to the petroleum industry and often composed of companies operating in both industries. The U.S. Census Bureau broadly classifies the sectors into a single grouping, Chemical Manufacturing (NAICS 325). The industry is intensely competitive, but it also commonly shares much information. The primarily large companies that comprise a majority share of the industry invest heavily in research and development. Several have divested themselves of basic chemical operations and moved to specialty products or pharmaceuticals (Backman, 1970, pp. 1-14; Bower, 1986, pp. 1-33; Chapman, 1991, pp. 13-34).

The petrochemical industry has not been labor intensive. Production is generally carried out through a continuous-flow process rather than through batch operations. Continuous-flow operations are highly automated, and thus require relatively few workers. These operations, however, use advanced technologies and therefore the employees generally have attained higher educational levels than many manufacturing workers. One consequence of this is that the workforce receives generally higher wages and better benefit packages than workers in many other industries. Nonetheless, labor costs account for less than 10% of total chemical industry costs. The rate of productivity per worker is high in comparison with that in other manufacturing industries. The industry has been highly profitable.[2]

In the early 1980s, petrochemicals were undergoing a major restructuring. Bower identified four significant trends that caused instability in the industry: increased feedstock prices, improved yields due to technological advances, a prolonged recession in the global economy, and product competition from countries that had rich oil and gas supplies (Bower, 1986, p. 19). The increase in feedstock prices reduced profit margins. Another factor that increased the industry's difficulties was the set of environmental laws that regulated the production of toxic substances and the disposal of toxic wastes.

The crisis facing both the petroleum and the chemical industries (particularly petrochemicals) in the early 1980s had a significant impact on OCAW's relations with the industry, the AFL-CIO, and the health and safety movement.

OCAW AS A PIONEER IN HEALTH AND SAFETY

OCAW was created in 1955 when the Oil Workers International Union and the United Gas, Coke, and Chemical Workers Union merged (Wooding, Levenstein, &

Rosenberg, 1997). Both unions had been created during the Congress of Industrial Organizations' (CIO's) organizing drives in the 1930s. Both were politically progressive and had higher-wage members than most CIO unions.

After the 1960s, OCAW became perhaps the leading AFL-CIO union in promoting health and safety as a central labor issue. Its status was achieved primarily as a result of the leadership and work of Tony Mazzocchi, who joined the union in the early 1950s and by 1956 was the youthful president of Long Island, NY, Local 8-149.

In 1956, Mazzocchi joined the movement opposing nuclear weapons testing. He attended meetings of scientists concerned about the testing issue (Mazzocchi, 1998a). (The group evolved into the Committee for a Sane Nuclear Policy.) Mazzocchi developed relationships with politically progressive scientists and their students, who were concerned about a range of threats to the environment and public health. Among the scientists were Barry Commoner and Glenn Paulson, a student of René Dubos of the Department of Environmental Biomedicine at Rockefeller University. As a result of these connections, Mazzocchi also learned about a group in St. Louis, the Committee for Nuclear Information (CNI). With CNI, Mazzocchi waged a campaign through his local in which union members collected the baby teeth of their children and grandchildren so that they could be analyzed for Strontium-90 uptake. This action, Mazzocchi said, gave him a vehicle for talking about the public health consequences of nuclear weapons testing with union members whose jobs helped develop nuclear weapons. "Without that, I think that I would not have survived politically in the union," he said (Mazzocchi, 1998a, p. 30).

In 1965, Mazzocchi was named OCAW's legislative director. He received inquiries from union representatives and officers about workers' health and safety. Apart from his work on nuclear testing issues, he had not previously been aware of these issues. "I really thought there were laws covering this stuff . . . [but I] found an unprotected worker population," he explained (Mazzocchi, 1998c).

Starting in 1967, under the presidency of A. F. Grospiron, OCAW became a force in the developing national health and safety movement. In 1967, Mazzocchi and others in the union presented a resolution to the union's 9th Constitutional Convention, which called for the union to (1) develop a health and safety program to be implemented by education, collective bargaining, and political action; (2) support each bargaining group in efforts to negotiate for a joint labor-management safety committee to police conditions in the workplace; (3) urge each local to develop relationships with the press and community leaders so that the public could be told about developing health and safety hazards, and urge the locals to consider hazards to the community as well as the workforce; and (4) urge the international union to work with the labor movement and other sympathetic organizations in support of federal, state, and local legislation and regulations to protect health and safety and to "place human values above property values" (Mazzocchi, 1998b). The resolution passed.

Between March 1969 and May 1970, Mazzocchi coordinated nine conferences presented at OCAW district councils in the United States and Canada, entitled "Hazards in the Industrial Environment." It was the beginning of a plan that became the mainstay of OCAW's health and safety organizing. Mazzocchi brought scientific experts to the workers so that the workers could give voice to their health and safety concerns and either receive scientific explanations or be provided with supportive research to empower them in their fight for workplaces that were safer and healthier. Accompanying Mazzocchi to the conferences were scientific and medical experts, including Paulson, Dr. William Nicholson of Mt. Sinai School of Medicine, Walter Bogan, field director of the Scientists' Institute for Public Information, and Leo Goodman, the UAW's atomic energy director. In addition, Mazzocchi secured help from a Johns Hopkins University doctoral student, Ellen Silbergeld, who developed information for the conferences. Workers, representatives, and officers of the union locals and district councils posed technical questions to the scientists, who tried to answer in lay terms. Paulson attended all nine conferences. The conference transcripts were published as a set of manuals for health and safety education.

By 1969, Mazzocchi had become part of a small group of activists from industrial unions and the IUD who organized and sought passage of the Occupational Safety and Health Act (OSH Act). Lobbying for the passage of the legislation was coordinated by these union leaders and representatives, Ralph Nader's Health Research Group, and other public health activists (Mazzocchi, 1982; Wooding et al., 1997). It was the birth of a coalition of labor, public health, consumer, and later environmental activists who supported each other in campaigns to achieve government action to protect workers, the public, and the environment. They focused primarily on the passage of federal legislation and regulations that would help develop local capacity for workers and citizens to use their federal rights.[3] After the OSH Act passed, OCAW president Grospiron created the Health and Safety Office at OCAW's headquarters in Denver, to provide technical support to OCAW members who wanted to use their new access to the law by seeking government aid to change dangerous workplace conditions.

The OSH Act became effective on April 28, 1971. On May 14, OCAW delivered the first health and safety complaint to the agency.[4] Steven Wodka, an assistant to Mazzocchi, along with Samuels of the IUD, filed a complaint requesting an inspection of the Allied Chemical Corp. facility in Moundsville, West Virginia (Mazzocchi, 1998).

In 1973, OCAW organized a strike against Shell Oil Co., which had refused to accept contract language that would have established joint labor-management health and safety committees and a network of union health and safety representatives in Shell facilities. Mazzocchi recruited support from scientists and physicians. He has discussed how his recruitment of scientists in some cases helped them to better understand and support the strategies of labor unions. Dr. Eula Bingham was one of the scientists recruited to support the Shell strike.[5] She later became the director of OSHA in the Carter administration and is well regarded among activists for her efforts on behalf of worker health and safety. Mazzocchi also recruited the support of 11 environmental organizations, which viewed this as an opportunity to bridge the gap between workers and environmentalists in order to gain support for effective coalitions to achieve government action (Lerza, 1973). With the aid of professionals and such organizations as those that have been mentioned, OCAW achieved success in its strike for health and safety protection measures against Shell.

OCAW fought many health and safety struggles during the 1970s and early 1980s. One major set of issues was workers' right to know about their exposures to hazardous substances and their right to act on the knowledge they obtained. OCAW also focused on the hazards faced by workers in the nuclear industry. Karen Silkwood, an activist from Local 5-283 at a Kerr-McGee facility in Oklahoma City, Oklahoma, helped OCAW raise these issues to a national level. Silkwood, whose efforts buttressed OCAW testimony at Congressional hearings on safety in the industry, met an untimely death during her activism against the company.

By 1976, OCAW had hired an industrial hygienist to provide technical input for the union's health and safety initiatives. Part of its health and safety education component was a tear-out section of its regular newsletter, called *Lifelines*. In 1976, the health and safety office was reorganized under the industrial hygienist. Educational activities comprised a third of the office's work; much of this was invested in a campaign to train OCAW local health and safety committee members.

OCAW also developed an internship program through which it educated medical students in occupational health. (Some industrial hygiene and law students also served internships.) About six interns worked with the union each year in plants throughout the country. It was an important step in linking the union's health and safety efforts with understanding professionals. In this case, the union developed future professionals as allies of the labor movement through participation in their education.

In 1976, Robert Wages, a former OCAW local president, was appointed assistant general counsel to the union. (In 1983, Wages was elected vice president of OCAW.) More than half of his time and effort was devoted to occupational safety and health matters. He worked with the health and safety office to develop the union's right-to-know campaign, and litigated cases against 3M and Colgate-Palmolive before the National Labor Relations Board and up to the DC Circuit Court of Appeals. Wages also handled the Title VII aspects of the lead exclusion cases the union brought against American Cyanamid for forcing several women to be sterilized so they could work in areas with potential exposure to lead pigments.

Mazzocchi was elected vice president of OCAW in 1977. He became responsible for the national union's health and safety efforts. One goal he pursued was the enhancement of training programs for members. In 1977, OCAW negotiated an agreement with the oil industry that established biennial training for health and safety committee members. It developed a training course called "The Hazards of the Petrochemical Industry" (Merrill, 1994). The biennial sessions came to be known as the "oil school."

OCAW encouraged OSHA director Bingham to back a grants program that would support occupational health and safety training. It became the well-regarded New Directions program. OCAW received its first New Directions award in 1979. Its program had two parts. It established a 2-week course, taught by OCAW staff and guest experts, to 11 rank-and-file members from its eight districts so they could become OSHECs. The workers would "pass on what they have learned to local union health and safety committee people as well as working with local unions on high priority health and safety problems" (OCAW, 1979). Glen Erwin, one of the OSHECs, said, "We were kind of like circuit-riding health and safety specialists."

The OSHECs coordinated training for workers, usually with the assistance of medical and other professionals. The OSHEC model was later incorporated into OCAW's hazardous waste worker training in the WETP.

The second part of OCAW's New Directions work continued the union's occupational physician training. OCAW supported medical student interns and physicians, many of whom became leaders in the field of occupational and environmental health. The interns and physicians were assigned to the eight OCAW districts, where they conducted health hazard evaluations, medical surveillance, and worker health education.

As an OCAW leader, Mazzocchi had reached out to the gamut of professionals who could be potential allies. In creating the space for professionals, union staff, and workers to cooperate, strategies were developed and implemented that likely would not have been considered otherwise. A network of creative and committed individuals and organizations successfully devised a national infrastructure to address occupational health and safety.

Mazzocchi unsuccessfully campaigned for the OCAW presidency in 1979. He lost the election but was appointed OCAW's director of health and safety. After a second unsuccessful campaign for the union presidency 2 years later, he returned to his local in New York as a rank-and-file member. But the health and safety groundwork that Mazzocchi had established would be evident in the union's eager grasp of the opportunities offered after 1986 by the WETP program.

THE LABOR INSTITUTE

In 1974, Mazzocchi created a small nonprofit organization called the Labor Institute to conduct research and education for labor struggles. The Labor Institute later became a key player in OCAW's hazardous waste worker training program under the WETP. The institute addressed a range of labor issues, including health and safety. The institute was not directly affiliated with OCAW. In fact, its only interaction with the union, apart from one economics training session in 1976, was with a local at a Merck facility in New Jersey. An intern in OCAW's legislative office, Les Leopold, who had recently graduated from Princeton University, was given the job of coordinating most of the institute's training work.

Throughout the late 1970s, Leopold and a doctoral student at Columbia University, Michael Merrill, conducted research and education for the labor movement. Leopold had developed training programs for workers, focusing particularly on devising training methods that were respectful and supportive of workers—considering their learning styles, their knowledge and experience, and especially the power relationships between labor and management.

The institute conducted economics training in 1976. Leopold began to notice that the institute had a "pedagogical problem," in that it was delivering the message that workers did not need conservative economists to run their lives, but instead they needed radical economists to do so (Leopold, 1998). Leopold came to believe that in order to help democratize the unions, workers' ability to take more control needed enhancement. Meeting that goal would require more than helping them to understand the ideas of progressive professionals.

Leopold began to explore participatory adult education methodology. With the support of several large grants, he developed curricula that employed multiple methods, including role plays, discussion groups, projects, games, videos, and music. But he found the approach exhausting for trainers and of limited value for trainees. The trainers were required to be expert in a range of topics—economics, labor issues, participatory training—and to have a strongly progressive perspective, which made recruiting difficult. The institute's training sessions at this point were teacher centered, with the trainers—their knowledge and performance—as the locus of classroom attention, rather than student centered, under which the goal would be facilitating dialogue between participants.

The Small Group Training Method

Leopold met Stan Weir, a rank-and-file longshoreman who was also a long-time union activist and agitator. He was an "old lefty" who had survived the McCarthy period's anticommunist purges of the CIO unions. According to Leopold, Weir used an "arsenal" of training methods as a way of organizing workers. Weir had studied Hawthorne's research on informal working groups. Unlike Hawthorne, who saw the potential to increase management control though manipulation of the groups, Weir believed that helping workers to use their informal groups and networks would be central to any effort to increase workers' power in the workplace. He used training methods whose roots were in the progressive education movement of the late 19th century. He organized his trainings so that workers held discussions in small groups. Leopold began to experiment with this approach (Leopold, 1998).

In 1980, Leopold attended a participatory training conference at the Highlander Research and Education Center in Tennessee. David Clemens was there, too. Clemens had worked for the British Trades Union Congress (TUC) and was visiting the United States to develop a manual with industrial hygienist Eileen Senn for the shipbuilders' union. Each conference participant presented samples of his or her training activities. Clemens was using small groups and, according to Leopold, Clemens's training was rooted in Freirian educational methods. Clemens invited Leopold to visit Bradford, England, to learn more about the TUC approach to worker training. Leopold visited with TUC leaders and members for a month and observed its "organized process of small-group education" (Leopold, 1998).

Training Trainers

The Labor Institute had been invited to assist a cooperative housing group in New York City to develop training that would help low-income people learn how to run cooperatives. Members of the group read an article that Merrill had written about the institute's work. As the institute worked with the group, Leopold was asked whether he wanted to conduct a training of trainers session for a national meeting of housing organizations to be held at the Wilder Training Preserve in Minnesota. He accepted.

Leopold designed this training so that people would have an opportunity to "learn by doing." The training involved several days of collective curriculum development. Then the group met with a low-income housing group in Minneapolis and conducted the training—as part of the group members' own training as trainers. The effort's success convinced Leopold and Merrill that they could develop curricula on technical subjects, since they had known nothing about housing prior to their Minnesota experience. Since he lacked expertise on technical health and safety issues, Leopold would be no more expert, and perhaps less, on the subject matter than the workers in training. This tactic, he believed, would facilitate a process to move training from being teacher centered to being learner centered.

The Labor Institute developed a small group activity method (SGAM) that it believed would help workers reflect on their shop floor experiences, apply past knowledge to new knowledge, and develop strategies for collective action against their employers. This was applied successfully with union locals facing concessions bargaining in contract negotiations. The locals wanted training that would help workers move beyond their fears of job loss so that they would not demand that the bargaining committee agree to a "give-back"—a critical issue across the manufacturing and chemical processing sectors. The training seemed to help workers buck national bargaining trends of agreeing to give-backs. Leopold was ecstatic. He believed that the training encouraged workers to talk with each other about the issues at hand, and helped a reform group win election in one local.

The Labor Institute next worked with Joseph Anderson and Paul Renner, the president and vice president respectively of an OCAW local at a Merck facility in New Jersey, to develop economics training for their members in anticipation of an upcoming battle with the company. This training helped the Merck Council of union locals, which was led by the New Jersey local, decide to conduct a national strike against Merck, which had locked out the union. The cooperation between Anderson, Renner, and the Labor Institute set up the leadership team that would later reunite to successfully develop the OCAW program within the WETP.

OCAW AND THE HAZARDOUS WASTE WORKER TRAINING GRANT

The union decreased its health and safety activities between 1980 and 1986, and did not continue the national leadership role it had assumed in the 1970s. The relationship with the medical interns who had worked with the union through its New Directions grant was discontinued. The union's industrial hygienist left his position under pressure. By several accounts, the health and safety activities maintained by 1986 were minimal. Multiple factors likely led to the weakening of OCAW's health and safety program. They included (1) the weakening of OSHA's New Directions program, including reductions in funding to grantees; (2) the shake-out in the oil and petrochemical industries, associated with a large drop in OCAW membership; and (3) the political fights for union control, leading to a near split in the union. By the end of this period, Bob Wages, then OCAW vice president, became increasingly frustrated with the union's direction. Among other things, Wages wanted to strengthen OCAW's health and safety program (Kieding, 1997; Leopold, 1998; Merrill, 1998; Wages, 1998).

OCAW made an effort to achieve Congressional action on worker health and safety in May 1985. The House Committee on Education and Labor held OSHA oversight hearings on worker health and safety in the manufacture and use of toxic and hazardous substances. Wages was the first person to testify and, among other topics, he addressed the topic of health and safety training in the oil industry. OCAW had commissioned scientists and public health professionals to analyze a videotape of an employer-selected training course. The reviewers found that the training was "largely irrelevant to oil refinery hazards . . . blatantly pro-management in its assumptions, was anti-OSHA, and often incorrect technically" (U.S. Congress. House of Representatives, 1985, p. 4). Wages testified that employers generally boycotted union-sponsored training courses. He criticized OSHA's promotion of voluntary health and safety efforts "with the keystone being a joint committee effort. Our experience has been that industry's definition of 'joint' is 'you agree with what I want to do'" (U.S. Congress. House of Representatives, 1985, p. 4).

None of the veterans of OCAW's health and safety program is aware of any OCAW involvement in the effort to gain worker protection language in SARA. When the WETP request for applications was released in early 1987, Sylvia Krekel, an occupational health specialist who had worked for OCAW's Health and Safety Department since 1973, was the sole staff person at OCAW working on health and safety issues. Krekel contacted Margaret Seminario at the AFL-CIO to talk about whether it would be appropriate for OCAW to apply for a training grant under the program. She also spoke with Mazzocchi, who then had an office at the Labor Institute. She asked him whether he was interested and how he thought a proposal should be organized. Krekel also discussed an application with Wages. Wages was interested, believing that a training program on hazardous waste issues could be a "precursor to a more sophisticated training program generally." The decision was made to apply for the funds. On Mazzocchi's recommendation, the Labor Institute was brought in to write the proposal and, if a grant was awarded, develop the program.

Leopold agreed to organize the program, as long as Wages was willing to have the worker-trainers conduct the training, and to have it based exclusively on the small group activity method that the institute had developed. Wages agreed, not knowing the institute's work well enough to be comfortable with it, but believing that workers required something other than a didactic training method. "It seemed that the interactive process that the Labor Institute was developing just made a lot of sense," he said. "I couldn't find any compelling reason not to embrace that."

OCAW Submits a Proposal to NIEHS

Michael Merrill wrote the proposal that OCAW submitted to NIEHS.[6] The goals of the program that OCAW proposed were as follows:

- To raise the standard of safety and health training throughout the represented industries;
- To ensure that OCAW members received the best possible training; and
- To seek to foster an active "culture of safety" in the workplace through the use of worker-trainers skilled in learner-centered, participatory teaching methods. (OCAW, 1992, p. BB)[7]

OCAW had other goals for its training program as well. The proposal suggested goals that project participants mentioned in subsequent interviews, which included the following:

- To protect workers from unsafe exposures to toxic materials;
- To develop the capacity for trained workers to become "watchdogs" over company safety programs and "systems analysts" who could analyze a system of safety and challenge its faults;
- To support the ability of a core group of workers in every facility to communicate, advocate, and mobilize around health and safety issues as they arose from time to time.
- "To challenge one of the most basic features of the organization of work in a capitalist economy—the separation of conception from execution, thinking from doing." (Merrill, 1995, pp. 42-43)
- To develop a program of excellence that would demonstrate to management the value of union-sponsored training and thereby receive management buy-in, facilitating program self-sufficiency through management purchase of courses. (Merrill, 1994)

The approximately 30,000 OCAW members who worked at hazardous waste treatment, storage, and disposal facilities (TSDFs) regulated in accordance with RCRA were the proposed target population. Under the plan, an 8-hour refresher course would be developed and taught by worker-trainers. The worker-trainers would be intensively trained and expand the existing group of OSHECs. They would teach the hazardous waste courses in teams. The OSHECs would maintain their jobs in the plants and work one quarter of their time as training instructors. The curriculum for the train-the-trainer course and the hazardous waste course would be developed by the Labor Institute (OCAW, 1987).

The Target Population

OCAW's targeting of RCRA facility workers for a grant from the Superfund was based on language in OSHA's interim final rule for hazardous waste operations and ER. The rule was issued in December 1986, several months before the due date for the proposals to NIEHS. OSHA had determined that because Section 126 of SARA was a freestanding statutory provision rather than an amendment to CERCLA, Congress intended to provide protection to all workers who dealt with hazardous wastes. OSHA listed workers at RCRA facilities. The targeted workers would be those who had hazardous waste operations duties or the potential for involvement in an emergency response to a HAZMAT incident.

The Refresher Training Course

The basis for the development and delivery of a refresher course was twofold: (1) employers in the oil and petrochemical industries were giving health and safety training, and (2) employer-provided training was generally inadequate. OCAW also believed, as did most industrial unions, that the employer had a responsibility to provide health and safety training for employees who were assigned to hazardous operations. Therefore, refresher training would add to the training workers received, and not just fulfill the employer's obligations.

Worker-to-Worker Training Using the Small Group Activity Method

OCAW had already developed its model of worker-trainers with the OSHECs under their New Directions grants. The Labor Institute had devised a system for training worker-trainers, and for developing a small group activity method-based curriculum that could be delivered by worker-trainers. A merging of the two models was proposed for the hazardous waste workers program. It would be substantially different from the training that OCAW members generally received from their employers. Employer-provided training rarely gave workers the information that they needed to improve their working conditions, and was usually delivered by professionals who often could not present information in a way that was comprehensible or relevant to workers. The format was almost always a lecture with no opportunity for workers to discuss how to change workplace conditions. Finally, employer-provided training usually had a "blame-the-worker" orientation implying that health and safety hazards exist because workers are not careful. In some of the most hazardous of all industrial sectors, such an orientation could generate cynicism, if not outrage (Anderson, 1998; Dodge, 1998; Erwin, 1998; Leopold, 1998). OCAW proposed a different model and orientation for its training.

The Labor Institute intended to develop high-quality materials that would explain health and safety issues in relevant, understandable ways. The curriculum would be developed by educational and technical experts, such as physicians and industrial hygienists. Workers would be recruited to become trainers. The worker-trainers would attend a comprehensive train-the-trainer session where they would learn how to facilitate training sessions incorporating the small group activity method. A workbook composed of a series of training activities would be supplied. The worker-trainers would learn the technical information in the workbook to the extent necessary to comfortably facilitate training sessions. It was not intended that they would become technical experts. Instead, they would rely on the technical expertise presented in the workbook and facilitate groups of workers through the workbook activities. As questions were raised in class, the worker-trainers would note them and refer them to technical experts associated with the program who would answer them for trainees at a later date.

> This active or participatory approach to teaching lifts the burden of needing to be an expert from the shoulders of prospective trainers. At the same time, it ensures that trainees have available to them all the best, and most accurate information relevant to the topics being discussed. (Merrill, 1991b, p. 7)

BUILDING THE PROGRAM

Mazzocchi confidently left the program's development and organization in the hands of Leopold, the Labor Institute, and Krekel at OCAW,[8] who would consult with him about the work. His one requirement in the beginning was that the program follow the guidelines established by NIEHS on target populations and the degree of expansiveness in program orientation. Mazzocchi was concerned that NIEHS would be under significant scrutiny because the WETP was a new initiative and it supported labor unions (Leopold, 1998; Merrill, 1998).

Twenty-four OCAW members were chosen to be OSHECs (OCAW, 1988). (The term worker-trainers later became more generally used than OSHECs.) Leopold visited some of the OSHECs who had been trained and active in earlier OCAW programs. He and a consultant discussed with them the roles of workers as trainers. Recruitment selections were based on several qualities, including regional, political (union), and gender-race-ethnicity considerations. The worker-trainers maintained their positions in the plants, taking negotiated leave time to train, for which the union supplemented their income. The majority of the worker-trainers were officers, stewards, or health and safety activists in their locals. At least 25% of them had some level of a college degree. Approximately one-third were women (OCAW, 1992).

Curriculum Development

In addition to interviewing the OSHECs, Leopold visited OCAW members around the country to talk about hazardous waste issues and to ask which production processes put workers at risk of exposure to hazardous wastes. He then sought professionals to assist on curriculum development. Dr. Steven Markowitz of the Mt. Sinai School of Medicine worked closely with Leopold on the curriculum. Leopold has described Markowitz as a confident professional who supported the notion of developing worker-trainers and eagerly assisted in developing an appropriate curriculum. Markowitz had experience talking to workers and community members about toxics and toxicology. He described some of the misconceptions, or myths, about toxic chemicals, human exposure, and how scientists assess health risks. Markowitz explained these areas to Leopold, and together they researched whether they were myths and then developed a curriculum activity entitled "Tackling Toxic Chemical Myths."

Leopold and Markowitz organized a curriculum that could be used both in training the worker-trainers and in the courses that these worker-trainers would teach. They sought other experts to assist them and consulted often with Mazzocchi. The curriculum took the form of a workbook of course modules and activities. The completed draft was given to the New York Committee for Occupational Safety and Health (NYCOSH) for review by its professionals. Some read through the materials. Others, who were worker health educators, tried out the activities. Leopold gained useful feedback from this "testing," which helped him prepare the curriculum for the first training of trainers.

The curriculum was developed for two purposes: its utility to teach the worker-trainers the material and how to present it; and its suitability as the basis for an 8-hour course that the worker-trainers would deliver. The curriculum included activities that would take up to 24 hours to complete. The worker-trainers would choose the modules they would use for any particular course.

The format of the training is the set of activities in the workbook. Each activity required an introduction by the trainer, and then the group read the supporting material in the workbook. Then the group collectively engaged in a problem-solving activity. One member of each group either volunteered or was selected to record the opinions, decisions, and strategies of all. When groups completed the activity, the trainers facilitated a "report-back" by each small group, where each presented to the larger group its ideas for solving the problems set forth in the activity. After all groups had presented their ideas and the larger group had finished discussing them, the trainers summarized the discussion, and highlighted the key points.

The Advisory Board

NIEHS required funded training programs to establish independent boards of advisors. OCAW organized a board of representatives from social sectors with whom the union's health and safety activities intersected. The advisory committee members were Ken Blehm, assistant professor, Department of Environmental Health, Colorado State University; Bart Chadwick, regional administrator, OSHA, Region VIII; Sharon Kercher, on-scene coordinator, EPA, Region VIII; Dr. Phillip Landrigan, director, Division of Environmental and Occupational Medicine, Mt. Sinai Medical Center; Steven Lester, science director, Citizens Clearinghouse for Hazardous Waste; John Marshall, captain and hazardous waste coordinator, Denver Fire Department; Tony Mazzocchi; and David Ortlieb, director of health and safety, International Chemical Workers Union.

OCAW built and maintained alliances with government agencies, other unions, and the largest national grassroots environmental organization addressing hazardous wastes. Its board membership also revealed the union's view of the importance of HAZMAT incident ER activities to its members and the training program.

THE FIRST TRAINING OF TRAINERS AT RUTGERS

In spring 1988, the two dozen OCAW members recruited to be worker-trainers gathered with Leopold, Merrill, and OCAW staff for the initial training. The draft curriculum workbook they used contained 24 hours of curriculum material. The goal was to develop the worker-trainers' ability to select from that basic curriculum 8 hours' worth of activities for the courses they would deliver to workers. Eventually, the full workbook would be used for a 24-hour course. At this point, though, Leopold and Merrill believed that going beyond an 8-hour period would overwhelm the worker-trainers. The training format was new to all of them.

Leopold introduced himself to the group and explained that the goal of the train-the-trainer course was to teach the worker-trainers how to teach. He said that after the first 2 hours, most of the talking that week would be done by them; he had not prepared expert presentations for them. Initially, the worker-trainers were upset and confused by what he said. The format was different from any they had ever experienced, either in previous schooling or in company training sessions. Even for those who had participated in the earlier OCAW training, it was a different experience. "But, by the end of the second day, they were walking on air," Merrill said. "They were floating because they were using and hearing their own voices."

The worker-trainers learned how to facilitate the small group activity training. The curriculum they learned to use also taught them what they needed to know in order to deliver the training. The workbook was not designed primarily for use as a reference manual, but rather as the actual curriculum of the training course. It was to be read by trainees as part of the training.

It was a learn-by-doing model, but the "doing" in this case was not using personal protective or monitoring equipment. Instead, the "doing" was actively participating in the study and discussion of health and safety issues and collective problem-solving. The worker-trainers learned how to help their fellow workers to become skilled at analyzing the health and safety risks they faced on the job and then to develop ways to reduce the risks.

Representatives of the international union (OCAW), various occupational health and safety organizations, and other unions attended the Rutgers training as observers. By the end of the first day, several health professionals and worker-health educators were discussing testing issues. Of particular concern to the educators was how Leopold and Merrill would know whether the worker-trainers had learned what they needed to know. They believed that some form of testing should be employed to make this determination. Leopold and Merrill made clear that they would not test the workers. They explained that the training was to teach workers how to analyze the health and safety systems in their workplaces, not to become health and safety experts. The testing question later became one of the main points of conflict for OCAW in the NIEHS program.

The worker-trainers left Rutgers and gradually took on their own courses. The train-the-trainer process included monitoring the worker-trainers once or twice at training classes. Leopold and Merrill went around the country to continue the "apprenticeship" of the worker-trainers (Leopold, 1998). They observed the trainers and "coached" them from the back of the room. Glen Erwin, an OCAW worker-trainer, said that his first class was recorded on videotape, which he watched later. "We had a video right in your face, and I guess every mistake made, I made," Erwin admitted. "Yeah, I think Les and Mike were there, but they weren't in there to pull us out of the fire." The process succeeded in helping the workers gain a sense of confidence about their competence as trainers.

THE WORKBOOK ACTIVITIES

OCAW had specific ideas about the nature of health and safety training, ideas that differed from those applied in most mainstream worker training. The dominant purpose of health and safety training was to inform workers of the work practices and behaviors that would ensure their health and safety. The training in most venues assumed that the workplace was inherently safe and that inappropriate behavior by workers was the primary cause of injuries and illnesses. In contrast, OCAW assumed that the workplace, for OCAW members, was inherently hazardous; that in most cases employers were not ensuring a healthy and safe workplace; and that the purpose of health and safety training was to help workers identify the weaknesses and failings of specific systems of safety in order to correct them.

A review of some activities from the *Hazardous Materials Workbook* will best demonstrate how these assumptions were applied during training. The workbook has 12 activity sections, each including a set of fact sheets with information that participants are instructed to read in order to engage in one or more tasks that comprise the activity. The activities address the following issues:

- Reducing job fear—workers' concerns about job loss due to environmental regulations;
- Assessing chemical hazards in the workplace;
- Tackling toxic chemical myths—introducing basic toxicological principles and the adverse health outcomes related to HAZMAT exposures;
- Explaining OSHA health standards, and understanding and using the material safety data sheets that manufacturers had to provide with chemical products;
- Evaluating employer exposure monitoring and medical surveillance programs;
- Assessing workplace H&S hazard controls, including respiratory protection;
- Understanding the limits and use of worker protections under federal and state laws;
- Making joint labor-management health and safety committees more effective;
- Understanding and applying emergency response plans; and
- Developing strategies for building toxic waste alliances with the community. (Labor Institute, 1992)

Tackling Toxic Chemical Myths

The "Tackling Toxic Chemical Myths" activity gives an insight into OCAW's perspective. The first task in this activity asks workers to assume that they have been asked by the union to respond to the worker who made the following statement:

> The danger of these chemicals is overstated. If you use your nose to warn you and don't breathe the stuff, it won't harm you. Of course, you must respect acids and avoid them. They can blow your lungs away. I don't buy this panic about cancer. I know some people who got cancer and never worked with chemicals. I also know people who work with chemicals and have not gotten cancer. It is obvious all cancer doesn't come from chemicals. The way they do lab tests is to shoot tons of chemicals into rats. How can they avoid getting cancer? In my opinion, I've worked with this stuff for twenty years and I'm okay. So, what's all the fuss about? (Labor Institute, 1992, p. 49)

In all likelihood, some training course participants will hold these views. The workbook helps them to analyze their own opinions in the light of new information. The participants read the fact sheets and then discuss in their groups how they would respond to the worker's comments. The fact sheets address such issues as the bodily routes of entry of toxic chemicals. They explain dose-response relationships, and the differences between chronic and acute health effects. Information is presented on how chemicals are tested and on the fact that the vast majority of chemicals have not been tested for exposure-related health effects. Of particular importance to OCAW members, the workbook discusses reproductive health effects. For this activity, 13 fact sheets are presented, along with graphs and charts. A great deal of information is offered in a simplified format. No worker need grasp all of the points. Working in groups, workers can take advantage of the variety of areas of interest and attention in order to discuss the issues.

Control of Toxic Hazards

OCAW's training does not simply explain to workers the different methods used to control workplace health and safety hazards. It helps workers to develop the ability to evaluate whether the controls in place are adequate to prevent "serious exposure to toxic hazards" (Labor Institute, 1992, p. 157). A case study of a hazardous wastes operation is delivered, detailing work tasks and established controls. Course participants are then asked to answer four questions: "1. What controls that are in place do you feel are proper? Why? 2. Which ones do you feel are inadequate? Why? 3. What controls would you recommend be requested for this situation? and 4. Now switching to real life, what is the most important hazard in your facility that you feel needs improved controls, and what controls would you recommend?" (Labor Institute, 1992, p. 159)

Again, fact sheets give information about work environment controls. The questions and fact sheets help workers to think critically about the controls in place, and whether they are adequate or inadequate. They are encouraged to think about the types of controls they would implement. Then, having examined a case study, workers are directed to apply their thinking to their own workplaces, to apply what they have learned to improving their own working conditions.

ISSUES FACING OCAW

As the core program elements were developed and the worker-trainers began to deliver courses, the program faced new challenges. The union anticipated that employers might initially be reluctant to accept the training. OCAW's plan was to deliver the training after shifts and on weekends in local union halls, and as word spread of its value and excellence, moves could be made toward gaining management acceptance and buy-in. OCAW members were not eager for the training at first. The numbers attending the classes were small. Workers were not willing to give up their time for a training course, assuming that it would be the same as an employer's training course. Also, the restructuring of the industries led to reduced employment levels in the plants, while at the same time, the remaining workers were working harder and longer. For an individual worker, time away from work became more limited (Dodge, 1998; Merrill, 1998). Gradually, however, workers who attended the courses encouraged others to do so based on their appreciation of the training.

Continued Curriculum Development

As OCAW health and safety personnel presented the training courses, they learned more about hazardous waste issues in the plants. Workers in the classes would raise technical issues that worker-trainers came to realize needed to be included in the curriculum. The OCAW training program hired an industrial hygienist, Joel Carr, who joined the Labor Institute's staff. He had worked in the labor movement for a decade, most recently addressing nuclear industry issues for the Workplace Health Fund.

With Carr's assistance, OCAW began the next phase of curriculum development. Some worker-trainers were extremely knowledgeable about HAZMAT ER issues. William Hoyle, in particular, was critical of the one ER activity in the workbook. He and others had read the ER regulations and available materials and they wanted a full emergency response course. Leopold and Carr worked with several worker-trainers to develop a curriculum. OCAW was ready to move beyond the 8-hour basic refresher course. It was also ready to incorporate the worker-trainers into curriculum development.

Personal Protective Equipment and Hands-On Training

ER training raised the question of how to address personal protective equipment. Leopold and Merrill had learned much of what they knew about health and safety from Mazzocchi. Mazzocchi had said for many years that there was no such thing as protective equipment; that some amount of hazardous material is bound to get beyond the equipment barriers to the worker. The established industrial hygiene hierarchy of controls placed personal protective equipment as a last resort, when engineering and other controls could not be implemented. For OCAW's team, this meant that when it came to ER activities in which no other controls were possible, the health and safety focus needed to be on how to prevent the emergency, not how best to equip workers who must jeopardize their health and safety in response to an emergency.

The agreed-upon message of the program was that if any worker was going to be assigned to HAZMAT response activities, he or she should have hundreds of hours of ER training before doing so.[9] OCAW's personal and respiratory protection activities in its HAZMAT and ER workbooks do not present personal protective equipment as the solution to hazardous waste operations and ER work. Instead, they approach these subjects from the perspective of how workers can determine whether their employers have implemented an appropriate and adequate personal protective equipment or respiratory equipment program. In this way, OCAW members learn to analyze whether the program complies with OSHA's requirements and whether the equipment provided is correct for the intended purpose. In the 24-hour ER course, workers performed hands-on activities with the equipment as a way of emphasizing these points.

> If you are respectful of people's desire to wear personal protective equipment and give themselves a slightly better chance of surviving in a hazardous environment, but also make the point that this is not the solution, this is a band-aid, then you get a lot more of them in the room paying attention to you. (Merrill, 1998)

Incident Tracking and Investigation

OCAW reported to NIEHS that compared with many other industries, the petrochemical industry maintained a low rate of lost workday injuries but a higher fatality rate (OCAW, 1992). The industry suffered catastrophic incidents, such as explosions, sometimes with severe injuries or loss of multiple lives, in the mid- and late 1980s and early 1990s. The Texas City local of OCAW, with 39 contracts and 2,500 members, asked the union to develop a preventive approach to catastrophic incidents. A plan was devised to record and evaluate near misses. The plan was reviewed by the OSHECs (worker-trainers) and labor-management attendees at an oil school session. It was dubbed an incident tracking, or near-miss, plan. Its purpose was "to discover what procedures and operations could contribute to a major catastrophe" (OCAW, 1992, Appendix F). OCAW used the information to plan action to prevent such incidents. An activity was included in the ER workbook in order to train workers how to implement the system in their plants.

OCAW sought funding from NIEHS in 1992 for the incident tracking and investigation system. To fully implement the plan, OCAW wanted to hire a full-time coordinator. The union proposed a 3-year pilot project to serve as an industry model for near-miss tracking. Thirty-six locals would participate. But NIEHS did not fund the effort, probably due to limited money rather than limited interest.

EVALUATION

OCAW implemented evaluation measures to determine the effectiveness and usefulness of its efforts. The worker-trainers were asked to evaluate and provide feedback on the curriculum in train-the-trainer classes. Merrill changed the activities as he and Leopold discovered that some were ineffective. In the first year, Merrill interviewed the 24 worker-trainers who had been recruited and trained. Their talks were tape-recorded and transcribed to maximize their value as a tool. The worker-trainers spoke to the effectiveness of the program.

Evaluation quickly became an important element for OCAW because of "some initial skepticism from those who believed safety and health too technical to be taught by anyone without an advanced degree" (Merrill, 1994, p. 350). Merrill volunteered to coordinate the evaluation process out of a concern that evaluation conducted by a health education specialist "could drive the program to a teacher-centered model . . . before we could get things going" (Merrill, 1998).

Since this was a new model, Merrill realized that it needed innovative evaluation methods that would capture the strengths and weaknesses of the program. "We got enormous pressure from the evaluation professionals to institute evaluation methods that would [require] conducting a class in a typical academic pattern." OCAW incorporated four aspects in its evaluation efforts: participant evaluations; worker-trainer evaluations and reactions; company evaluations; and impact evaluations.

The OCAW program incorporates an annual refresher training course for all worker-trainers, including evaluation of the curriculum and program so that information can be collected from the worker-trainers, who are interviewed during breaks. The information has demonstrated that the program "not only provided important safety and health education to the union's membership, it also enriched the lives of the worker-trainers" (Merrill, 1994, p. 351).

In the first 2 years, 17 company managers attended at least one 8-hour course. Merrill interviewed as many as possible for two reasons. First, OCAW needed to know what the health and safety professionals and management thought of the training. Second, if they found it acceptable, the union could use the feedback to build stronger ties with management in an effort to get companies to purchase courses. Repeatedly in his writing, Merrill pointed to the willingness of construction contractors to accept worker training from building trades unions and said that OCAW hoped to encourage petrochemical employers to do the same.

Leopold and Merrill worked with the worker-trainers to develop mechanisms for evaluating the impact of training. Many of the worker-trainers volunteered to collect data from participants; two volunteered to design a common survey instrument. The survey results showed that the course was well liked and that the training helped them to be "more effective advocates of safety and health at work, and it contributed directly to positive changes in the workplace" (Merrill, 1994, p. 352). Several years later, OCAW recruited an evaluation specialist who expanded the effort to assess the impact of the training upon working conditions.

EXPANSION IN 1990

In 1990, when NIEHS requested applications for new and supplemental program funding, OCAW submitted a successful proposal. Several of its proposed program expansions were denied, such as funding for the incident tracking and investigation program and a proposed component designed to use medical interns. The main request for funding to expand the program was approved. One major OCAW issue was its continuing difficulty in recruiting workers to its courses. The union decided to offer stipends to workers for the courses that were conducted outside workers' shifts.

OCAW also had to expand its base of worker-trainers if it was going to conduct more training. The union successfully argued that program expansion would provide strong support to the goal of achieving collective bargaining agreements with companies to purchase OCAW's training for their workers. NIEHS's proposal review committee commented, "Overall this is an excellent application" (NIEHS, 1990).

Program Administration

OCAW hired Joseph Anderson as a program specialist. His initial role was to negotiate with interested companies to purchase training from the union. He quickly moved into the role of grant administrator, directing the program. Anderson had been the president of the Merck local in New Jersey that had worked with the Labor Institute. He had been a strong supporter of the SGAM and the worker-centered training approach since 1979. Anderson oversaw the expansion of the number of worker-trainers. By 1992, the program had recruited 10 more of them, bringing the total to about 30, after some of the original recruits dropped out.

The program had developed quickly and successfully, but as many NIEHS awardees discovered, rapid development often came at the expense of cohesive administration. By 1991, a major curriculum development project was stalled and financial administration was inadequate. OCAW, like several of the other union WETP awardees, was not accustomed to operating in the manner required for a large federal grant. Between 1990 and 1992, OCAW mounted a major effort to develop the competency required to manage such a program. By the end of 1992, OCAW had not only an exemplary training program but one that was appropriately managed.

OCAW's emphasis on a worker-trainer-based program created a contradiction in terms of managing the program, in that strong management seemed to oppose the idea of permitting workers to take charge. Anderson soon realized, though, that in order for the worker-trainers to be able to assert control, strong administration was required. "To keep the thing moving, you have to administrate in a very hands-on fashion," he said. He gradually took charge, demanding the completion of the set of curricula and appropriate financial accounting.

New Recruits and Changing Roles for the First Worker-Trainers

The recruitment of new worker-trainers created the need for a more developed train-the-trainer and apprenticeship process. A second train-the-trainer course was scheduled, again at Rutgers University, where Merrill was on the faculty. Leopold recruited four of the original worker-trainers to lead it, using an updated version of the original curriculum. Glen Erwin was one of the four. "The thing that's really been used to develop the skills the most is that trainers are used to train other trainers, training the next group," Erwin said.

Bradley Dodge was one of the new recruits. He was a pipe fitter-welder at a Chevron plant near San Francisco. Dodge was already an activist in his local, serving as a member of the joint labor-management health and safety committee and as a shop steward. He remembered going to the train-the-trainer class, fearing that people would not welcome him. Instead, he was instantly helped to feel as though he was a valuable part of the program. In his view, the trainer training provided a chance to "participate in the methodology as well as begin to understand the materials and to understand some of the bigger themes that we were trying to get to." Dodge had been a college student and had been through an apprenticeship and employer-provided training. In these courses, an instructor would tell the students how to do things. At the trainer training, Dodge learned about centering the training around the workers. By the end of the training, he recognized that "[t]his is the only way in the long run that the message can truly be carried."

After the second train-the-trainer class, the more experienced worker-trainers began to mentor the newer trainers. A veteran trainer attended sessions conducted by the newer trainers. The veteran would provide "training tips"—suggestions based on the veteran's own experience—and assist if the new trainer needed help with a difficult situation. For the worker-trainers, it was much like the way that learning takes place on the job. "Traditionally, when we go to work, workers learn from workers. We call it 'tag-along training' in the plants. You spend so many weeks of tag-along training with somebody that knows the job" (Erwin, 1998).

The Curriculum Action Team

Developing a curriculum is not a simple process, but it was one that Les Leopold did well. He did not realize, however, how difficult and intimidating that task was for others, especially workers. This created a problem for the OCAW program because few worker-trainers volunteered for the curriculum development team, and those who did were often not comfortable with the work. (It took 8 years—until 1995—for OCAW to develop a strong, competent, and confident curriculum development team from among the worker-trainers.)

Nonetheless, by 1990, all new curricula developed for OCAW came from a curriculum action team (CAT). Writers' classes were held to support the team's development. The CAT got involved in curriculum development for the oil school classes, which were being changed to the SGAM format as well. The team also developed smaller curriculum activities addressing new health and safety developments, such as process hazard analysis (which was required under OSHA's Process Safety Management standard).

Some professionals aided the worker-trainers in curriculum development. Paul Renner, who had been an officer of the Merck local in New Jersey, was hired as the curriculum development coordinator. Renner had put himself through college and then law school while working at the plant. A radiation health physicist and industrial hygienist named Mark Griffon worked as a consultant to OCAW. Griffon helped Renner with the CAT in developing curricula for training courses conducted in the nuclear industry. Curriculum development became a collective process in which the CAT was central.

Outreach, Marketing, and Self-Sufficiency

Most employers resisted contracting with OCAW for health and safety training. Consequently, gaining access to the numbers of workers the union wanted to train remained difficult. OCAW offered a $40-$50 stipend for course attendance. Since OCAW members earn considerably more money than that represents, it was a limited incentive for attending training. After Anderson was moved to overall program coordination, Erwin took over outreach and marketing to employers.

The cooperative agreement with NIEHS required all awardees to incorporate plans that would help them become financially self-sufficient. OCAW wanted employers to purchase health and safety training from the union, as a way to open joint labor-management dialogue to improve conditions in the plants.

A number of companies purchased training from OCAW. They included British Petroleum, Whitco, Axel Nobel, Mobil Oil, Ethel Corp., and Goodyear. Their purchases did not necessarily indicate a willingness to work jointly with the union on health and safety issues. Often, a contract resulted when a company was issued citations by OSHA. Some companies were willing to accept the decisions of health and safety managers who genuinely believed that OCAW's training was better than other available courses and was worthwhile because it created openings for joint labor-management actions to improve health and safety conditions.

In 1993, OCAW received WETP permission to assign Erwin the position of self-sufficiency outreach coordinator, to provide "a concentrated effort toward self-sufficiency in the Gulf Coast Region . . . Texas, Louisiana, Oklahoma, Alabama, Kansas, and Missouri" (OCAW, 1993).

OCAW and the DOE's Nuclear Facilities

In 1993, the WETP received funds from Congress, through the DOE, to give grants to awardees to train workers at the DOE's nuclear facilities. The facilities were managed by private corporations under contract to the DOE. OCAW received some of these funds. While coverage of this work by OCAW is beyond the scope of this research, the DOE program created difficult conflicts for OCAW.

The justification for these grants was the need to address the training of workers who might be involved in environmental remediation programs as the facilities underwent end-of-the-Cold-War restructuring. A major conflict for OCAW was the issue of which workers should be employed for clean-up work. OCAW wanted to see any of its members who faced job loss due to the closing of operations given the option of clean-up work, for which OCAW would provide training. The union, on occasion, found itself at odds with building trades unions, particularly the Laborers, who claimed that clean-up work came under their jurisdiction. OCAW, and all NIEHS awardees, had been in conflict with the contract companies' training departments, which had lost a significant portion of work to the awardees. As a result, OCAW's approach to training came under attack in the DOE effort. OCAW assigned a staff person to serve as a liaison to the DOE and Congress on these issues. By 2007, the union had provided more than 2,000 training courses to its members at six facilities.

Post-Training Testing of Workers

The WETP's effort to develop a set of minimum criteria for programs developing and delivering training for hazardous waste operations and ER workers forced discussions among the awardees about the testing of trained workers. Merrill took the lead on the issue for OCAW, which opposed testing workers attending training courses. Merrill drafted an article on testing at a point when OCAW was being pressured by employers to test workers at the end of a course (Merrill, 1989, 1998).

Merrill's criticism was directed at the proposed rule issued by OSHA, dealing with the accreditation of hazardous waste operations training programs. OSHA proposed to require that worker certification should be based on the ability to pass a 50-question test. Merrill and OCAW argued that the emphasis should not be on whether workers had learned how to work safely but on the degree of responsibility assumed by employers. Merrill and OCAW argued that the NIEHS program and its awardees were undermining the model established by the program. He called for a requirement for employers to

> demonstrate that they have provided their employees with training from a nationally recognized, fully accredited safety and health training program. And before they are accredited, training programs should be required to submit to a full-scale peer review by an independent panel of health professionals and training experts no less comprehensive and rigorous than that used in the competition for federal grants. (Merrill, 1991a, p. 52)

In the oil and petrochemical industries, accidents and excess exposures are common. Merrill and OCAW argued against the explanation that these resulted from system failures alone, alleging instead that systems failures were the effects of normal operating procedures. Using accident literature, they argued that accidents were the result of a particular organization of work in a set of industrial processes. Merrill argued that in order to change the organization of work, workers must be empowered through education with the right to express and enforce their concerns, supported by mechanisms for doing so (Merrill, 1991a, p. 57).

Merrill and OCAW never argued against educating workers so that they could engage in appropriate work practices. They were committed to worker health and safety training. They argued, however, that testing workers to determine how well they had learned the information in training was a way to obfuscate the imbalance of power in labor-management relations that ensured that workers in the oil and petrochemical industries would remain at risk of injuries, illnesses, and fatalities.

OCAW believed that it lost the argument. The Minimum Criteria Document developed through the NIEHS-sponsored consensus process, however, did not call exclusively for testing workers. It contained a detailed section titled "Proficiency Assessment" (NIEHS, 1991, p. 6). But a compromise was reached, accepted by OCAW, to set criteria for a written test, *if* a written test were to be used. Regardless of the practical outcome, OCAW presented an alternative discussion of worker testing that was given enough consideration to warrant a compromise. This suggested the strength of its arguments, support from the ICWU led consortium, and respect for the need of these programs.

TAKING LEADERSHIP IN THE NATIONAL PROGRAM

OCAW gave strong leadership in the NIEHS program, largely due to its commitment to the worker-to-worker and small group activity-based training. From the outset, NIEHS encouraged and supported the use of participatory training methods. The Laborers-AGC took a strong lead in developing hands-on training using mock waste sites. OCAW led in developing training rooted in popular education methodology and principles. Three other awardee organizations also developed similarly oriented training curricula: the California Consortium (CAC), a university program based at the Labor Occupational Safety and Health program at the University of California Los Angeles; the New England Consortium (TNEC), a program at the University of Lowell (which later became the University of Massachusetts Lowell); and the ICWU consortium, which included several major manufacturing industrial unions. All of the organizations adopted elements introduced by OCAW, although none adopted the worker-to-worker, small group activity method outright. Together, though, they formed a solid block of training organizations with foundations in popular education.

OCAW also played a leading role in supporting the training and protection needs of workers for whom ER activities are a "collateral duty." That is, they were not hired to serve as emergency responders but in the event of a HAZMAT incident they would be expected to support the ER effort in some manner.

OCAW's leadership on evaluation has been innovative and consistent. It has been central for the NIEHS awardees, who wanted to focus on how training supports workers' abilities to effect change in the workplace.[10]

Support for Other Programs

The OCAW program worked with SEIU to create a worker-to-worker, small group activity-based training program. It became the second such program among the awardees. OCAW provided significant resources for the training of SEIU's worker-trainers and helped develop its curriculum. SEIU also incorporated OCAW's evaluation methods and approach.

By the mid-1990s, the UAW had begun to collaborate with OCAW to strengthen its hazardous waste worker training. The George Meany Center for Labor Studies, which was the WETP awardee that coordinated a training program for a network of rail worker unions, also collaborated with OCAW. In both cases, the focus was on strengthening worker-trainers' positions in the programs and on evaluation methods.

In 1992, OCAW conducted two training courses in Chicago in which both workers and community residents participated. The training was done cooperatively with the National Toxics Campaign as a forum for workers and community residents to collectively review local hazardous waste issues. Individuals from the two groups engaged in small group activities together. According to Mary Elsner, of the Chicago Area Committee on Occupational Safety and Health (CACOSH), "Workers and community activists got to know one another, shed stereotypes they held about the 'other' group, and found common ground" (Elsner, 1992).

At its October 5, 1993, program advisory board meeting, OCAW was advised to request NIEHS to support the inclusion of community activists and environmentalists as participants in training courses addressing issues that affect both workers and community residents. By this time, a "Jobs and the Environment" curriculum had been developed by the Public Health Institute and OCAW. On December 9, 1993, a project justification was submitted to NIEHS. OCAW proposed an 8-hour course on a Saturday in a local union hall for an audience of environmental activists and union members. WETP administrator Dobbin approved the request, largely due to the relationship between Section 126 of SARA and the provisions of Title III of the act, which justified the use of a worker training program to train nonworkers in the adjacent concerned community. For the next decade, OCAW would continue these efforts. A particularly strong relationship was developed with the Southwest Network for Environmental Justice.

DIRECTIONS PURSUED

The incident tracking system that was denied funding in 1992 remained an OCAW program goal. The chemical industry, through the Chemical Manufacturers' Association, had rolled out its Responsible Care® program—a voluntary effort in which companies would demonstrate their commitment to continuously improving their compliance with existing environmental and health and safety regulations. From OCAW's point of view, the industry's lackluster goals were established mainly to improve the industry's public image, and amounted to no more than stonewalling. OCAW's frustration led the union to develop its own comprehensive health and safety program, which it hoped would push the industry to take health and safety and environmental protection seriously.[11] The Triangle of Prevention (TOP) program was established. It consisted of three independent components: (1) measuring and tracking incidents; (2) implementing an OCAW Systems of Safety and Incident Investigation training program; and (3) implementing a union-led health and safety program with a full-time health and safety (H&S) representative responsible for program implementation and oversight (working with a joint labor-management H&S committee.)

TOP came to be included in the grant program, primarily to cover the costs of curriculum development. Employers, however, must agree to pay for the program—with release time for the H&S representative and mutually agreed upon training hours. By 2007, 10 years after the program's initiation, the union has gotten it implemented at 41 sites. Employers enter into 3-year contracts with the union to engage in the TOP program (at $150 per employee for the first year). Although it is a joint labor-management program, the union must usually remain vigilant in moving management to adopt its H&S orientation. The program has had some exceptional successes, but it also has been implemented in an equal number of facilities at which little progress has been made. The majority of TOP sites have a progress record somewhere between exceptional success and contentious noncooperation. For the most part, TOP has enabled the union and workers to more fully participate in facility health and safety program development and implementation, providing them with a previously unavailable platform. The program focuses on its successful achievements, or "lessons learned," and maintains a Web library of cases explaining dangerous problems and how they were solved. These cases are used in the training courses as well as by committees seeking examples to provide to management.

The program builds upon the requirements of OSHA's Process Safety Management standard and EPA regulations for chemical accident prevention and risk management mandated under the Clean Air Act Amendments of 1990. The union seeks to demonstrate reductions in both the injury rate and the process incidents that result in safety system failures. By 2007, the union had found that when TOP was introduced at one facility belonging to a corporation, it tended to be adopted at other facilities throughout the corporation (USWA, 2007). Program successes have included TOP facilities taking the lead in safety records within the corporation. A Chevron site in Richmond, California, has successfully integrated the TOP program so that each investigation is followed by a meeting in the affected area at which a discussion of the findings and recommendations takes place. The TOP representative then sends out an "email flash" to all refinery employees, informing them of the investigation and the planned next steps. The TOP program at a 3-M facility has included a focus on musculoskeletal injuries and making ergonomic improvements to prevent them—defining process hazards beyond a limited chemical focus. Where the program is succeeding, the union has demonstrated that its approach to training helps members to get management to commit to workplace improvements and to focus on building effective safety systems rather than blaming workers for system failures.

In 2004, the union (OCAW was part of the United Steel Workers at this point) built on the TOP program's systems of safety emphasis to address the potentially catastrophic vulnerability of chemical facilities to terrorist attacks and natural disasters. Concerns were heightened due to the union's experiences with chemical facility and oil refinery damage during Hurricane Katrina, as well as with post-September 11, 2001, national efforts to prevent chemical facilities from being blown up by terrorists. As part of its expanded evaluation efforts, the union conducted a nationwide survey of 125 local union leaders at sites with very large volumes of hazardous chemicals. Respondents reported that voluntary industry safety efforts were not creating secure facilities (Lippin et al., 2006, p. 1307). The study was conducted by an evaluation group that included two public health researchers and worker-trainers who had been trained to be "worker-evaluators," an emphasis in the union's evaluation efforts since the late 1990s. The scientifically valid study, which included sound recommendations, was published in *Environmental Health Perspectives,* a highly regarded international environmental health journal published by NIEHS (Lippin et al., 2006).

A final example of the training program's progress is its actions in the aftermath of Hurricane Katrina. The union's near-decade of successful joint worker and community training conducted in collaboration with environmental justice groups enabled it to collaborate with the Deep South Center for Environmental Justice (DSCEJ) at Dillard University (a WETP awardee). Dr. Beverly Wright, DSCEJ executive director and a lifelong resident of New Orleans, along with other community organizations and leaders, was tired of waiting for government assistance to remediate New Orleans communities and facilitate the return of displaced New Orleanians. In March 2006, a demonstration project to remediate residential properties and renovate and rebuild damaged houses—"A Safe Way Back Home"—was inaugurated (Deep South Center for Environmental Justice, 2007; USWA, 2006).

The union provided training and health and safety equipment to community volunteers and union members who then removed contaminated soil from a block of Aberdeen Road, in a New Orleans East community. The project involved six community-based organizations from New Orleans. The union obtained funding support from four corporations that employ union members. Additional funding was obtained from six foundations and government agencies. Though this project was limited in its extent of remediation and labor/community coalition building, it facilitated the ability of some displaced New Orleans residents to return to their homes and provided a remediation and rehabilitation model to the government agencies whose efforts were failing to produce the results desired by the affected communities.

CONCLUSION

The OCAW project was established in the belief that in order to achieve management buy-in for its strategy, its training program had to demonstrate excellence in content, delivery, and impact on workers' analytical skills. Internal and external reviews have consistently validated the achievement of this degree of excellence. Nonetheless, the various industries' organization and structure presented formidable barriers to the program's success. Due to the elaborately bureaucratic and hierarchical organization of the industries represented, management supporters of the union's program are often overruled. The dominant industry paradigm of placing responsibility for injuries, illnesses, unexplained catastrophic incidents (that is, "accidents"), and fatalities on workers' behavior has blinded much of management to the excellence of OCAW's training program, which develops workers' ability to think critically and analytically about health and safety issues. From the beginning, OCAW regarded its industrial sectors as inherently dangerous. Mike Merrill's statement of the OCAW belief that " employees can only be safe . . . when they are directly and constantly involved in preventing accidents" (Merrill, 1991a, p. 52) remains a core program principle. That is, workers must have shop floor control in order to prevent accidents and create a safe workplace—exactly the opposite of dominant management beliefs and practices.

The case study of OCAW reveals a strong relationship between the organization of the industries, at a point of economic and political industrial crisis, and the political strategies of the union, particularly the set of health and safety activists in and affiliated with the union. OCAW developed a program that addressed the structural and political dynamics of the industries whose workers it represented. The OCAW program's greatest impact in the union has probably been the development of a network of competent worker-trainers. The network has provided a base of trained health and safety activists who CAN work together in their union's efforts to prevent work-related health impacts and deaths.

The training program has helped sustain the union's health and safety activism. It has helped identify and develop leaders. Many of the first worker-trainers became international representatives or leaders in their locals. The program has given the union the ability to "place" its natural leaders. It has created a union career path for some members.

> A lot of times the company steals away our good leaders within the union. The biggest trick the company does is they look at the stewards and health and safety committee members and they see their leadership qualities, and then the company comes and gets them, pays them more than they're making, and gives them a chance for advancement. This has been a chance for advancement for union people through the union. (Erwin, 1998)

The program has provided a forum for workers to talk with one another about issues that are often too frightening to discuss anywhere else. Workers fear that they can lose their jobs by raising serious health and safety issues. They also know that the chemicals to which they are exposed may have the potential to cause cancer or chronic, often fatal, diseases. "You know, washing your parts off in benzene 20 years ago and you just, every time you go to the doctor you're afraid that, every ache and pain you get, you know it's the cancer's developed" (Erwin, 1998).

Where the program has been successful, trained workers are less accepting of the "inherent" dangers of the industry. Bradley Dodge, a worker trainer, told me the program creates "activism throughout the system. By taking on campaigns effectively against the employer. Individuals taking on campaigns, working with specific issues." Early evaluation found workers who received the training reporting that they subsequently had a different set of expectations about their relationship to their employer. Workers got used to proposing solutions and sometimes actually achieving positive change (Merrill, 1998).

The balance of power between labor and management in the industry sectors represented by OCAW was never favorable to workers and has shifted even more to management since the early 1980s. Some facilities have been moved out of the United States, while others have been bought by larger corporations that have downsized the production force. Jobs have been lost and the union's diminished strength has led it to merge with larger unions. Each of these mergers has created challenges for OCAW's health and safety program. The labor/management history and conditions of the paper industry created an orientation to health and safety that differed from OCAW's. The emphasis was on professional staff response capacity rather than on supporting health and safety activism in plants. The coming together of these orientations created a period of conflict within the program. The steelworkers' union has had an activist orientation similar to that of OCAW and has been more cooperative with the environmental movement. It has a health, safety, and environment department. The merging of the steelworkers' and OCAW's health and safety programs and approaches was in its infancy in 2007 but appeared to be moving in a direction that would build on the strengths of each.

After 20 years, the training program developed by OCAW has proven to be a strong model, addressing critical issues and needs in dangerous industrial sectors. It hasn't led to a health and safety revolution in those sectors. Plants still blow up and workers are still killed. Toxic and hazardous spills and releases occur regularly at a time when sector profits are soaring but are advancing neither workplace health and safety nor environmental protection. Program evaluation has shown, though, that union members are more aware of the hazards around them and the ways to use their union to make their working conditions less hazardous. Many have used the TOP program to gain greater participation in process decision making to advance health and safety. This is no small victory in the post-"social contract" era of U.S. capitalism.

ENDNOTES

1. In 1999, OCAW merged with the United Paperworkers International Union and formed the Paper, Allied-Industrial, Chemical and Energy Workers International Union (PACE). In April 2005, PACE merged with the United Steel Workers of America to form the United Steel, Paper and Forestry, Rubber, Manufacturing, Energy, Allied Industrial and Service Workers International Union. These mergers have shaped the directions taken by the health and safety training program. For the most part, this chapter will not address the consequences of these mergers.
2. See Wooding, Levenstein, and Rosenberg (1997) for a fuller discussion of the industry and its relationship to OCAW. For a discussion of the health and safety hazards of the industry, see Merrill (1994).
3. By 1982, some 24 of the 28 standards that had been promulgated by OSHA were being fought for by Nader's Public Health Interest Group, the AFL-CIO, the IUD, OCAW, USWA and other CIO unions, including the Rubber Workers Union. OCAW was responsible for 15 of the 24 standards (T. Mazzocchi, 1982).
4. Hours later the IUD delivered another complaint addressing a problem at the Omaha, Nebraska, ASARCO smelting facility represented by the USWA. Sheldon Samuels, then health and safety director for the IUD, reported that as he handed the complaint to Assistant Secretary of Labor George Guenther (DOL), he warned Guenther that shortly the IUD would push OSHA to promulgate standards in accordance with Section 6 of the act.
5. According to Tony Mazzocchi, Dr. Bingham had not previously supported labor strikes.

6. The information on the initial proposal submitted to NIEHS was collected through interviews and from a progress report submitted by OCAW to NIEHS in a later proposal for additional funding. Neither OCAW nor NIEHS could provide a copy of the original proposal. Individuals who wrote and submitted the proposal, and who worked to develop the program, have described the contents of the proposal and the program's goals.
7. OCAW listed the same specific aims in both its 1987 and its 1992 proposals. The earliest proposal available at the time of this research was the 1992 proposal.
8. In 1988, Mazzocchi was elected as the secretary-treasurer of the union. Misbrener was still president and Wages was vice president. In 1991, Robert Wages was elected president. Wages appointed Mazzocchi as a special assistant to the president. Mazzocchi was involved in the formation and organization of the Labor Party.
9. OCAW was consistent with OSHA, the National Fire Protection Association, and other ER organizations on the matter of ER training. OSHA had conducted a review of the recommended training requirements for offensive ER activities (that is, acting to abate the hazard and correct the damage causing the emergency): a minimum of 140-160 hours of training was required.
10. OCAW's effectiveness in incorporating the experience of worker-trainers and workers into the evaluation process led in 1998 to the development of a joint evaluation effort by a number of NIEHS union awardees. OCAW was also a driving force behind an NIEHS technical workshop on the evaluation of worker health education programs.
11. The Environmental Working Group's Chemistry Industry Archives project reviewed industry documents and critiqued the Responsible Care program. The group asserts that the program's primary goal is to improve the industry's public image. "During the 1990s, CMA spent $1 million to $2 million a year on implementing Responsible Care at its member companies, but more than $10 million a year on advertisements about the program. . . . Since Responsible Care is voluntary, participating companies do little more than comply with current environmental laws. In effect, the industry did not bother to develop new programs for Responsible Care." Retrieved July 4, 2007, from the Environmental Working Group's Web site, http://www.chemicalindustryarchives.org/dirtysecrets/responsiblecare/2.asp

REFERENCES

Anderson, J. (1998). Interview by author, tape recording, RTP, NC (August 1).

Backman, J. (1970). *The Economics of the Chemical Industry*. Washington DC: Manufacturing Chemists Association.

Bower, J. L. (1986). When Markets Quake: The Management Challenge of Restructuring Industry. Boston: Harvard Business School Press.

Chapman, K. (1991). The International Petrochemical Industry: Evolution and Location. Cambridge, MA: Basil Blackwell.

Deep South Center for Environmental Justice. (2007). *Project: A Safe Way Back Home*. Retrieved July 4, 2007, from http://www.dscej.org/asafewayhome.htm

Dodge, B. (1998). Interview by author, tape recording, Raleigh, NC (August 1).

Elsner, M. (1992). Memo to Stan Holt, National Toxics Campaign, from CACOSH (November 24). From NIEHS files, RTP, NC.

Environmental Working Group. (2007). *Chemistry Industry Archives Project*. http://www.chemicalindustryarchives.org/dirtysecrets/responsible.care/2.asp (Retrieved, July 4)

Erwin, G. (1998). Telephone interview by author, tape recording (August 7).

Kieding, S. (1997). Interview by author, tape recording, Denver, CO (July 18, 1997).

Labor Institute. (1992). *OCAW/Labor Institute. Hazardous Materials Workbook* (6th ed.). New York: Apex Press.

Leopold, L. (1998). Interview by author, tape recording, New York City (July 9).

Lerza, C. (1973, March 3). Giving Shell Some Gas: Environmental Issues Reaching the Bargaining Table. *Environmental Action,* 3-6.

Lippin, T. M., McQuiston, T. H., Bradley-Bull, K., Burns-Johnson, T., Cook, L., Gill, M. L., et al. (2006). Chemical Plants Remain Vulnerable to Terrorists: A Call to Action. *Environmental Health Perspectives, 114*(9), 1307-1311.

Mazzocchi, S. (1998). The First Complaint Filed and the First Citation Issued Under the Occupational Safety and Health Act of 1970: Filed by the OCAW, AFL-CIO, on Behalf of Local 3-586, Involving Allied Chemical Corporation, Moundsville, WV. In S. Mazzocchi (Ed.), *A Collection of Documents From the OCAW Struggle for Worker Health and Safety*. Washington, DC: Alice Hamilton College.

Mazzocchi, T. (1982). Speech and discussion transcript (April 19). From files of Michael Brown,.

Mazzocchi, T. (1998a). Crossing Paths: Science and the Working Class. *New Solutions, A Journal of Environmental and Occupational Health Policy, 8*(1), 27-32.

Mazzocchi, T. (1998b). Letter introducing the OCAW history binder. In *A Collection of Documents From the OCAW Struggle for Worker Health and Safety*. Washington, DC: Alice Hamilton College.

Mazzocchi, T. (1998c). Telephone interview by author, tape recording (August 8).

Merrill, M. (1989). *Deficiencies of the Proposed OSHA Standard on the Accreditation of Training Programs for Hazardous Waste Operations*. Unpublished draft that was later published by *New Solutions* (see 1991a). Institute for Management and Labor Relations, Cook College, Rutgers, New Brunswick, NJ. (May).

Merrill, M. (1991a). No Test Know-How: Deficiencies of the Proposed OSHA Standard on the Accreditation of Training Programs for Hazardous Waste Operations. *New Solutions, A Journal of Environmental and Occupational Health Policy, 2*(2), 47-58.

Merrill, M. (1991b). An Overview of the OCAW/Labor Institute Worker-to-Worker Training Program in Hazard Communication, Hazardous Waste Operations, and Emergency Response, Appendix A of *OCAW Proposal in Response to NIEHS RFA ES-92-1, Worker Health and Safety Training Cooperative Agreement, January 23, 1992*.

Merrill, M. (1994). Trust in Training: The Oil, Chemical, and Atomic Workers International Union Worker-to-Worker Training Program. *Occupational Medicine: State of the Art Reviews, 9*(2), 341-354.

Merrill, M. (1995). Sharing Power: OCAW Worker-Trainers and the Small-Group Activity Method. *New Solutions, a Journal of Environmental and Occupational Health Policy, 5*(2), 39-50.

Merrill, M. (1998). Interview by author, tape recording, Princeton, NJ (July 9).

NIEHS. (1990). Summary Statement by the Special Review Committee. OCAW Application number 3 D42 ESO7218-04S1 1990/5/29.

NIEHS. (1991). Minimum Criteria for Worker Health and Safety Training for Hazardous Waste Operations and Emergency Response: NIEHS Training Grant Technical Workshop on Training Quality. Second Printing. 1991/12. Washington, DC: National Clearinghouse on Occupational and Environmental Health, Workplace Health Fund.

OCAW. (1979, March). OSHA Grant Training Program Set for March 12-13. *Lifelines: OCAW Health and Safety News, 6,* 1.

OCAW. (1987, July-August). OCAW Applies for Hazardous Waste Grant. *Lifelines: OCAW Health and Safety News, 13,* 5-6.

OCAW. (1988, January-February). 24 HAZMAT OSHECs Selected. *Lifelines: OCAW Health and Safety News, 14,* 11-12.

OCAW. (1992). Grant Application to NIEHS RFA ES-92-1, *Worker Health and Safety Training Cooperative Agreement* (January 23).

OCAW. (1993). OCAW. Request for Use of Carryover Funds. Letter from OCAW to NIEHS. (December 9).

Samuels, S. (1998). Interview by author, tape recording, Solomon's Is., MD (January 16).

U.S. Congress. House of Representatives. (1985). Committee on Education and Labor. Subcommittee on Health and Safety. *Worker Health and Safety in the Manufacture and Use of Toxic and Hazardous Substances.* 1st sess., 99th Congress. April 16. Washington, DC: GPO, p. 2.

USWA. (2006). Residents to FEMA: This Is How to Clean Up Tainted Properties in New Orleans: Steelworkers and Deep South Center for Environmental Justice Demonstrate How to Conduct Environmental Clean Up and Safety Training. Retrieved July 4, 2007, from http://www.uswa.org/uswa/program/content/2830.php

USWA. (2007). Report on TOP: 2006-2007. Presentation to Training Program Advisory Board. January. Pittsburgh: Tony Mazzocchi Center.

Wages, R. (1998). Telephone interview with author, tape recording (August 11).

Wooding, J., Levenstein, C., & Rosenberg, B. (1997). The Oil Chemical and Atomic Workers International Union: Refining Strategies for Labor. *International Journal of Health Services, 27*(1), 124-139.

Workers in Chemical Protective Equipment
Sampling Hazardous Waste Stored in 50-Gallon Drums.
Courtesy of the U.S. EPA

Hazardous Waste Site Remediation Workers Decontaminate after Site Work.
Heavy Equipment Operator in Background.
Courtesy of the U.S. EPA

CHAPTER 7

The L-AGC: "Training Is the Blood That Runs Through Our Veins"

A central reason for the WETP's success was John Dement's decision to "let 100 flowers bloom." This approach acknowledged that the structure and organization of each industry would likely necessitate different intervention strategies.[1] The largest program in the NIEHS network is the one run by the Laborers—Associated General Contractors (L-AGC) Education and Training Fund, a joint labor-management training and education trust fund between the Laborers International Union of America (LIUNA) and the contractors' association. LIUNA pressed hard to secure the worker training protections in SARA and was better prepared than other awardees to start up its training program. It was eager to expand union construction work to the environmental remediation market through health and safety excellence. An examination of this program will show contrasts with the OCAW program described in chapter 6, but will also show similarities in its WETP leadership and dedication to arming workers with essential information about their health and safety.

The worker health and safety movement that developed during the 1970s paid close attention to the health effects of workers' exposures to hazardous and toxic materials. Alliances were built among scientists, medical professionals, and unions to meet workers' health and safety needs—through training, fights for regulation, and developing easy-to-understand resource materials. In large part, the building trades were not part of this effort, as safety issues remained their primary concern. Also, many in the health and safety movement came out of the New Left and had been involved in the struggles to end the Viet Nam War. Construction workers had put on their safety helmets in those times to show their support for President Nixon rather than to be safe at work. By the end of the decade, though, the economic restructuring that was squeezing manufacturing and processing workers, like OCAW's members, was also hitting building trades workers. Employers wanted to gain concessions and to get out of union contracts. For OCAW, health and safety had been viewed as a way to mobilize resistance to employers' demands. LIUNA also saw health and safety as a way to push back against the pressures from contractors, but as a way of showing the value of maintaining union contracts rather than mobilizing workers to resist demands for concessions. The difference lies in the organizational structure of the construction industry.

DYNAMICS OF THE MODERN CONSTRUCTION INDUSTRY

Labor-management relations in the U.S. construction industry are different from those in other industries.[2] Silver has discussed the fact that the demand for construction in any period depends on the strength of the overall economy at the time. Consequently, employers, for the most part, insist on being able to employ workers on a per-job basis. Per-job hiring results in transience among construction workers, who may work on a variety of sites and for a variety of contractors. A union construction worker usually works for as many as three employers in a single year, and some workers may work for more than six employers (Allen, 1998; Bergfeld, 1998; Halpin & Woodhead, 1980, p. 249; Lange & Mills, 1979, pp. 1-9, 60-61; Thursby, 1998a). Per-job hiring also results in regular periods of unemployment for individual workers. The building trades' local unions have adapted by maintaining hiring halls. The halls serve as a referral service; workers are assigned to jobs from the hiring hall, once the labor-management contract has been signed.

The average laborer works 1,400 hours a year, or 35 weeks (40 hours a week). Full-time employment in other sectors tends to be 50 weeks a year. Two reasons for the difference with regard to construction workers are employment on a per-job basis and seasonality. Construction is often too difficult to perform during periods of inclement weather, since much of it is done out of doors. Employment variability results in unemployed union construction workers seeking other means to support themselves and their families. They may choose self-employment, often doing residential construction work. Some workers grow weary of the limited financial security they receive from construction work, particularly in periods of a weaker economy with limited construction work available, and leave the industry to seek other work. Some workers, both younger and older, decide that they want less physically demanding work, and they too quit the industry (Allen, 1998; Bergfeld, 1998; Thursby, 1998a).[3]

Such conditions cause a building trades union to lose membership. Turnover in union membership averages about 20% annually (Allen, 1998; Thursby, 1998a). Unless the union can continually maintain and even increase its membership, it lacks the strength in numbers required to support the activities that help secure better working conditions and higher compensation for workers. Consequently, the building trades are inclined to work cooperatively with employers as a mechanism for union organizing and maintaining union strength, that is, ensuring union jobs for members.

Union Organizing in the Building Trades

The term "organize" may have a different meaning in the building trades than it does in the industrial and service sector unions, which usually organize existing employees so that the union can represent them in collective bargaining with their employers. In the construction industry, the primary mechanism for union organization (that is, increasing and maintaining membership) is through negotiations with contractors or employers, usually prior to the hiring of workers by a particular employer. This mechanism was legally established in the Taft-Hartley Act in 1947 (Knack, 1980, p. 588). The conditions of employment in the industry supported this type of union-contractor labor agreement. Once relationships are established, larger contractors may be encouraged by the union to bid on jobs that they otherwise might not have pursued. The unions may employ contracting specialists who review databases of both private and public construction bids and then communicate with contractors to see if the union can help the contractors meet the requirements for a successful bid (Allen, 1998). Thus, central to any organizing in the building trades is the development of relationships with contractors and their associations.

The building trades unions have sustained long-standing relationships with Congressional public works committees in order to encourage the expansion of union construction work on public sector projects. They have also secured "prevailing wage" laws requiring contractors that have been awarded contracts to pay the construction wage that unions have negotiated in a given geographic area. The Davis-Bacon Act offers this protection to union workers at the federal level (Halpin & Woodhead, 1980, p. 228). These political strategies are central components of union organizing in the building trades (Allen, 1998; Mallino, 1997; Warren, 1998).

The Open-Shop Movement

Halpin and Woodhead have discussed the construction industry changes that began to develop in the early 1970s. Throughout the 1960s, contractually determined wage increases and restrictive work rules reduced the competitiveness of union contractors. An "open-shop movement" was organized by contractors during the 1970s. The movement was supported by nonunion contractors, who were able to leverage larger shares of the construction market. They were able to underbid union contractors and offer higher productivity due to the absence of obligations to restrictive negotiated work rules. Associated Building Contractors has been the primary industry association representing nonunion contractors. The union contractors were able to use the open-shop movement to make concession demands of unions at the job site and in collective bargaining (Silver, 1986, p. 163). In 1969, the Laborers Union and the Associated General Contractors of America established a partnership that set up a trust fund to support training and education, in part to advance the capacity of union contractors to compete against open shops. The Laborers-AGC pursued grants to support their training programs.

THE LABORERS UNION

The Laborers International Union of North America (LIUNA)[4] is the current configuration of the building trades union that was established in 1903 as the Laborers International Union of Hod Carriers. The union was established in its current form in 1966, with three divisions: construction, industrial, and public service. In 1974, a health care division was added. Over the century, smaller craft unions—including those of compressed air workers, pavers, stonecutters, and mail handlers—merged with the Laborers' union. By 1979, LIUNA was the fifth largest AFL-CIO union with more than 500,000 members.

LIUNA has described its mission as follows:

> to empower working men and women, especially those starting out on the lowest rungs of the economic ladder. To raise Laborers' living standards . . . To give them a strong voice in the workplace . . . To provide skills so that members can achieve their full potential . . .To protect members' health and safety . . . And most of all, to ensure dignity, respect, and security. (LIUNA, 1998)

In its 1903 charter, the AFL assigned the union jurisdiction over a range of construction tasks.[5] The union's jurisdiction currently includes wrecking and excavating buildings; digging trenches, piers, foundations, and holes; engaging in concrete work for buildings; shoring, underpinning, and razing old buildings; and clearing debris from buildings (Thursby, 1998b). Historically, the Laborers' jurisdiction on construction sites has included manually digging dirt, demolition, and the full range of site clean-up work.[6] The union's expansion into hazardous waste site cleanup and environmental remediation work stems from this jurisdiction, on the grounds that it is "clean-up work" (Bergfeld, 1998; Thursby, 1998a; Warren, 1998).

Opportunities for work are a strong priority for the Laborers. They face two sets of challenges to their jurisdiction over construction sites. Technological advances in materials and processes may provide wider opportunities depending on the skill level and training of laborers, but they also can warrant the assigning of tasks to other trades. The processes resulting from new technologies are not as easily distinguished by trade: that is, the processes are not easily identifiable as tasks "belonging" to a specific trade. Therefore, several trades can legitimately be assigned the tasks. The other challenge results from the wage increases secured for laborers over the last two decades. Higher wage rates for laborers provide a disincentive for employers to assign work to laborers rather than to those pursuing another craft, such as carpenters, who may already be on-site for other tasks. This problem is particularly acute in an industry like hazardous waste remediation, in which jurisdiction over some aspects has not been assigned or arbitrated (Allen, 1998; Thursby, 1998a).

The Laborers, the Teamsters, and the Operating Engineers were confronted with all of these issues as they eyed the emerging hazardous waste remediation industry. The new industry supplied opportunities for organizing in each union. That is, it was a new industry that required construction work (digging, erecting structures, staging of materials, transporting materials, and suchlike) using existing skills, but it also required training and new skill development as technologies and processes evolved. For the Laborers, their established jurisdiction for clean-up work at construction sites, combined with the historical assignment to them of tasks that "no other trade wanted" (Warren, 1998), constituted fresh opportunities to gain members.

ROOTS OF THE LABORERS' TRAINING PROGRAM

A consequence of the construction tasks assigned to laborers, as well as the lack of an apprenticeship program, is that, until recently, when skill assessments were conducted by the U.S. Department of Labor,[7] laborers were not considered to be as skilled as other construction industry workers. The union has worked to defend the right of the less-skilled laborer to job security and a union-scale wage and benefit package. Laborers have received lower wages than workers in most other crafts, but this trend has changed in a positive direction for members during recent years (Bergfeld, 1998; Thursby, 1998a).

The building trades have a tradition of apprenticeship training of new workers who develop the skills to become journeymen. The Laborers were one of the few building trades unions that did not offer apprenticeship training.[8] Laborers' work traditionally was considered unskilled, although that label is now deemed inappropriate. The ditch diggers, hod carriers, and so forth could have been any workers willing to take on the task. Skilled trades, such as those of carpenters, plumbers, and operating engineers, all have training programs through which new workers learn the craft and practice for a time on the job until they qualify as journeymen.

About 1966, Jack Wilkinson, LIUNA's first director of education and training, and Robert Connerton, LIUNA's general counsel, submitted a proposal for federal funding that would support basic construction training for laborers. A grant was awarded through funding authorized by the Manpower Development and Training Act, and several pilot programs were established around the United States. The programs were successful and were used to negotiate contracts that included "cents-per-hour" contractor contributions to a training fund. The training funds were local or regional and supported the establishment and maintenance of training centers. Laborers began to receive education and training aimed at construction skill development. Until that happened, training was given by one laborer to another, and often by father or uncle to son or nephew. In the words of a now-retired laborer,

> I can go back in ancient history[,] back in the early '40s when we used to have a training program in the basement of my union hall to train hod carriers on how to climb the ladder with a hod. That was about the extent of any training we had up until in the '60s. It was just "pass it on." That's how I learned my craft. I had to learn it from all the other laborers. (Thursby, 1998a)

The L-AGC Education and Training Fund

The formation of the L-AGC Education and Training Fund in 1969 stemmed from the efforts of Wilkinson and Connerton to put in place a network of training centers. The L-AGC's fund is a nonprofit labor-management trust fund and is responsible for "developing programs that enhance the skills of Union Laborers, while expanding the competitiveness of their employers" (LIUNA, 1997, p. 9). LIUNA and the AGC each have an equal number of trustees on the board. The national L-AGC acts as an umbrella organization for the 74 state and regional training funds (including those in Canada), providing the independent operations with significant support for program development. This apparatus represents the horizontal structure of the unions. The fund supports the centers' delivery of the training needed in their service areas.

L-AGC has a programs department composed of two departments that had been set up earlier, construction and environmental, and trains in each of these areas of work. The fund has matured into one of the most comprehensive training organizations in the building trades. By 1997, 50,000 laborers each year were trained through the fund. James (Mitch) Warren, who was the L-AGC director through the first 15 years of the group's WETP participation, was quoted in a LIUNA information brochure about the Tri-FUNDS, stating that

> Lifelong learning is the key to increased employment opportunities, productivity, and contractor competitiveness and profitability. The Fund's mission is to provide LIUNA members with the opportunity to prepare themselves for this challenge. (LIUNA, 1997, p. 8)

Warren started to work for the L-AGC as an assistant director in 1975. His family urged him to do something different from following in his laborer father's footsteps. He went to college and became a school teacher, but within several years was offered work by the Construction, Production, and Maintenance Laborers Local 838 in Arizona in 1969. The Laborers' Arizona training fund started up at that time and Warren became a trustee for it. In 1975, Warren Anderson, the director of the L-AGC, appointed Mitch Warren as an assistant director. The fund was then based in Washington, DC, but later moved to Pomfret, Connecticut. Warren was appointed director of the L-AGC in 1985 (Warren, 1998).

The L-AGC Education and Training Fund received funding through OSHA's New Directions program, but it was the new asbestos removal industry that pushed the union into developing strong health and safety training. The first health and safety training modules addressed issues such as respiratory protection for pavement breakers. The modules were presented by instructors at the training centers. It was asbestos training, developed by the New England Training Fund, that broadened the scope of health and safety presentations (L-AGC, 1987b, p. 113). It was also the first time that the union used health and safety professionals to assist in training workers (Warren, 1998). HAZMAT exposures in environmental remediation pushed the Laborers' health and safety training into a new dimension.

Although LIUNA and the L-AGC had begun some efforts at basic construction skill and health and safety training, they did not have the training apparatus and infrastructure of other unions that had longer-established apprenticeship programs. Nevertheless, both organizations made a commitment to health and safety training and a commitment to research, outreach, and political organizing that was without parallel in the building trades, and even in much of the labor movement.

In 1980, William Bergfeld became the first Laborers' training director in Iowa. The son of an operating engineer, Bergfeld went to work "the day after I graduated high school." He worked from 1974 to 1980 as a construction craft laborer. In 1978, Bergfeld served on the negotiating committee for Laborers Local 659 in Dubuque. LIUNA had suggested that every local should negotiate employer contributions to a training fund. Bergfeld brought this to the negotiating committee and won a 5-cents-per-hour contribution. By 1980, this training fund had grown enough to warrant hiring a director.

Bergfeld and the trustees of the Iowa Laborers' Heavy Highway Training fund received $224,000 from the U.S. Department of Labor to establish a training course for environmental remediation workers. They developed a 4-week course on lead, asbestos, and hazardous waste remediation issues. A manual was developed for the course, *Toxic and Hazardous Waste: Handling, Control, Removal and Disposal* (Iowa Laborers' Heavy Highway Training Fund, 1980).

L-AGC DEVELOPS A PROPOSAL FOR NIEHS

In 1985, Mitch Warren and Donald Elisburg discussed the idea of securing funding for worker training in the Superfund reauthorization bill. Later that year, at an L-AGC conference in Hawaii, Warren Anderson talked with James Merloni, director of the New England Training Fund, about the idea of hazardous waste worker training. Merloni formed a committee with several other training fund directors.

In 1986, the L-AGC drafted a proposal for a hazardous waste handling training program for Laborers (Dime, 1986). The proposal was developed by an environmental consultant who worked with the training center in New Jersey. He stressed that many laborers might not easily absorb large amounts of information in short periods of time, and therefore the training should combine classroom instruction with hands-on activities, field drills, and hazardous waste site simulations. The proposal raised issues of literacy levels, using participatory methods, and meeting and/or exceeding regulatory standards and criteria. The committee used the proposal to further develop ideas about hazardous waste worker training.

LIUNA holds a convention every 5 years. At the 1986 convention, a resolution was passed mandating that the L-AGC become involved in hazardous waste worker training. Elisburg urged that the focus of the training be health and safety.

> We were building interest and consensus and bringing people along out in the field who were thinking about new areas, new markets really. We were looking at worker health and safety training at the same time we were looking at a new market for the international [union] to expand into. (Warren, 1998)

The committee of training directors formed to consider a hazardous waste worker program evolved into a committee of the L-AGC board. On the committee, Wilkinson, by then a regional manager from the mid-Atlantic states, represented LIUNA. The panel also included a contractor representing the AGC, and Sheldon Samuels from the Workplace Health Fund (WHF). Individuals with technical expertise were gradually added.

Employers were supportive, but they also had a common strong concern: liability for harms claimed as a result of remediation work. Most of the trustees on the management side of the L-AGC were principal owners of their own contracting firms. They were less than eager to pursue remediation work, even if it represented a new market, due to concerns that they might "hang their company out to dry over some problem that they dug up" at a remediation site (Warren, 1998).

The L-AGC fund's hazardous waste committee met on February 8, 1987. Warren reported that the final program notice from NIEHS "largely reflect[s] the concerns of the LIUNA-AGC Fund" (L-AGC Education and Training Fund, 1987a). Connerton spoke about the liability issues facing both the L-AGC and the contractors. He urged the L-AGC to "proceed with due diligence in connection with all aspects of developing and implementation of this program" (L-AGC Education and Training

Fund, 1987a). The committee agreed to recommend to the L-AGC board that it should submit a letter of intention to NIEHS, develop a proposal, and search for a program director.

Connerton strongly believed that the union should pursue environmental remediation work. He also had been a vigorous proponent of worker training in LIUNA, and supported the formation of the L-AGC Education and Training Fund. According to Elisburg, who worked closely with him, Connerton saw economics as the primary motivation for entrance into hazardous waste remediation work. The union and its contractors had already begun performing asbestos removal work (and training for this work), which was providing new jobs for laborers.[9] It was clear that large numbers of workers would be needed for hazardous waste remediation work. To Connerton, Elisburg, and others, it was also clear that the health and safety issues that became problematic with asbestos removal were more than likely to be an issue for hazardous waste remediation work as well. "So the health and safety issues just flowed from the decision to get into the work. If you're going to get into that work, you're going to have to deal with those health and safety issues big time," Elisburg said.

The proposal that the L-AGC submitted to NIEHS was developed by a committee of individuals who had a range of areas of expertise. Many of them were included in the proposal as the technical experts and professionals who would form a team of "master trainers" for specific curriculum areas. Samuels and Elisburg took lead roles in developing the proposal. Samuels represented the Workplace Health Fund (WHF), a nonprofit organization created in 1983 by the AFL-CIO's Industrial Union Department as "labor's own health agency for occupational disease and safety" (L-AGC Education and Training Fund, 1987b, p. 114). The WHF collaborated with other organizations that were included in the proposal: the Workers' Institute for Safety and Health (WISH); New York University (NYU) Medical School; Mt. Sinai Medical School; and Clean Sites, Inc.

WISH was directed by Matthew Gillen, a certified industrial hygienist, and its board of trustees was composed of labor leaders. The NYU group (Drs. M. Lippmann and R. Jaeger) provided support for the occupational health curriculum. The Mt. Sinai group (Drs. Philip Landrigan and Steven Levin) provided medical support. Clean Sites, Inc. (CSI) was a private nonprofit corporation that had been established to accelerate the cleanup of hazardous waste sites. The vice president of CSI was Glenn Paulson, PhD, former assistant commissioner of the New Jersey Department of Environmental Protection, responsible for directing the agency's hazardous waste clean-up program. Paulson had supported labor unions for many years on a range of issues. The CSI board of directors was chaired by Russell E. Train, U.S. EPA director from 1973 to 1977. Its technical advisory board was chaired by Dr. Mort Corn, a former head of OSHA. This network of organizations was established and brought into the project by Samuels.

The L-AGC proposed an 80-hour hazardous waste training program that would be delivered at six regional training centers in the first year. Three more centers would be included in the second year. Nine thousand workers would be trained during a 5-year period (L-AGC Education and Training Fund, 1991, p. 1). The

L-AGC emphasized excellence and competence for all proposed staff positions, the curriculum development team, the instructor training, and the training center capacity development. The professionals in the network would take responsibility for curriculum development and instructor support in each of their areas of expertise. Elisburg would be the master trainer who addressed pertinent laws and regulations as well as the rights and responsibilities of workers and supervisors.

The proposal provided a justification for an 80-hour course, rather than the 40-hour minimum established in the OSHA interim rule. The L-AGC noted that laborers at hazardous waste sites face graver hazards than other workers, including higher concentrations of exposure for a longer time. The proposal also stressed the need to accommodate the general educational level of laborers, which would require "repetitive educational techniques" (L-AGC Education and Training Fund, 1987b, p. 126). The proposal stated that 80 hours of training were necessary to "effectively limit potential liability—of the training program, contractors, and the government" (L-AGC Education and Training Fund, 1987b, p. 127).

The proposal presented the L-AGC's goals: to prepare laborers for remediation work; to provide construction contractors with training centers that could produce qualified workers; and to provide a certification mechanism that would make it easier for contractors to comply with federal regulations. The training would be performed away from hazardous waste sites, but it would include mock site training. The L-AGC program was awarded $8.6 million for a 5-year period.

BUILDING THE PROGRAM

NIEHS notified the L-AGC on September 4, 1987, that its application would be funded. Ten days later, Neil Thursby was hired as associate project director. He would be responsible for running the project. A committee of the L-AGC board of trustees, composed of a contractor, a LIUNA officer, and Warren, selected him.

Thursby was the son of a heavy and highway construction worker and had worked for 16 years as a construction laborer in Kansas City; for four years, he was a local union representative. In 1966, he became an international union representative. He became a key person in establishing the initial training centers with the U.S. DOL funding. He worked closely with the Illinois training center to make certain that training courses were taught "on a level that our laborers could get some benefit out of." He was the trainer in an 8-hour course informing laborers of their responsibilities to the contractor and to the union. He believed, as did other key proponents of the training effort, that "laborers ought to be teaching laborers." In the mid-1970s, Thursby was selected to work with the L-AGC to develop training for new-entry laborers. It was during a period of low unemployment in the construction sector (about 2% in some areas), creating a strong demand for new laborers. Thursby stressed that LIUNA "believed in giving a fair day's work for a fair day's pay." Workers were to start work on time and work until quitting time and not take 40 minutes for a 30-minute lunch break. Such were the values he brought to the training program.

Thursby immediately began to organize the program. Support staff members were hired. He began a search for health and safety training equipment, such as chemical protective clothing and respiratory equipment. He consulted representatives of the EPA and NIOSH, Richard Duffy of the IAFF, and equipment manufacturers' representatives. He received advice from Paulson and Stuart Allen from CSI and Bergfeld from the Iowa Training Fund.

On December 1, 1987, Bergfeld was hired by the L-AGC as a training and education specialist to work with Thursby to develop the 80-hour hazardous waste course. Because of his experience in establishing and running the first hazardous waste training courses in Iowa, Bergfeld became involved in much of the program's development. He also acted as a master trainer and backed up the instructors at each regional center.

Donald Elisburg and Sheldon Samuels

Elisburg helped guide the L-AGC program. He pushed the L-AGC to pursue excellence in its health and safety training. He helped to organize the proposal that was sent to NIEHS. He reviewed the program's needs and moved staff for the purpose of program development. Elisburg understood the workings of federal bureaucracy and helped the L-AGC in its relationship with NIEHS. He also worked carefully to make sure that NIEHS came to understand the needs of unions and how best to work with them. Elisburg assisted the L-AGC with audit issues and financial management. He stressed strong professional and technical credentials. Elisburg urged that the L-AGC training program should represent the state of the art in training, health and safety, and hazardous waste remediation methods and should always be technically correct. He wanted to make sure that the program could defend itself against any challenge to its standard and operations (Bergfeld, 1998; Dobbin, 1997; Elisburg, 1997; Matheny, 1998; Thursby, 1998a; Warren, 1998).

Samuels is a public health activist who early developed a strong interest in the labor movement. He began his career in New York, a state where strong alliances between labor unions and medical professionals had developed earlier than in many other states. He worked closely with Dr. Irving Selikoff of Mt. Sinai Medical Center in New York and others in the effort to identify asbestos as a carcinogen. Samuels served as a liaison with labor for the Public Health Service. Immediately following passage of the OSH Act, Samuels left the PHS to work for the AFL-CIO's IUD. From the IUD, Samuels coordinated the OSHA Environmental Network, which was instrumental in passing the Toxic Substances Control Act of 1976. He created the WHF as an occupational health research organization affiliated with the IUD. Samuels worked to build links between the labor movement, public health and medical professionals, environmentalists, and government. He brought his connections with him when he joined the L-AGC's effort to develop its training program.

Curriculum Development

Samuels recruited a team of professional experts who became the master trainers of the L-AGC's program. The primary members included Paulson, Stuart Allen, and Charles Glore (CSI); Dr. Jerry Rosenman (WHF), and Gillen (WISH). Elisburg worked for the WHF and as a consultant to the L-AGC. Their first task was to tackle the curriculum. Each expert was responsible for specific elements. The team that organized the proposal to be sent to NIEHS established a nine-task work plan for each course module; 12 modules were listed as a minimum in the NIEHS request for applications, and two additional modules. The process of curriculum development included evaluation of existing educational materials; observation of laborers at hazardous waste sites to identify laborers' operations tasks; curriculum development; pilot testing; training of instructors; identifying and procuring needed equipment, reference books, and materials; monitoring and evaluating instructors and offering them assistance; developing and conducting a 1-week refresher training course for instructors; and giving technical assistance through master trainers.

Responsibility for the tasks associated with each subject area was assumed by one of the organizations at which a master trainer was based. Elisburg developed the module dealing with the rights and responsibilities of workers under OSHA and assumed the oversight and coordination responsibilities related to the training. He also directed the process designed to meet all the requirements established in the regulation, which at that time was an interim standard. He stressed the importance of strict adherence to the mandate of Section 126 of SARA and the OSHA standard, both as a principle for participation in a federal grants program and as a means to avoid liability and challenges from unsupportive employers.

Lectures, Hands-On Training, and 80 Hours

The L-AGC had proposed an 80-hour training course for hazardous waste workers rather than the 40-hour minimum set in the legislation and adopted by OSHA. Samuels agreed to work with the L-AGC because he wanted to use the additional 40 hours for a "science literacy" curriculum. Samuels had already developed this type of curriculum through the IUD. His goal was to "free workers of dependence on the intelligentsia of the professionals." Samuels's notion of incorporating "science literacy" lacked support from other curriculum development team members, who saw the need for extensive hands-on activities and repetition of subject matter as more essential aspects of training for laborers. To Samuels's disappointment, the "science literacy" approach was not adopted.

Laborers' literacy was an important general issue, though. The L-AGC began to address it even before the beginning of the training program. Hazardous waste, however, posed more literacy issues than did basic construction training. Due to the technical nature of the training, the L-AGC decided that workers in the classes would be required to be able to read technical material. Recruiting materials made this requirement clear. L-AGC offered literacy classes separately from the hazardous waste training. The promise of environmental jobs led increasing numbers of workers into those courses (Warren, 1998).[10]

The curriculum development team was responsible for compiling a training manual. The manual and curriculum were to be completed by February 21, 1988, when the first pilot training for instructors was scheduled. As the team completed sections of the manual, Thursby reviewed the material to determine whether it could be understood by laborers. "If I could understand it," he said, "I knew they could."

Repeatedly the L-AGC insisted to OSHA and NIEHS that 80 hours of training were necessary to accommodate the amount of hands-on training that would be most useful to laborers. Eighty hours permitted the repetition and review of information, along with adequate classroom discussion. The L-AGC wanted to develop a new model for construction worker education that provided ample time to learn by doing. "Perhaps the major innovation of the L-AGC program has been the emphasis on hands-on training of workers" (L-AGC Education and Training Fund, 1988, p. 6). Each training center established a simulated hazardous waste site. The sites replicated the work activities of an actual toxic site. The L-AGC was so committed to this approach that each local training fund center donated labor to construct the sites "as part of their contribution to the program" (L-AGC Education and Training Fund, 1988, p .6).

WORKERS AND PROFESSIONALS

By February 1988, 4 months after its NIEHS award, the L-AGC had made its initial training equipment purchase in preparation for a scheduled instructor training. The master trainers presented a 120-hour course to 19 instructors from the six regional hazardous waste training centers. This was regarded as a quick program start-up, and it was one that NIEHS had not expected (Matheny, 1998; Thursby, 1998a).[11]

Nearly all of the 19 instructors in the training centers were former laborers with years of experience. Many had also served as union stewards or had been labor foremen. They had come up through the ranks (Thursby, 1998a). They had all been construction laborers, and had never done environmental work (Bergfeld, 1998). Nonetheless, throughout the course, the instructors participated in a critique of the manual, the supporting materials, and the course schedule. In addition to the training provided by the master trainers, instruction was provided by representatives of two equipment supply companies, HAZCO and Interspiro. A primary goal of these sessions was to develop competence in teaching the hands-on aspects of the course.

The first pilot class started in March 1988 at the training center in Connecticut. By the end of June, pilot classes had been presented in five other training centers: Belton, Missouri; Kingston, Washington; Anza, California; Livonia, Louisiana; and Jamesburg, New Jersey. Each pilot class was conducted by a combination of master trainers and local instructors. Each training center then scheduled courses regularly with 2–3 weeks between courses. Local instructors discussed issues with master trainers through regularly scheduled telephone conferences. By July, more than 300 laborers had been trained in 19 classes at the regional centers.

NIEHS required funded programs to have independent boards of advisors. The L-AGC had formed a hazardous waste committee in 1986. That committee gave its function of overseeing the development and implementation of a training program to the L-AGC program's newly formed advisory board. Some committee members were appointed to the board. Then, largely at Elisburg's urging, scientists and professionals with national standing were invited on to the board.

The scientists and professionals on the board demonstrated the importance placed on associating expert credentials with the L-AGC program. The scientists and professionals became active participants; they were not merely names on the organization's stationery. The board also included employer representatives, providing a direct mechanism for employer feedback and support. The advisory board members were Dr. John Finklea, MD, professor of preventive medicine, University of Alabama, and former director of NIOSH (Dr. Finklea was elected chair at the October 1988 meeting and has been the chair ever since then); Glenn Paulson, PhD, director of the Illinois Institute of Technology's Center for Hazardous Waste Management; Jack Wilkinson, the regional manager of LIUNA; James Merloni; Diane Morrell, CIH,[12] Envirosphere Co.; Mitch Warren; John Gibbons, vice president, Guy F. Atkinson Co.; Knut Ringen, DPH, Laborers' National Health and Safety Fund; Dr. Morton Lippmann, Institute of Environmental Medicine, New York University Medical Center; and Frank Radomski, Jr., of Frank V. Radomski & Sons. Later, Francis J. Mastropieri, cochairman of the L-AGC, joined the board. "It wasn't a committee that you put your friends on," Elisburg said. "It was a committee [for which] you got people who really knew what they were doing."

The combination of the master trainers (some of whom were brought on to the board) and the advisory board represented the successful adoption of a strategy to join professionals interested in occupational health and safety with labor. Bringing professionals to the side of labor strengthened labor's political power for raising health and safety issues in the workplace and at the level of national policy. It supplied credentials and scientific legitimacy. The strategy was implemented during the 1970s by such industrial union leaders as Mazzocchi of OCAW and Samuels of the IUD. Little attention, however, had been paid to the health and safety needs of building trades workers before the early 1980s. Warren, Elisburg, Samuels, and others succeeded in bringing professionals into an effort to improve the health and safety conditions of construction workers. The advisory board was a way to accomplish this.

The Tri-Funds

The effort to incorporate professionals into the unions' health and safety activities occurred during a period when LIUNA was developing ways in which the international union could strengthen the ability of locals to secure union construction work. In 1988, the union established two new funds, which joined the L-AGC Education and Training Fund as bulwarks of cooperation between the union and the employers who hired its members. Referred to as the Tri-Funds, the three funds are central aspects of the health and safety strategy for securing environmental remediation work. The success of the L-AGC's training program was largely due to the commitment and support received from these funds as well as the federal fund awards.

The other two components of the Tri-Funds, in addition to the L-AGC, are the Laborers' Health and Safety Fund of North America (LHSFNA) and the Laborers-Employers Cooperation and Education Trust (LECET). The purposes of each of these funds are rooted in providing job security, in the fullest sense of the term, by supporting ways to lower construction labor costs and increase worker efficiency and productivity (Allen, 1998; LIUNA, 1997; Warren, 1998). As Arthur A. Coia, LIUNA general president in 1997, expressed it,

> In today's highly competitive global economy, North America must collectively pursue a pro-active strategy. The reality is that neither workers nor employers

> can do it alone. The key is to combine our strengths, talents and skills to fortify our position in the marketplace. Cooperation between labor and management increases productivity, efficiency, and job security. It will enable us to compete effectively, raise our living standards, and create more just societies. (LIUNA, 1997, p. 2)

The Laborers-Employers Cooperation and Education Trust (LECET) was established in 1989 to "generate market opportunities for employers and job opportunities for LIUNA members" (LIUNA, 1997). LECET is a partnership between LIUNA and its affiliated construction and environmental employers. LECET uses marketing and communications mechanisms to expand the union-sector market share for these employers. Through a tracking system, LECET obtains and maintains information on more than 20,000 construction and hazardous waste clean-up projects and more than 50,000 construction firms. The information is used to encourage construction contractors to bid on posted projects and to hire Laborers. LECET interacts with the L-AGC Education and Training Fund to ensure that a contractor has access to trained, skilled workers (Allen, 1998).

The Laborers' Health and Safety Fund of North America (LHSFNA) was, established in 1988. It is "committed to creating safer, healthier and more cost-effective work places" (LIUNA, 1997, p. 7). LHSFNA maintains three program areas: occupational safety and health; health promotion; and research. The fund provides technical assistance in support of preventing job-related injuries and diseases. The Health and Safety Fund, along with the Hazardous Waste Worker Training Program, was the result of union decisions to build strong relationships with scientists, medical professionals, and health and safety professionals. These relationships were focused on helping LIUNA move construction health and safety issues to a position of greater importance.

The environmental training programs provided by the L-AGC have resulted in the Environmental Partnering Agreement, which assures to signatory contractors highly trained workers and access to the resources of the other two funds. The L-AGC's program department coordinates the Construction Skills Training Program and others in a range of environmental remediation areas. The program department's goals are to support the union, contractors, and individual workers. A major interest of the L-AGC is in providing career paths for laborers. The L-AGC successfully sought accreditation through the American Council on Education in order to offer college credits for several of its environmental courses. The goal of providing career paths was stated repeatedly in interviews with individuals involved in the hazardous waste worker training program. It is the purpose of the literacy programs. Learning to read can provide opportunities for laborers to take other training courses that can lead to different job options.

THE TRAINING PROGRAM'S EARLY GROWTH

In September 1988, The L-AGC received its second year's funding from NIEHS, based on its fulfillment of commitments and the stated goals for a second-year award. That fall, 17 new instructors were trained. The L-AGC expanded its program to four more training sites. The new trainers instructed at those sites served as supplemental or replacement instructors for the six initial training centers.

The Instructor Development Program

In October 1988, The L-AGC conducted its first annual instructor refresher course—40 hours of training for the original instructors. The class trained on technical issues as well as methodology and adult education principles and techniques. Leopold, of the Labor Institute in New York, was invited to teach on using the worker-to-worker, small group activity method. Leopold had been coordinating curriculum development for OCAW's training program.

While the L-AGC did not adopt a "worker-to-worker" training method, it did employ instructors who had done construction work earlier in their careers. Thursby explained that the "worker-to-worker" method did not seem appropriate in this case since laborers often do not work with the same coworkers for very long, depending on the amount of work in a given locality. For the L-AGC, the important relationship to develop through training was the one between the laborer and the regional training center instructors. The L-AGC developed the instructors as a local resource for laborers who attended the training.

The L-AGC program supported large group discussions during the training. Instructors learned how to facilitate classroom activities that included lectures and discussions. Through the less structured conversations, the class addressed questions about the application of the training to specific work sites and conditions.

According to its evaluation by participating instructors, the refresher training class was extremely successful. The L-AGC has repeated it yearly to support growth in its instructors. The course came to be called the Instructor Development Program (IDP). The instructors have gathered each year to collectively enhance their training skills and discuss successful training approaches. The exchange has enabled instructors to work on the curriculum and the more accomplished instructors to train the new trainers. The program has also allowed instructors to receive certification for their work and even earn college credits. IDP includes more than 100 presentations over a 6-day period. The L-AGC supports more than 140 hazardous waste health and safety instructors nationally.

Evaluation

The L-AGC included the Building and Construction Trades Department (BCTD) of the AFL-CIO in its work plan to evaluate its training. Les Murphy and James Lapping, two BCTD staff members with substantial construction safety and health backgrounds, coordinated the evaluation. Their initial efforts included participation in the first instructor training class and observation of at least the first class at each training center.

Workers joined in the evaluation process as well; trainees were given evaluation forms for each module of the course. The forms allowed trainees to comment on the aspects of the course that worked well for them and those that needed improvement or did not "work" at all. A report submitted to the L-AGC by Murphy showed that substantial comment and criticism were forthcoming, even about the order of the modules. The L-AGC made the training more worker centered by seeking and using trainees' suggestions. The BCTD produced thorough reports of the evaluation results, which were then reviewed by the master trainers. The reports also went to the advisory board.

The evaluation served two purposes for the L-AGC. It was an instrument for collective worker feedback and input, thus serving as a basis for the assessment of course relevance. It was also a mechanism to assure employers that the trained laborers they hired for hazardous waste operations were "knowledgeable about safety and health aspects of their work and knowledgeable about how to do the work" (Finklea, 1998).

INPUT FROM THE ADVISORY BOARD

The 9-member advisory board met semiannually. The board was the most direct means through which AGC member-contractors guided and participated in the training program. Board members remained actively involved between meetings through communication with the program's managers. Some members participated in a medical committee of the board. Others visited the training centers. Members reviewed the curriculum, assisted in the training of collaborating medical and health care professionals, or assisted in the program's marketing and outreach, which gave broader employer exposure to the program (L-AGC Education and Training Fund, 1990a).

In October 1988, the advisory board established a medical committee to determine the necessary medical examinations and the procedures for maintaining medical records for laborers who performed hazardous waste work. The members included five physicians from the Centers for Disease Control, the Tennessee Valley Authority, ATSDR, the New York State Health Department, and George Washington University Medical Center. The committee also included an environmental health engineer, a biostatistician, a certified industrial hygienist, and the director of LHSFNA's Occupational Health and Safety Division. It designed a medical monitoring protocol for hazardous waste workers. The committee recommended to the L-AGC that workers should receive a medical examination prior to training and then subsequent monitoring at their annual refresher training.

Some members had participated in earlier government efforts to develop health guidelines for hazardous waste workers, which recommended liver function testing. As the committee explored this, too many difficult issues were raised. The committee decided against including liver function testing in its guidelines. The medical committee completed guidelines for the medical monitoring of workers, detailing the examinations and tests required before starting hazardous waste work. The guidelines were piloted by Dr. Christine Oliver, an occupational physician from Boston, during a training course at the Connecticut center.

The committee also discussed the need for baseline medical data on hazardous waste workers. Members wanted to create an "early-warning system—to find and correct any health problems early" (LIUNA, 1990). Medical committee members, along with LHSFNA, approached ATSDR for funding to conduct a medical surveillance project based on the population of hazardous waste workers trained by the L-AGC. ATSDR awarded a 5-year $1.8-million contract for the study.

Employer members of the board raised certain issues. A recurring concern for them was whether the cost of the program was appropriate, especially as it compared to the costs of programs run by other NIEHS awardees. Employers were interested in various aspects of program evaluation. They wanted some kind of testing that showed how well trainees retained the course information. Employer representatives asked that the evaluation effort survey contractors who had employed trainees to discover what they thought of the program. Employers also encouraged the administrators to make observations at actual hazardous waste sites to ensure that the training program addressed the tasks and conditions of the work. In general, however, the employers on the board were highly supportive of the program.

The issues that professionals raised, other than medical issues, were often the same as the concerns of the union representatives (usually the employers were in agreement as well). Testing of workers' knowledge was a key issue. At one point, someone questioned whether testing was necessary, since the EPA did not test participants in its courses. Most board members agreed that the discontinuation of testing could result in the "degradation of the program" (L-AGC Education and Training Fund, 1992, minutes of meeting, June 7, 1991). Addressing laborers' literacy issues was another common concern of professional and union committee members.

The issue of program cohesiveness was raised, particularly in relation to consistency between training centers. These concerns recognized the horizontal structure of the union and the potential for resistance by regional training center directors to directives from the national office. Efforts were taken to address "we" and "they" attitudes in some training centers, according to Thursby. The administrators' efforts were successful and the centers all came to regard the program as "ours" (L-AGC Education and Training Fund, 1992, minutes of meeting, December 6, 1989).

Training program indemnification was a major concern of all the advisory committee members, as well as the L-AGC trustees. No appropriate liability insurance was available to either the training program or the contractors. Indemnification concerns ranged from employer indemnification, which was needed to encourage contractors to enter the market, to training program indemnification, which addressed training program quality assurance and control. Even after the EPA agreed to indemnify the WETP awardees, many doubted that this provided adequate protection from potential liability. Discussions about certification of trained workers were often directly related to liability concerns. Certification was viewed as a vehicle for the provision of a reasonably level playing field in the job market. It would be a way to determine who had received high-quality training and who had not. If the standards for laborers' certification were sufficiently rigorous, they would establish a level of training quality that few nonunion employers could obtain for their employees.

Consequently, curriculum issues were also matters of great and common concern. All agreed that the focus of training should be on teaching proper work methods for hazardous waste operations. Emphasis was placed on extensive hands-on activities.

By spring 1990, the L-AGC Hazardous Waste Worker Training Program was well established. More than 3,000 laborers had been trained and certified, and nearly all had been employed on hazardous waste jobs (L-AGC Education and Training Fund,

1990b). The L-AGC had trained 65 instructors. In the spring and summer of 1990 NIEHS conducted site reviews at two of the training centers—Kingston, Washington, and Pomfret, Connecticut, respectively.

The L-AGC reported to NIEHS review teams on the progress and status of the program. In addition to the mock site at each training center, CSI had developed a "site safety and health plan" for each site, which was used as a teaching tool. Each site delivered hands-on exercises with apparatus set up for operations involving confined spaces, buried drums, simulated wells, and decontamination.

The NIEHS review team was impressed with the L-AGC's program accomplishments. "This is one of the strongest grantees observed in terms of the basic commitment by the union and employers; as a joint labor-management grantee this is inherent in the grant and training activity. . . . There are no significant weaknesses in the program" (NIEHS, 1990, p. 3).

LEADERSHIP IN THE WETP

The WETP increasingly relied on the L-AGC to provide supportive leadership in the national Superfund training effort. Thursby volunteered for such tasks as coordinating the purchase of training equipment for multiple awardees. Elisburg helped devise strategies for gaining the support of Congress and other federal agencies. Another key professional who helped the L-AGC was John Moran.

Moran had directed NIOSH's Division of Safety Research between 1983 and 1988. Late that year, the L-AGC wanted to hire an industrial hygienist for its training program. Elisburg urged the L-AGC to hire Moran, who, though not an industrial hygienist, had extensive expertise in occupational health and safety. Moran reviewed the trainee and instructor manuals for the 40-hour course and wrote the first refresher manual.

In furtherance of the leadership role of the L-AGC in the WETP, Moran worked with Denny Dobbin in 1990 to coordinate and facilitate the national workshop to develop minimum criteria for the hazardous waste worker training programs. Moran later went over to the Laborers' Health and Safety Fund as director of its occupational health and safety program. He remained closely involved in the WETP, organizing and facilitating two technical workshops on new technologies, and helping to plan a second workshop addressing the minimum training criteria, which resulted in interpretive guidance on the original Minimum Criteria Document (Bergfeld, 1998; Elisburg, 1997; Finklea, 1998; L-AGC Education and Training Fund, 1991; Moran, 1998).

GROWTH OF THE LABORERS' PROGRAM

After Congress doubled the WETP's funding, the L-AGC submitted a successful supplemental proposal for the expansion of its program. Six more training centers were established, doubling their number. The L-AGC also developed a 45-hour hazardous waste operations course targeting contractor supervisors, union leaders, and government compliance personnel.

The L-AGC steadily increased its number of hazardous waste training instructors. Each new trainer attended an 80-hour worker course and a 40-hour new instructor class. Existing trainers attended the annual Instructor Development Program.

Developing Instructors, Including Medical Professionals

As the program progressed, so did the instructors. Instructors became more expert in their understanding of hazardous waste operations, health and safety issues, and training delivery. Some instructors became curriculum developers, building on their experience as instructors and workers. Reliance on the master trainers for the instruction of new trainers diminished as the pool of instructors grew in competence and ability.

The health effects sections of the courses were taught by medical professionals at each training center. This created some difficulties. Many medical professionals, due to their training, focused on how workers could reduce their lifestyle risks. Workers who engaged in activities with the potential for exposure to a wide range of toxic chemicals were generally not interested in learning to change the way they lived. The workers came to the classes to learn about the nature of the chemicals to which they were exposed on the job.

The L-AGC established an annual medical conference to discuss medical issues. At the conference, the instructors who taught the Instructor Development Program taught the medical professionals how to train adults (Bergfeld, 1998).

Practicing Principles of Adult Education

Over time, it became increasingly apparent to the instructors and program administrators, and even to the advisory board, that the application of adult education principles was essential for success in training. This discussion took place mostly among the instructors. The instructors "recognized early on that presenting material in lecture form wasn't in the long run the best way to go" (Finklea, 1998). Instructors were encouraged to innovate to find better methods for teaching laborers. Innovation raised concerns about program consistency between centers, but Thursby and Bergfeld understood that flexibility was necessary to permit innovation, and that they should strive for a balance between flexibility and consistency.

Beyond the First 5 Years

The L-AGC, as much as any WETP awardee, experienced frustration at the failure of the federal government to move forward with the cleanup of hazardous waste sites. Workers were trained and prepared to engage in hazardous waste operations. Although the L-AGC had strong contractor support for the hazardous waste worker training program, for many of the smaller contractors the environmental remediation market did not appear strong enough to warrant the initial investment necessary to establish themselves and start work. Nonetheless, at the point at which the federal and state governments made a commitment to the national clean-up effort, trained laborers would be needed. For the L-AGC, the plan was to continue developing its training program and pursuing work in environmental remediation.

The Tri-Funds matured and coordinated their efforts to support an expansion of environmental work for LIUNA members. LECET played an important role. It sponsored conferences on work in the environmental sector. For example, a New England conference was entitled "New Business Opportunities for Union Contractors" (LECET, 1991). In 1994, Ken Allen coordinated research for LECET on wages, productivity, and highway construction costs. Allen's report was released by the National Alliance for Fair Contracting, a nonprofit labor and management organization "dedicated to the advancement of fair competitive contracting in the public-sector construction industry" (National Alliance for Fair Contracting, 1995, inside cover).

The report documented attempts between 1993 and 1995 to convince Congress to repeal the Davis-Bacon Act. The report gathered data from a study commissioned to analyze the costs of building a mile of highway, utilizing Federal Highway Administration data. The research sought to determine whether a correlation existed between wages, man hours, and highway construction costs. It compared highway construction costs in high- and low-wage states, and then compared them with the national average. It demonstrated that construction cost savings are related to both wages and productivity, not only to wages. It showed that "states associated with higher hourly wages have lower labor hours per mile of highway and overall highway costs which are below those of lower wage states" (National Alliance for Fair Contracting, 1995, p. 2). The report refuted the arguments against requiring those awarded federal construction contracts to pay the prevailing wage.

Ken Allen came from a family of construction workers. He started as an operating engineer in 1956. He worked 42 years continuously in the construction industry. He was an active member of the IUOE and served as a national representative. In addition to his IUOE service, Allen also worked for the Teamsters' union as a program manager for its hazardous waste worker training program. Shortly after that, he was hired by the Laborers to serve as the national field coordinator for the L-AGC in coordination with LECET. Allen tracked work, particularly environmental work, by reviewing published reports of construction bids. He researched the names of bidders and contacted them about the training program. Allen gave contractors information about the increased efficiency that can be gained by using a trained work force. He also maintained a database of trained workers from the locals and could determine whether the L-AGC would have to provide additional training in order to meet contractor needs for trained workers. Finally, Allen encouraged district councils and locals to participate in the training program.

The DOE and the Minority Worker Training Program

The L-AGC expanded its effort in two other directions after 1992. It trained workers for hazardous and nuclear waste clean-up work at DOE facilities. In most years the largest DOE program awardee, the L-AGC has provided training to thousands of workers involved in the cleanup of the nation's nuclear energy and weapons research and development facilities. One of the worst of these is in Hanford, Washington, comparable in size to the state of Rhode Island and practically entirely contaminated with radioactive and chemical contaminants.

The L-AGC also became active in the national environmental justice movement and helped NIEHS develop its Minority Worker Training Program (MWTP). Don Elisburg became an early member of the National Environmental Justice Advisory Council and helped the L-AGC engage in the national environmental justice dialogue. By 2005, the L-AGC had participated in the WETP's core MWTP and its Brownfield MWTP, having coordinated projects in Massachusetts, Michigan, Ohio, Louisiana, and California, demonstrating significant success in training young people from minority and underserved communities to work in the environmental remediation sector. Many of these trainees became union members.

Cleanup by Skilled Support Personnel

September 11, 2001, demonstrated the strength and success of the L-AGC training program. More than 3,000 Laborers worked 12-hour days to clean up Ground Zero at the World Trade Center site in New York City. The L-AGC worked closely with the WETP to ensure that construction workers at the site had appropriate training and adequate protective equipment and measures in place. Following this experience, the L-AGC used WETP funding to develop an array of training courses for laborers and others with potential for working as skilled support personnel at future disaster sites.

Following the discovery of ricin in Senator Frist's Congressional office on Monday, February 2, 2004, the L-AGC and the West Virginia Laborers' Training Trust Fund mobile unit provided this training to law enforcement agents in the Washington, DC, area. These included the U.S. Capitol Police, the DC Metro Police, and the Federal Protection Service. A 50-hour course had been developed for workers who would be engaged in response, recovery, and cleanup after incidents involving weapons of mass destruction. It included "special equipment training, information on explosives, biological and chemical WMD's, health effects, decontamination, monitoring and sampling, and field exercises and dressouts" (L-AGC Education and Training Fund, 2007). The Laborers had established sufficient expertise to be prepared for these new kinds of hazardous waste sites and to demonstrate the need for worker health and safety protections in the heightened national emphasis upon homeland security and disaster preparedness, response, and recovery.

The Program's Overall Impact

The L-AGC's program has affected the L-AGC, LIUNA, Laborers, and their work. Much of its model has been applied to all the other training programs organized by the fund. In 1995, LIUNA established a formal stewards' training program, largely due to the success of the training implemented through the hazardous waste program.

> With a national stewards program, we stand a better chance of having qualified front-line support when our trained and certified workers reach the job site: an individual that knows the regulations and how to approach management to help make the work site safer. (Warren, 1998)

Challenging an employer's organization of the work site may leave a worker vulnerable to being labeled a troublemaker, jeopardizing future employment opportunities. An educated and supportive steward can be the front line in support of a trained worker.

Workers also need educated employers who will protect their health and safety. Contractors have taken the course and learned that health and safety can support their work and help them succeed in the environmental market. Additionally, the combined efforts of the Tri-Funds have raised employer awareness about joint labor-management initiatives to create healthy and safe job sites.

The L-AGC training program is shaping the next generation of LIUNA leadership. After 10 years, the program had trained a large percentage of the leadership of the local unions, as well as most of the training center instructors. Many of the trained Laborers have moved into positions of authority in the locals, the district councils, and the international union. The union leadership has grown increasingly committed to protecting workers' health and safety.

> You have a workforce that knows that OSHA is supposed to be there but is never there. And so they have to try to fend for themselves. And with no real training they have to accept sometimes what other people tell them. . . . We're still not to the point where a laborer can say no, refuse to work and not have some repercussions for it at some point. (Bergfeld, 1998)

Once trained and hired on an environmental remediation job, Laborers not infrequently found that they had more field and health and safety knowledge than others already in the employ of a contractor. This "edge" often meant that Laborers were assigned responsibility for contaminant monitoring and sampling or promoted to the position of site health and safety officer. The range of training offered gave Laborers the skills to take on many construction tasks. Some in L-AGC believed that helping members have a variety of careers, all within the construction industry, would help the union retain members. Trained Laborers sometimes left the union when they became health and safety officers. "But that's still beneficial to us, because we trained them" (Bergfeld, 1998). Employer trustees of the L-AGC were also eager to recruit trained laborers to help manage their companies and supervise construction sites.

During case study interviews, several program leaders used the "lifeblood" metaphor when referring to the Laborers and their training. Thursby said that he modified an old Laborers' expression, "Jurisdiction is the blood that runs through our veins," to "Training is the blood that runs through our veins." Dr. Finklea, of the L-AGC's advisory board, said that the Laborers "feel that an educated productive work force is a key to maintaining the strength of the union and growing the union. . . . They view training programs as . . . the lifeblood of the union" (Finklea, 1998). The L-AGC program presented a model for worker health and safety training in the union sector of the construction industry. As Bergfield said, "It's better to train people and be pro-active than not to be" (Bergfeld, 1998). His comment captured the L-AGC's viewpoint.

The program has definitely had an important impact upon the Laborers' union, which underwent significant changes in the first decade of the 21st century. The union's president, Terence O'Sullivan, has promoted efforts to mobilize the membership. LIUNA was one of seven unions that moved six million workers out of the AFL-CIO to form Change to Win, a new labor federation with a stated commitment to increasing the size of the labor movement. Perhaps indicative of the HAZMAT training program's impact and the new directions being taken by the LIUNA leadership is a news flyer from the Regional Organizing Coordinator's Committee of the LIUNA Organizing Department. Under the headline "Using Health and Safety in Organizing," the short piece describes how the Laborers' Health and Safety Fund "is providing training to regional organizing committees on how to use health and safety effectively in organizing campaigns" (LIUNA, 2004).

CONCLUSION

The L-AGC has established a training program that specifically addresses the needs and conditions of environmental remediation construction work. The program incorporates a curriculum appropriate for the learning styles and needs of laborers. An emphasis has been placed upon hands-on training. Provision of training at off-site training centers fully equipped with simulated hazardous waste sites helps to ensure a consistent core of training that prepares Laborers uniformly for hazardous waste operations. In this way, the union and the employers can be confident of the knowledge and skills possessed by trained Laborers.

The LIUNA and L-AGC leadership have pursued strategies to organize the emerging hazardous waste remediation industry so that a significant percentage of the industry's workforce would be union Laborers. Entrance into this industry, however, brought the realization that construction workers would be at risk of chemical exposures as great as those of any chemical worker. Therefore, health and safety issues became key components of their efforts. The L-AGC strategies included several integrated components: regulatory requirements for safe and healthy work practices, worker training, legislative action, and marketing and outreach to contractors and government agencies responsible for hazardous waste site remediation. The L-AGC was determined to establish benchmarks for training quality and comprehensiveness that would translate into benchmarks for Laborer skill levels.

It was believed that, if successful, these measures would encourage union construction contractors to enter the hazardous waste remediation industry and also create competitive barriers to nonunion contractors. The L-AGC and LIUNA have achieved considerable success with these strategies, despite unfavorable political and economic pressures and circumstances that are beyond the control of any single union or set of contractors.[13] The combined forces of the insurance, real estate, finance, manufacturing, and petrochemical sectors, as well as recalcitrant governments at all levels, have thwarted the broader hazardous waste remediation strategies of the environmental, labor, public health, and civil rights movements.[14]

The union's efforts have been less successful within the context of the larger battles of control over public policy, development, and production. The union's difficulties are not dissimilar to the obstacles facing workplace-specific worker training strategies within the context of employer control of production in the workplace, including health and safety measures. When an employer evades its responsibility to maintain a safe and healthy workplace, and the government's health and safety protection apparatus is weak, then workers may not be able to act on the knowledge gained through training without risking potential discriminatory action by the employer. This is the political context within which worker health and safety education strategies operate.

Through the L-AGC training program, LIUNA has elevated Laborers' status from that of low-wage, low-skilled workers to that of highly skilled construction workers. The Laborers have advanced their goals of expanding union construction work in the hazardous waste management industry, and making it safe. They have also greatly advanced construction workers' health and safety, both for Laborers and for many other building trades workers.

ENDNOTES

1. Denny Dobbin (1997) later commented that NIEHS let the 100 flowers bloom, but then "kept them in the same flowerbed to help their survival."
2. See Silver (1986) for a discussion of the impact of market and organizational conditions on construction workers and unions. Silver provides a class analysis of labor-management relations in the construction industry, as well as a detailed discussion of the organization of local unions in the building trades.
3. LIUNA eventually negotiated a "national reciprocity agreement," which permitted an individual laborer to have all of his or her pension and health and welfare fund contributions pooled. Regardless of the number of employers a worker has had, and the number of funds to which he/she made contributions, the Laborer receives a full payout representing all contributions.
4. For a history of LIUNA and an explanation of its strategies and goals as a union of laborers, see Goodman, *Working at the Calling* (1991). This history is largely told through the voices of LIUNA officers, staff, and members and provides a rich sense of one of the largest AFL-CIO international unions. Much of this history is also available on the LIUNA Web site at http://www.liuna.org/about/history.html.
5. The assignment of building trades' work at a construction site is based on a system of craft jurisdiction. Jurisdiction for construction tasks was originally established in the union's charter with the AFL-CIO, which held to the principle that each trade would be represented by a single union (Halpin & Woodhead, 1980).
6. Some specific tasks stipulated in Laborers' contracts include the following: handling and carrying concrete reinforcing bars; grading, setting, and laying street, slab, and road forms; wrecking, stripping, removing, or dismantling forms used for concrete construction; excavation, site grading, clearing, backfilling and compaction; and the following aspects of building construction—docks, pile driving, piers, tunnels, retaining walls, sidewalks, sewers, water mains, black topping, parking lots and facilities, and sodding. These are taken from contracts with the Heavy Constructors' Association of the Greater Kansas City Area (August 1, 1994), and the Builders Association of Missouri (expired March 31, 2000).
7. The U.S. Department of Labor makes available a list of job titles in U.S. industries, the Dictionary of Titles (DOT). The list, developed by a committee of the National Academy of Sciences, maintains 110 separate titles that represent "laborer" classifications. Twenty-one of them are construction industry titles and nine are titles classified as "any industry." A review of the titles indicates the broad set of skills represented by members of the Laborers' union.

8. At its national convention in 1996, LIUNA passed a resolution urging all affiliate locals to establish apprenticeship training. Three programs had already been operating for 5–15 years: two in the Northwest and one in Kansas. The programs had not identified themselves as apprenticeship programs because of the lack of support from the international for apprenticeship training. Since the passing of the LIUNA resolution in 1996, the L-AGC and the local training funds have worked diligently to establish apprenticeship training programs. By the end of 1998, 53 training funds had received either State Apprenticeship Council or U.S. Department of Labor Bureau of Apprenticeship and Training approval for their programs.
9. Construction workers, including Laborers, had worked with asbestos for many years. Asbestos was used largely as a building material, in building, ships, pipelines (as piping and pipe insulation), and so forth. Many of the workers who developed disabling and often fatal asbestos-related illnesses were construction workers. The LIUNA and L-AGC officers and staff were well aware of the cost to workers who had never received proper training and protection for asbestos work (Allen, 1998).
10. Most of the workers who have attended the hazardous waste training courses have completed 12th grade. Gradually, the L-AGC was able to rewrite the manuals so that they could be understood by individuals with a 10th-grade reading level.
11. Carol Matheny, former NIEHS grants and contracts manager for the WETP, explained to me that Thursby would proudly tell the story of meeting with John Dement, who asked him whether the L-AGC really believed it would be training laborers by February. Thursby affirmed that it would happen. Connerton broke into a wide grin because he knew that Thursby would do it.
12. Certified Industrial Hygienist
13. For discussions of these barriers, see Barnett (1994) and Hird (1994).
14. Though it is outside the scope of this book, an important focus of the civil rights movement has been directed toward "environmental justice." The environmental justice movement represents a convergence of the labor, environmental, public health, and civil rights movements. As early as 1976, a conference entitled "Working for Environmental and Economic Justice and Jobs" was hosted by Environmentalists for Full Employment, the UAW, and the Urban Environment Conference, and more than 100 other organizations. For further discussions, see Dowie (1997), Gottlieb (1993), Kazis and Grossman (1991), and Szasz (1994).

REFERENCES

Allen, K. (1998). Interview by author, tape recording, Severna Park, MD (May 6).

Barnett, H. C. (1994). *Toxic Debts and the Superfund Dilemma.* Chapel Hill: UNC Press.

Bergfeld, W. (1998). Interview by author, tape recording, Pomfret, CT (July 17).

Dime, R. A. (1986). *Proposed Hazardous Waste Training Program for Laborers,* prepared for the Laborers-AGC Education Training Fund (August). From L-AGC files, Pomfret, CT.

Dobbin, D. (1997). Interviews by author, tape recording, Los Angeles (April 10).

Dowie, M. (1997). *Losing Ground: American Environmentalism at the Close of the Twentieth Century.* Cambridge, MA: MIT Press.

Elisburg, D. (1997). Interview by author, tape recording, RTP, NC (October 21).

Finklea, D. J. (1998). Telephone interview by author, tape recording (July 27).

Goodman, J. F. (1991). *Working at the Calling.* Hopkinton, MA: New England Laborers' Labor-Management Cooperation Trust.

Gottlieb, R. (1993). *Forcing the Spring.* Washington, DC: Island Press.

Halpin, D. W., & Woodhead, R. W. (1980). *Construction Management.* New York: John Wiley & Sons.

Hird, J. A. (1994). *Superfund: The Political Economy of Environmental Risk.* Baltimore: Johns Hopkins University Press.

Iowa Laborers' Heavy Highway Training Fund. (1980). *Toxic and Hazardous Waste: Handling, Control, Removal and Disposal. A Resource and Information Manual.* Des Moines, IA: Iowa Laborers' Heavy Highway Training Fund.

Kazis, R., & Grossman, R. L. (1991). *Fear at Work: Job Blackmail, Labor and the Environment* (New Edition ed.). Santa Cruz, CA: New Society Publishers.

Knack, L. E. (1980). Labor Relations and Their Effect on Employment Procedures. In J. P. Frein (Ed.), *Handbook of Construction Management and Organization* (2nd ed.; pp. 587-600). New York: Van Nostrand Reinhold.

L-AGC Education and Training Fund. (1987a). Minutes of Hazardous Waste Committee, Hollywood, Florida (February 8). From L-AGC files, Pomfret, CT.

L-AGC Education and Training Fund. (1987b). Proposal submitted to NIEHS for Superfund Worker Training Programs (April 30). From L-AGC files, Pomfret, CT.

L-AGC Education and Training Fund. (1988). Noncompetitive renewal application submitted to NIEHS. Progress report (July 1). From L-AGC files, Pomfret, CT.

L-AGC Education and Training Fund. (1990a). Application submitted to NIEHS for supplemental funding, Progress report (July 1). From L-AGC files, Pomfret, CT.

L-AGC Education and Training Fund. (1990b). Summary Report for NIEHS Review Team: Kingston Site Visit (May 7). From L-AGC files, Pomfret, CT.

L-AGC Education and Training Fund. (1991). Board of Trustees Meeting: 4-Year Chronological Progress Report, Hazardous Waste Worker Training Program, March 30, 1987 Through March 30, 1991 (April 25). Laborers-Associated General Contractors. Pomfret, CT.

L-AGC Education and Training Fund. (1992). Hazardous Waste Worker Training Program Advisory Board Meeting Minutes, May 13, 1988-December 3, 1992. From L-AGC files, Pomfret, CT.

L-AGC Education and Training Fund. (2007). *Spring '04 Laborers' Training . . . Helping to Keep Our Nation Safe.* Retrieved July 6, 2007, from http://www.laborers-agc.org/recentarticles_helpingtokeep.asp

Lange, J. E., & Mills, D. Q. (1979). *An Introduction to the Construction Sector of the Economy. The Construction Industry: Balance Wheel of the Economy.* Lexington, MA: Lexington Books.

LECET. (1991, Spring). Labor Management Update. *LECET Newsletter,* Vol. 2.

LIUNA. (1990, December). Special Report. *Health Lines Newsletter.*

LIUNA. (1997). *The Tri-Funds.* LIUNA Informational Brochure. 905-16th Street, NW, Washington, DC, 20006, Laborers International Union of North America.

LIUNA. (1998). *Change at the Speed of Light.* Retrieved September 1998, from http://www.liuna.org

LIUNA. (2004). *ROCC On! News of the Regional Organizing Coordinator's Committee, LIUNA Organizing Department.* Retrieved July 6, 2007, from http://www.laborersinternational.com/marketshare/stories/rocconmarch04.pdf

Mallino, D., Sr. (1997). Interview by author, tape recording, Washington, DC (December 10).

Matheny, C. (1998). Interview by author, typed responses by the interviewee, and notes from interview, Durham, NC (July 29).

Moran, J. (1998). Telephone interview by author, tape recording (July 27).

National Alliance for Fair Contracting, (1995). *Wages, Productivity, and Highway Construction Costs.* Washington, DC: Author.

NIEHS. (1990). L-AGC. *Site Review Visit Report; Laborers-AGC Educ. & Trng. Fund* (July 23-25). NIEHS WETP files, RTP, NC.

Szasz, A. (1994). *EcoPopulism: Toxic Waste and the Movement for Environmental Justice.* Minneapolis: University of Minnesota Press.

Silver, M. L. (1986). *Under Construction: Work and Alienation in the Building Trades.* Albany: State University of New York Press.

Thursby, N. (1998a). Interview by author, tape recording (June 22).

Thursby, N. (1998b). Laborers health and safety training class presentation outline. Provided by Mr. Thursby.

U.S. DOL. (1991). *Dictionary of Occupational Titles* (4th ed.). Revised. Washington, DC, retrieved from, http://www.oalj.dol.gov/libdot.htm

Warren, M. (1998). Interview by author, tape recording, Pomfret CT (May 28, 1998).

Workers at a Hazardous Waste Site Sampling Drums.
Courtesy of the U.S. EPA

Worker in Protective Gear Opening Barrel with Bung Wrench.
Courtesy of the U.S. EPA

CHAPTER 8

The Political Economy of Labor's Policy Initiative and Regulation

The goal of most occupational health and safety intervention programs is to prevent workplace-related injuries, illnesses, and fatalities. As a member of a history panel on the WETP's tenth anniversary, Donald Elisburg told the NIEHS awardees that the program had succeeded in preventing the adverse health and safety outcomes among workers that otherwise would have been predicted for such industrial operations. "The key thing . . . is this great statistic that is not there. We've changed the safety and health culture on these environmental clean-up sites." This statement gains additional weight when it is compared with a report from Shirley Miller of the Chemical Workers' Industrial Union of South Africa, stating that "clean-up contract workers have the highest fatality rate in the South African chemical industry" (ICEM, 1996). The combination of a specific OSHA standard for hazardous waste operations and emergency response and a training grant program whose awardees have either trained workers or influenced their training by other providers through the program's high quality standards seems to have led to safer HAZWOPER work in the United States.

Labor unions responded to the rise of the hazardous waste management industry with its inherent dangers for workers by pursuing public- and private-sector measures to protect their members. Their multiple policy initiatives led to the setting up of the WETP at a time when, paradoxically, labor's own power was declining relative to that of the employing class.[1] This analysis asks how this happens.

Wooding and Levenstein (1999) have argued that an analysis of the political economy of the work environment requires an examination of the location of various actors within the system of production. They present four broad categories: workers, managers, health professionals, and the state and the governance system. In this study, because of the central role played by organized labor, it is useful to specify "unions" in place of "workers." Likewise, the health professionals group has been expanded to include a wider range of professionals and scientists. Finally, the category of social movements has been added.

UNIONS

A study of the hazardous waste worker health and safety policy initiative and its implementation requires an understanding of unions and provides lessons about how unions approach these issues. A key element of the WETP has been the fact that unions have used government support as a vehicle for communicating with workers about health and safety issues.

Regardless of the power of a union, or of organized labor nationally, within the context of the existing political economy of the work environment, labor's power is overshadowed by the clout of employers. Labor's health and safety strategies, then, will generally reflect their relative strength in comparison with that of employers. The strategy of aiming for a federal mandate for worker training and of gaining support for it reflected a number of areas of limited strength. First, labor did not have the strength to negotiate adequate training provisions in individual labor-management contracts. Regardless of the industry, management will rarely voluntarily give adequate release time from industrial operations for health and safety training. Second, labor did not have adequate funds to support such training on its own. Even in the case of LIUNA, which had established a joint labor-management trust fund with the Associated General Contractors, external start-up funds were needed. Third, and most important, the political and economic reorganization of the U.S. economy during the 1980s generally left labor without the ability to deploy the power of strikes (work stoppages) to achieve employer agreement to health and safety interventions. (With the exception of certain unions, under specific circumstances, labor in the United States has made limited use of strikes to achieve health and safety improvements. It has relied more on the contract negotiation process for such purposes.)

Labor has exercised its strength to improve health and safety conditions. Some unions have built strong alliances with supportive professionals who have helped them fight for improved health and safety conditions. OCAW represented one example, with its network of occupational medicine interns and physicians, one of whom helped the union locals in Niagara County, New York, to raise important health and safety issues about hazardous waste exposures. Health and safety and other professionals were also employed by individual unions and the AFL-CIO. These relationships expanded after the passage of the OSH Act. The professionals in the AFL-CIO and affiliated unions have developed health and safety policy initiatives and legislative strategies. During the Carter administration, with Eula Bingham directing OSHA and Anthony Robbins directing NIOSH, labor gained greater support from these agencies. OSHA's New Directions program helped to build health and safety competency in the unions and nurtured a network of supportive professionals (including labor educators) and activists in academic institutions and coalitions on occupational safety and health (COSHes).

Hazardous waste exposures became a health and safety issue for much of labor. It was a broad issue initially, which caught the attention of the AFL-CIO Safety and Health Department, after OCAW and USWA succeeded in bringing it to national attention. OCAW's reduced emphasis on health and safety, resulting from a leadership change in the union and growing fears of job loss among its membership, led the union to abandon the issue, at least at the national level. Next, the IAFF became actively involved over firefighters' HAZMAT exposures during ER operations. Its activities in cooperation with NIOSH were incorporated into the AFL-CIO's general legislative and regulatory strategies in the early phases of the initiative. The issues were part of labor's overall health and safety approach: that is, to use the regulatory and research structures that were won through labor's efforts to achieve the OSH Act.

Then the building trades became interested in securing hazardous waste worker protections through the Superfund reauthorization bill. Although the building trades sought to continue these industrial hygiene and regulatory plans (standards, enforcement, and certification, similar to the mechanisms established pursuant to the federal Coal Mine Health and Safety Act of 1969), they were also developing organizing tactics that would incorporate health and safety measures. LIUNA, which had a joint labor-management trust fund for education and training, worked for a federal training grant program and mandated training as a basis for organizing—these were creative ways to gain power in an emerging industry.

The staff and professionals working on the effort to achieve protective language in SARA consisted of representatives from three AFL-CIO departments—Safety and Health, Industrial Union, and Building and Construction Trades—and individual national unions: the IAFF (firefighters), LIUNA (laborers), and the IUOE (operating engineers). Although the IUD was directly involved and permitted David Mallino to direct the legislative effort, Mallino saw this primarily as a building trades initiative for work in the hazardous waste remediation industry. He was willing to work with AFL-CIO staff and the IAFF (both had early roles in the policy initiative), but he never moved too far from his original focus.

The IAFF's role was critical. Richard Duffy's testimony at Congressional hearings helped turn hazardous waste and ER worker protections into a "Mom-and-apple-pie issue" (Mallino, 1997). Firefighters put their lives in jeopardy to protect property, the environment, and public health. The nation had an obligation to provide some basic protection measures, such as health and safety standards, enforcement, and training for these heroic workers. This logic transferred well to the many hazardous waste management and remediation workers who risked their lives to rid the nation of its hazardous waste crisis. Although the IAFF supplied the moral high ground for labor, it ultimately failed to achieve what it sought most: protections for public-sector workers.

The story of the hazardous waste initiative and its implementation, then, is the story of the strengths and weaknesses of labor. Labor had the strength to achieve a legislative victory that mandated OSHA to promulgate a standard and the EPA to provide $10 million for worker training. Additionally, the EPA was required to promulgate a standard to protect public-sector HAZWOPER workers. This was achieved by a Democratic House of Representatives and moderate Republican senators in the middle of a 12-year period of control of the executive branch of the federal government by basically antiunion Republican administrations that opposed placing health and safety and environmental regulatory burdens on industry. Labor had friends on both sides of the aisle.

Labor lacked the strength to force the regulatory agencies to adequately fulfill their Congressional mandate under Section 126 of SARA. Neither OSHA nor the EPA provided strong enforcement of their respective HAZWOPER standards.

Public-sector workers, such as firefighters, have received inadequate support for their protection during HAZMAT ER. OSHA has failed to promulgate an effective rule for HAZWOPER training program certification.

Although it has not been an explicit labor policy, what has emerged from labor's strategies for health and safety education and training has been a reliance on benevolent and labor-supporting agencies and bureaucrats to provide coordination and to distribute resources to the national health and safety movement. Federal government training programs, during both relatively benign and hostile regimes, have been the closest that labor has been able to get to coordinating a national health and safety movement.

MANAGEMENT

The almost unique aspect of the hazardous waste management industry, when it is compared with most others, is that it developed in direct relationship to federal environmental laws and regulations. Unlike other employers, waste management employers generally regarded environmental regulation as benefiting their competitiveness and profitability. Limited evidence indicates that hazardous waste management employers opposed legislation and regulation to protect their employees. However, they mounted no opposition to the worker protection provisions in SARA. They did not oppose the OSHA regulatory requirements, but they did seek less stringent language that would permit them greater control over the amount of training they would offer.

Mallino's legislative plan for achieving the passage of SARA's worker protection provisions was to maintain a low profile. He stayed clear of the labor and environment coalition fight for the emergency planning and community right-to-know provisions. He believed that this low-profile strategy and a general lack of understanding of which employers would be affected by the regulations were the reasons for the lack of employer opposition. This may be so, since employers in the oil, petrochemical, and manufacturing sectors were more forceful in their opposition to OSHA's proposed HAZWOPER regulation.

Employers were fighting much more important battles during the effort to reauthorize the Superfund law. The oil industry was lobbying to spread the Superfund tax burden to include the industrial sectors that generate hazardous waste. The manufacturing industries, the hazardous waste generators, were fighting for Congress to keep in place the tax burden on the oil industry. Despite their interindustry conflicts, the producers of both oil and chemicals as well as the hazardous waste-generating industries were lobbying Congress and the Reagan administration for the weakest possible Superfund. The Congressional debate, except for remarks by a small number of legislators, provided evidence of broad agreement on the need to pass a Superfund reauthorization bill. Worker protection provisions in the bill were of little concern to the few industries and employer associations that were aware of them.

Employer and industry concerns during the struggles over SARA were supported by labor in some specific industries. For example, construction contractors and their associations sought liability waivers. The building trades unions also encouraged

Congress to allow such waivers, fearing that their plans to expand labor market opportunities for construction workers would not be realized if contractors believed that hazardous waste remediation work would pose excessive liability risks and costs. Similarly, unions representing workers in the heavy manufacturing sectors, out of fear of job losses, aligned with employers in cautioning Congress against imposing a tax on hazardous waste generators that would put U.S. firms at a competitive disadvantage against foreign firms. The ability of employers to win labor support for measures opposed to labor's best interests demonstrated the strength of the employers' collective power relative to labor.

Management may work in cooperation with labor to pursue mutual goals, such as the L-AGC training program. The Laborers' union took the initiative to raise the skill level of Laborers through training. By the 1980s, the success of their strategy became evident enough to encourage the AGC to agree to bargaining proposals for a "cents-per-hour" contribution to the L-AGC Education and Training Trust Fund. The focus on health and safety training as a means of support for entrance into the environmental remediation market, which began with asbestos and lead training, received backing from the employer representatives on the L-AGC's executive board. It built on the industry's tradition of labor-management cooperation on apprenticeship training.

The oil and chemical industry employers do not have a history of joint labor-management training programs. Merrill wrote in 1991 about the employers' unwillingness to let "the unions that represent their employees . . . provide the training required on the job." Several key informants of the present author discussed the problem of layers of management in the vertical organization of the oil and chemical industries. At times, a health and safety manager might have been eager for OCAW to provide health and safety training, but too often another manager in the hierarchy refused to approve a request to permit it. Decisions by management to permit OCAW to deliver its training have often been related to a safety system failure that strengthened the union's position in negotiating worker access to the training. Such situations resulted from a serious injury or fatality, an accident that alarmed the surrounding community, or an OSHA citation.

Another key difference between the construction and the oil and petrochemical employers was their use of the workforce. Construction employers rely on a contingent workforce, since they do not provide year-round, full-time employment. Construction employers who are willing to negotiate with building trades unions have come to rely on the union hiring halls for access to the labor force. The oil and petrochemical employers provide full-time, permanent jobs. These industries are both profitable and hazardous, with well-developed health and safety departments that protect their turf against encroachment by the union. These industries have also demonstrated a half-century of successful maneuvering for steady workforce reductions. The industries automated and, in addition, contracted out maintenance work. As documented in a 1991 John Gray Institute study, contracting out maintenance without demanding contractor health and safety compliance increased the number and severity of such accidents (Wells, Kochan, & Smith, 1991). Employers in such a setting may find themselves facing a confrontational union that demands job and health and safety protection. Employers in the oil and petrochemical industry willing to form cooperative labor-management partnerships are rare, but as OCAW's TOP program demonstrated, such partnerships can succeed with mutual commitment.

PROFESSIONALS

The hazardous waste problem arose and continues in some part due to two major weaknesses of the industrial hygiene profession. One is its general inability to consider and recommend pollution prevention and clean production strategies as mechanisms for worker protection. The other is its general alliance with management rather than workers. Although industrial hygienists are trained to protect workers, far too often they provide greater protection to the interests and property of management. More generally, Levenstein and Tuminaro (1991) have located health and safety professionals primarily as allies of management, due to their employment or contractual arrangements with company managers. Levenstein and Tuminaro note that even those who are positioned independently of industrial employers, for instance, health care personnel, generally lack the training in occupational health and safety that would help them better understand workers' perspectives when it comes to health and safety. However, the story of the WETP demonstrates that health and safety and related professionals may also ally with and be located in labor and government. The WETP has allied workers and unions with more progressive industrial hygienists in an effort to give workers training that helps them understand the limits of health and safety protection. The WETP's emphasis on developing model training programs has helped to establish the social infrastructure necessary to change traditional ideas and practices.

In fact, the success of labor's initiative and its implementation as an OSHA standard and the WETP rests largely on the helpful integration of labor and professionals. Many professionals were situated as union staff, consultants to labor unions, or in government. Others were located at academic and scientific or medical institutions, law firms, or health and safety advocacy organizations. Many were or had been "middle-class activists" in the labor, health and safety, public health, environmental, and civil rights movements.[2] The WETP attracted education professionals, including proponents of popular education and researchers. Some union staff professionals were former workers who had attained higher education.

Professionals in the AFL-CIO Safety and Health Department and the IUD, in their pursuit of protective standards for workers, acted on the industrial hygiene and regulatory principles that had molded the federation's health and safety activities for a decade. Thus, language in RCRA and CERCLA mandated action by the EPA, OSHA, and NIOSH that could lead to directives for the application of existing standards or the development of new ones for new industrial operations. Despite the frustration over Reagan's obstruction of prior Congressional worker protection mandates, a plan to achieve a new Congressional mandate for OSHA to promulgate a standard was devised. During the hearings, professionals working with national unions (and some from government agencies) delivered strong supportive testimony. Professionals from public interest organizations also testified.

Professionals played central roles in each WETP effort and at NIEHS. As the L-AGC prepared to submit a proposal for a grant-funded Superfund program, it was urged to adopt a strategy that industrial unions had used for worker training about chemicals. The unions had established alliances with scientists and professionals who were willing and able to present technical information in ways that were comprehensible to workers. The unions relied on experts to develop education, industrial hygiene, and medical surveillance. The L-AGC incorporated and expanded on the plans, developing a network of "master trainers" and an expert and active advisory board. LIUNA adopted a similar approach in its Health and Safety Fund activities, recruiting leading scientists, industrial hygienists and engineers, and health and medical professionals to shape comprehensive worker health initiatives for the construction industry.

OCAW was the industrial union leading the labor movement in these areas during the 1970s. The union had allied with scientists and professionals in a key labor struggle against Shell Oil. It pursued innovative legal approaches to defend workers' rights to know about chemical hazards in the workplace. By 1979, OCAW had developed an active network of medical professionals who worked with local unions in each of the union's national regions. Intraunion political struggles no doubt played a major role in OCAW's abandonment of several key health and safety efforts. By the time NIEHS issued its request for applications for the WETP, OCAW was not as strongly associated with its former network of professionals.

But the union renewed its former strategic model in developing its training program. Instead of relying on scientists and health and safety professionals, this time OCAW recruited labor education experts (the Labor Institute). It pursued a training model whose goal was to create expertise in a network of union members. The assistance of scientists and medical and health and safety professionals was requested when specific expertise was needed, but except for a select group, no network was reestablished. As a consequence, according to some key informants at the time of the present author's research (the late 1990s), the union found itself somewhat removed from any strong network of health and safety professionals.

A near-midnight decision by legislators to transfer the WETP away from NIOSH and reestablish it under the umbrella of NIEHS, a biomedical research institute, made the institute the federal agency directing the most substantial worker training program of the time. A small group of public health scientists and professionals committed to both supporting the interests of labor unions and developing effective health and safety education interventions conducted a participatory planning process for the program.

The professionals applied a comprehensive process to the task of creating a program. A needs assessment was conducted to determine the degree of competency that had been established in the union and university programs over the previous decade, particularly through OSHA's New Directions. They reviewed the worker health and safety education literature to gain a more thorough understanding of the issues related to effective training. They also engaged in an assessment of New Directions to determine how to expand on its successes and avoid its failures, the primary failure being its inability to create an effective activist constituency for OSHA. They used the NIH process for the scientific peer review of grant proposals, and purposefully selected reviewers who were knowledgeable about worker health and safety education and supportive of the goals of labor and the health and safety movement. Their application of professional principles and methods was expansive and inclusive, respecting the interests and approaches of the unions as well as the integrity of health and safety activists.

NIEHS initially funded five union programs, five university consortia, and a public-sector employer. In this way, it supported a network of professionals and activists. The choices broadened the constituent base of the program. Although it has meant that unions have received a smaller percentage of the total funds than they expected, at key times the broader constituency has helped to win continued Congressional support for the program. The NIEHS administrators have also been receptive to unions representing industrial sectors other than construction, oil, chemicals, and firefighting. The professionals interpreted the "intent of the Congress" to have been that all workers engaged in a hazardous waste operation or emergency response to HAZMAT incidents should be covered by programs and standards set up pursuant to Section 126 of SARA. As a consequence, training program grants have been awarded to organizations that train workers in the transportation, service, public, heavy and light manufacturing, and paper and pulp processing sectors. In addition, training funds are used for a fairly broad range of workers with HAZMAT ER responsibilities in both the private and public sectors.

Given the limited financial resources available for unions that represent workers facing potential hazardous waste exposures, the AFL-CIO Safety and Health Department would have been in a politically awkward position if it had been responsible for the funding allocations. Ceding this responsibility to professionals in the government was a politically safer and a necessary option. In fact, the department largely removed itself from involvement in the WETP. Perhaps at a point when labor's relative power expands or if health and safety issues come to be viewed as potentially strong bases for organizing, the AFL-CIO and Change to Win may well be willing and able to coordinate and provide stronger leadership to the national health and safety movement. In the meantime, in 2007, neither had a health and safety department and both left health and safety to their affiliated unions. Professionals allied with labor provided health and safety leadership from within those unions, academic institutions, labor-based centers, and the government.

The professionals involved in this work environment intervention have played significant roles. Their flexibility in the intervention systems makes it difficult to identify their specific roles as actors. For example, a person who appears as a labor actor is actually a lawyer, and an industrial hygienist functions as a government bureaucrat. Some professionals have allied themselves with unions in different industrial sectors. Others have been located within both government and labor. Figure 1 shows some of the broad categories of professionals involved with the WETP.

Scientists	Lawyers	Administrators
Industrial hygienists	Engineers	Economists
Health and safety professionals and educators	Medical professionals	Labor educators
	Lobbyists	

Figure 1. Types of professionals involved with the WETP

THE STATE

The hazardous waste worker health and safety policy initiative has had two basic implementation points, each located in the state: (1) OSHA has promulgated a regulation mandating employers to provide specific training to workers who are or may be exposed to hazardous waste materials in a range of operations; (2) the Superfund has supported an NIEHS training grant program that funds a network of organizations for the development and delivery of the mandated training. SARA established both elements.

The focus of the present author's research has been on the training program, limiting the study of its interface with the regulatory functions of OSHA to those aspects that demonstrated relatively cohesive action by the network of awardees in using rulemaking hearings as an arena of conflict over adequate regulation. Central to the policy initiative and the strategies that resulted in the WETP was the mandate that OSHA require health and safety training. There were specific requirements about content, number of hours, and provision of training to employees before they were permitted to do the work. OSHA's mandate for employers was that training be delivered to employees and that workers receive wages for the time they spend in training.[3] Such rules were critical for the successful implementation of the training requirements. Figure 2 shows the role of the state with regard to establishing the WETP.

Securing government funding was essential for the success of the WETP. Considering the reduction in OSHA New Directions funding to labor and allied institutions by the Reagan administration, it is difficult to imagine that labor could have achieved funding for the worker training program through general funds during that period. Levenstein and Tuminaro have duly noted that "[d]uring periods when the underlying political-economic climate is concerned with fiscal austerity, cost-effectiveness and deregulation, erosion of . . . gains can and does occur" (1991, p. 30). Labor's training program strategy depended on the success of the environmental movement in securing substantial increases in the Superfund tax. Congress could easily agree to a request for an appropriation of less than 1% of a fund that was separate from the general revenues.

The state serves as an arena for class conflicts. The government is not monolithic and has various points from which conflicts can be mediated.

Labor's Dual Strategy

Legislation	**Regulations**
SARA 126 (worker protection provisions, including training program); and separately, 110 (funding); and 119 (contractor liability)	29 CFR 1910.120: mandates employers to provide specific training (hours and content) 40 CFR Part 311: for public-sector workers

Executive Branch

Reagan administration seeks regulatory relief for industry: wide discrepancy between this and the public's desire for vigorous environmental protection (Florio, 1986). It underestimates strength of environmental movement's demands for hazardous waste remediation and management.

Legislature

Elected representatives responding to various constituencies: must use the "mystification of policy" to appear pro-environmental while still supporting corporate funders.

Political parties: Democrats control House and use environmental issues as political wedge against the Republicans who control the presidency and the Senate. Moderate Republican senators, with concerns for protecting the environment and workers, oppose Reagan and conservatives in party. Republicans in House, facing a midterm election, are concerned about Republican party losses due to appearance of being against environmental protection.

Congressional Staff: can act independently and shape policy and compromises.

Congress becomes "reluctant regulator" in absence of strong regulatory means to manage the hazardous waste crisis (Barnett, 1994; Florio, 1986; Wooding, 1990).

Regulatory Agencies

Unelected bureaucrats: primary responsibility is to the constituency of the executive branch, in this case, industry rather than workers/unions and environmentalists.

Nonregulatory Agencies

NIEHS: health research institute: has broad constituency and relatively stable budget; uses NIH peer review process.

NIOSH: faces industry opposition; has middle-class, professional orientation; does not see workers as core constituency.

State and Local Governments

As employers, they resist health and safety protections for public sector workers. Congress is aware that state and local governments will demand federal funding to support the mandate.

Figure 2. The state.

Many conflicts between labor and management that are mediated by the state occur in the regulatory arena. The WETP was established in the legislative arena—by Congress. Whereas regulatory bureaucrats serve the function of shielding politicians, legislative struggles place politicians in the awkward position of having to commit to their various constituencies. Their constituents include the powerful interests of the corporate class as well as the vast voting public from the working and middle classes. The timing of legislative struggles with regard to elections is critical.

Congress failed to pass SARA in 1985, leaving the bill to be shaped and voted on during a crucial election in the midterm period of a popular Republican president. The Senate had come under the control of the Republicans in 1980 but was likely to be returned to the Democrats in 1986. The House remained under strong Democratic control, and the Republicans wanted at least to retain the seats they held. The Reagan administration's mismanagement of the Superfund program resulted in a political scandal. The public wanted stronger environmental protection and was concerned about the possibility that a Bhopal-type disaster could occur in the United States, especially following a similar chemical release at a Union Carbide facility in Institute, West Virginia.

The Democrats were generally willing to expand the provisions of the Superfund law to demonstrate their commitment to public health and the environment. Many Republicans, particularly in the Senate, wished to demonstrate to the public that their party was not opposed to environmental protection.

Even in this setting, though, Republicans objected to the hazardous waste worker health and safety initiative. The administration was committed to an anti-regulatory agenda and declared that additional regulatory measures were unwarranted. This stance was probably ideological and not taken at the behest of a specific industrial constituency, since in this case, the regulated industry was not opposing the initiative. Several Republicans allied with the administration raised two substantive issues. Both were related to the perception that labor was attempting to amend the OSH Act.

The Republicans in question opposed legislation mandating OSHA rulemaking and insisted that regulations be developed through the mechanisms of Section 6 of the OSH Act. They also opposed the extension of OSHA protection to public workers by amending the OSH Act through an environmental law. The administration and its House and Senate supporters were rightly wary of labor's use of legislative amendments to subvert the regulatory constraints imposed by the administration.

The compromise over the protection of public-sector workers demonstrated what Barnett has referred to as the manipulation of public perceptions "through the mystification of policy" (Barnett, 1994, p. 47). Senator Hatch, who raised the above-mentioned issues in the Senate, was concerned to ensure that labor did not establish a mechanism for amending the OSH Act. Anecdotal evidence indicates that he was at least sympathetic to the health and safety concerns of the IAFF, though he clearly stated his opposition to OSHA coverage of the public sector.[4] The House-Senate conference committee compromise requiring the EPA to adopt OSHA's final HAZWOPER rule demonstrated commitment to the IAFF but preserved the stance against broad public-sector worker health and safety protection.

If the EPA enforced the rule, the policy precedent would not exceed a specific set of justifiable protections, and it could be argued that these provisions were warranted as a component of measures to protect public and private property from major environmental hazards.[5]

The members of the Congressional staff have received little attention in the health and safety literature. They are often professionals whose employment depends on the reelection of the congressperson for whom they work. Therefore, they are likely to espouse political expediency. Yet, those directly involved in the efforts to pass SARA's worker protection provisions acted as middle-class activists and social reformers. Some were committed environmentalists, health and safety activists, or supporters of labor. Obviously, the political makeup of the staff depends on the affiliation and orientation of the members of Congress. Still, in this story, key staff members acted independently in the interest of workers' health and safety.

The House Committee on Government Operations staff members, with the support of their respective representatives, independently organized OSHA oversight hearings. They were the ones who decided to conduct the hearings on hazardous waste worker protection. They provided critical independent support for labor's initiative, which resulted in a bipartisan report criticizing OSHA's failure to protect waste workers.

Finally, the role played by NIEHS needs to be considered. Several key informants, from labor, academia, and government, stated their doubt that NIOSH, the agency originally targeted to run the program, would have been as effective as NIEHS in promoting a training program that would establish models of excellence. They believed that the NIOSH staff were probably too rigidly constrained by their professional and/or scientific ethics, and likely would have had difficulty supporting labor's pursuit of worker health and safety education interventions. What permitted NIEHS to act differently? Why wasn't it constrained as NIOSH was?

NIOSH had critical institutional constraints. It was established pursuant to the OSH Act, a construct of health and safety strategies for state intervention on behalf of workers' need to identify the hazards and risks in the work environment and the ways to control and prevent them. NIOSH was mandated as a means to counter the control that the corporations held over industrial hygiene and toxicology from the 1920s through the late 1960s. As such, industry tended to view the agency antagonistically. NIOSH is constrained in its support of workers' and unions' needs by measures that encourage the agency to give greater consideration to industry concerns, for example, by executive branch or Congressional dictates limiting the agency's research scope and funding. Additionally, NIOSH provides funding to train occupational health and safety professionals and carry out occupational health research at academic institutions. Consequently, its core constituency is a network of public and occupational health programs, academic and medical, which tend to be of marginal importance in their institutions and politically weak.

NIEHS, on the other hand, is a biomedical research institute serving as a component of NIH, which supports the medical-industrial complex. NIH institutes often conduct research that serves the broader needs of key health-related industrial sectors, such as hospitals and medical research centers and the pharmaceutical industry, as well as the finance sector. Some institutes, such as NIEHS, may do research that could threaten industrial sectors with a direct causal relationship to a major health problem, such as the tobacco industry and its relationship to lung cancer. Most, though, reinforce the reliance on the scientific, technological, and ideological dominance of industry over health care in the United States. Although NIEHS can be a threat to some industrial sectors (the chemical industry particularly), NIH is generally supported by a broad constituency stretching across social and industrial sectors, making it an unlikely target for budget reductions, though specific institutes might be targeted.[6]

NIEHS's management of the WETP demonstrated the capacity for, and impact of, autonomous action by bureaucrats. The agency lacked experience in addressing either health and safety or worker health education and training issues; therefore, a new division was established to run the program. This permitted the development of fresh approaches. The institute's director was receptive to supporting the goals of labor. To run the program, he appointed an individual who was grounded in the scientific practice of occupational health and safety and who maintained a strong public health ethic. Together, the two worked closely with labor to shape the program. They also recruited a staff member who was strongly grounded in occupational health and safety, with firm ties to the health and safety movement, and who was an experienced bureaucrat familiar with NIOSH, OSHA, and the EPA. Working with a creative and supportive grants manager, they applied administrative procedures with the intention of strengthening the health and safety movement, providing high-quality health and safety training for workers in a range of industries, and establishing models for effective educational interventions.

The last-minute unilateral decision to locate the WETP at NIEHS may have been the single strongest factor in shaping its direction. The decision was not arbitrary; in the view of Sheldon Samuels, Rall respected labor's intentions. The agency's location in NIH probably constituted the political and bureaucratic basis for sustaining program autonomy. A key factor is the NIH tradition of providing long-standing grants to its awardees, often establishing research centers. The decision by Rall and Dement to award grants with the intention of maintaining awardees in the program over the long term, rather than establishing time limits as the OSHA New Directions program had done, was easily supported in the NIEHS environment.

The relationship of OSHA and the EPA to their labor and environmental constituencies changed significantly between the time of the Carter administration and the time of the Reagan administration. The Reaganites underestimated the public's concerns about environmental protection and the threats to the public health posed by hazardous wastes. The hazardous waste crisis was not as easily managed by the state as some other crises had been. Barnett has noted that "Confronted with a 'wide discrepancy between the public's desire for vigorous environmental protection and the Reagan administration's ideological preferences for regulatory relief' Congress was forced, in the words of James Florio, to become a 'reluctant regulator'" (Barnett, 1994, p. 232).

SOCIAL MOVEMENTS

Discussion of the role of social movements, aside from that of the labor movement, in the political economy of the work environment has been limited. Yet the work environment in the U.S. setting directly reflects the impact of social movements on working conditions. The OSH Act and most major federal environmental laws passed during the 1970s resulted from coalitions of the labor, environmental, public health, and public interest and consumer rights movements. Elements of the civil rights movement were also involved in some efforts, and the civil rights movement in general moved public opinion to more strongly support the rights of workers. Despite the institutional, ideological, and organizational barriers to the coalescence of these separate movements into a united progressive front, they were able at least to unite around a set of legislative strategies. Following the passage of the OSH Act, a labor-environment network was gradually established. One of that network's last major efforts was the successful inclusion of the emergency planning and community right-to-know provisions in SARA.

Labor's pursuit of health and safety protections for hazardous waste workers and emergency responders advanced on the coattails of the environmental movement. The hazardous waste management industry was created in direct response to environmental movement demands. Each stage of the initiative took advantage of legislation fought for by the environmental movement. Labor, however, faced (and still faces) a major contradiction that inhibited united action with the environmental movement. The contradiction stems from the role of workers in producing the products that are the basis for environmental degradation.

Too often, the demands of the environmental movement are framed in a way that results, unintentionally, in job losses for workers in polluting industries. In efforts to prevent unity between the labor and environmental movements, industry and government often frame environmental issues in terms of "jobs versus the environment." Some environmental issues provided opportunities for jobs through environmental remediation and hazard abatement. The environmental movement, in conjunction with the health and safety movement, pushed the development of state-forced measures to abate the health risks posed by hazardous materials, such as asbestos, lead, and hazardous waste. The building trades unions have taken the lead in many such strategies. The Laborers and the Carpenters have pursued environmental jobs strategies with environmental justice organizations as ways to address the hazardous waste remediation and urban development needs of minority communities in depressed urban areas. The affected areas have been identified as "brownfields."

The segment of the environmental justice movement that was particularly active on brownfield issues won a Congressional appropriation for NIEHS to provide grants for minority worker training programs. The programs aimed to help young adults develop the skills needed to acquire either environmental technician or remediation jobs at brownfield sites.

The environmental justice movement emerged from the civil rights movement in general and the anti-toxics wing of the environmental movement (which evolved from the hazardous waste movement) and the labor, public health, and civil rights movements.[7] Its development is strongly related to the efforts of the hazardous waste management industry to establish facilities. Szasz (1994, p. 106) has discussed the decisions by the industry to site facilities in those communities "least able to resist," which were usually poor, either rural or urban, communities of color. In response, the EPA established the National Environmental Justice Advisory Council (NEJAC).

The WETP exists because of labor's ability to perceive the need for worker protection strategies related to the state's responses to environmental movement demands. The state's responses held the potential for the creation of large numbers of new construction jobs. At the same time, industry responses to the same demands attempted to alienate workers and their unions from the environmental movement by threatening industry dislocation and relocation with resultant job loss and community disinvestment. The efforts of LIUNA, OCAW, and the WETP itself to develop coalitions with environmentalists demonstrate the potential for labor and other movements to promote policies that may lead to a more sustainable future.

The relative power of either labor or environmentalists (or other social movements) in broader class struggles bears directly on their ability to sustain their mutual successes. The power of both labor and environmentalists may be temporarily affected should either succumb to requests for collaboration by industrial or corporate powers. Short-sighted goals, which may even seem to be based on a moral imperative—such as legislative victories or the elimination of a harmful product (such as cigarettes)—can have the long-term impact of creating intermovement conflict and antagonism, weakening relative power. Chemical-related work environment issues will always interface with issues confronting movements addressing environmental, public health, and public interest and safety concerns. The interfaces require investigation in order to achieve a full understanding of the historical relevance of movements as actors in the political economy of the work environment.

THE POLITICAL ECONOMY OF REGULATION

The strength and limitations of the factors that led to the passage and implementation of the WETP are made even more clear by the process by which OSHA developed its standards for HAZWOPER work. In doing their jobs, regulators must consider how new rules affect industry, which means, Levenstein and Tuminaro argue (1991, p. 32), that "the fundamental rule of profit-making will be protected."

The hazardous waste management industry was created as part of a regulatory strategy to address the externalization of environmental protection by other industries. In this economic setting, the costs of regulated hazardous waste management practices can be passed on to those purchasing the industry's services. Data provide evidence of environmental-sector employers urging extensive training requirements, even after noting their high cost per worker. It was the regulatory agencies, OSHA and the EPA, that recommended against strict legislative requirements for worker training. Why then, with no hazardous waste management industry opposition, was labor unable to achieve more stringent training requirements through the OSHA rulemaking process?

Hazardous wastes, hazardous waste operations, and HAZMAT incident ER are endemic in a range of industries. The hazardous waste management industry was not the only industry that would be affected by the regulation. It may also be that waste generators were interested in minimizing their costs for hazardous waste management, even while the management industry may have been willing to have OSHA mandate practices with costs that could be passed on to its clients. The environmental consulting sector of the hazardous waste management industry was the one sector that objected to some requirements. It might not have been able to pass along training costs as easily as could the treatment, storage, and disposal facilities and the remediation sector. On the other hand, the relatively few remediation contractors in existence had already given training to their workers, much of it through the EPA's program. If new contractors entered the industry, the training requirements would serve as a leveler in bidding competitions.

During the rulemaking hearings, the oil and petrochemical industries raised a number of concerns. Unrelated to training, but significant in demonstrating how the regulations affected industries other than hazardous waste management, was their opposition to OSHA's proposal to include petroleum and petroleum products in its definition of hazardous substances. Repeatedly, the oil industry had successfully persuaded Congress and the EPA to exclude petroleum and petroleum products from hazardous waste categorizations. OSHA believed that SARA's Section 126 called for protecting workers from all hazardous waste spills. "Petroleum products create significant health and safety hazards. . . . Spills [that] involve petroleum products . . . present both health and safety risks" (54 Federal Register, 1989, p. 9302).

The forces of industry won victories in a number of critical areas connected with the specification of which workers would or would not be protected. OSHA originally proposed to cover actions at all hazardous waste sites, including voluntary clean-up operations. But OSHA had not been given the "statutory responsibility to identify hazardous wastes sites" (54 Federal Register, 1989, p. 9296) and was forced to exclude the protection of workers at clean-up sites that had not been designated as hazardous waste sites by some government body. Since 94% of hazardous wastes had been managed on-site by industry, this provision could exclude a substantial number of workers if voluntary clean-up actions were undertaken.

OSHA also decided that small-quantity hazardous waste generators would not be covered, as long as they relied on external ER services rather than requiring ER to be taken by their own employees. OSHA noted that the types of facilities that would be excluded from coverage were small businesses such as gas stations and dry cleaners. It argued that these types of facilities "do not present the relatively high exposure to a number of hazardous health risks to employees that hazardous waste sites typically do" (54 Federal Register, 1989, p. 9299). It was a remarkable comment, since benzene and perchlorethylene, substances likely to spill at gas stations and dry cleaning businesses respectively, are carcinogens. OSHA's history is full of strong opposition from associations of small businesses. OSHA does not report opposition from them, but likely made this exclusion to avoid such opposition.

OSHA yielded to an industry argument for a reduction in training hour requirements that labor opposed. Industry argued for fewer than 40 hours of training for hazardous waste site workers who would visit sites only occasionally and would not be exposed to hazardous substances above the permissible levels. Unions in several industrial sectors vigorously opposed this decision. OSHA not only failed to include their opposing statements in its record but also failed to include a request from the L-AGC for a specific statement that laborers who would be engaged in hazardous waste site remediation should receive 80 hours of training, as opposed to the minimum 40 hours.

OSHA also hedged on requiring protection for all workers who would be exposed to hazardous waste materials during HAZMAT incident ER actions. OSHA cited the broad definition of ER workers in Section 126 (d)(4) of SARA, and also asserted its belief that Title III of the act indicated Congress's intention "that any employees participating in an ER to the release or potential for release of a hazardous substance be covered by this rulemaking." Following a lengthy justification of its argument, OSHA provided the following qualification: "only employers whose employees have the reasonable possibility of engaging in ER are covered" (54 Federal Register, 1989, p. 9298). This led to the aforementioned exemption for small-quantity generators. Many workers in industry are assigned a "collateral duty" to respond to HAZMAT incident emergencies on the job. OSHA's limitations on its ER provisions exclude these workers from protection and free employers from the cost of training and protective measures.

The final training issue on which OSHA bowed to employers' demands concerned the certification of workers, trainers, and training programs. While noting that SARA had recently been amended, with a mandate to OSHA to develop a certification system, OSHA declined to address certification issues in CFR 1910.120, stating that it would issue a new rule pursuant to the amendment. OSHA later issued a proposed rule, which produced strong resistance from industry and led to the proposal of a set of minimum criteria by NIEHS and its awardees that OSHA realized would cause conflict with industry. In the following decade, OSHA never promulgated the rule.

Labor's power relative to industry's was sufficient to achieve the most stringent training requirements issued by the agency up to that time. It was able to sustain OSHA's support for relatively broad coverage of ER workers. Labor lost on two critical issues, though: the length of the training requirement for some hazardous waste workers and strong training program certification provisions. The certification issue has had the consequence of weakening OSHA's ability to enforce the standard in the way that labor had intended. It forced labor and its allied WETP professionals to promote nonregulatory strategies such as the use of the Minimum Criteria Document as a model for employer consideration. The document was intended for use as an aspect of a regulated strategy—that is, inclusion in an OSHA training certification rule. OSHA only later included portions of a subsequent document as a nonmandatory appendix to 29 CFR.1910.120 (59 Federal Register, 1994b).

Telling evidence on the political economy of regulation, directly related to training, is found in the 1994 preamble to OSHA's final rule for Personal Protective Equipment for General Industry (29 CFR 1910.132, for which see 59 Federal Register, 1994a). In 1994, the National Solid Waste Management Association, which included hazardous waste management employers among its members, opposed the promulgation by OSHA of training provisions similar to those in the HAZWOPER standard. Instead, it urged that OSHA "consider a training requirement more closely aligned with the concepts of its Hazard Communication Standard" (59 Federal Register, 1994, p. 16334). That standard established neither minimum durations of training time nor certification requirements for workers, trainers, or the program. By 1994, the industry that had emerged in the early 1980s as a result of regulations had undergone changes that led it to oppose its own further regulation.

The rulemaking process has evolved as a central arena for "conflict and compromise between economic and political actors" (Levenstein & Tuminaro, 1991, p. 32). The hazardous waste worker health and safety policy initiative demonstrated that conflict and compromise occur between and among class actors and regulators. Labor's achievement of a legislative victory was tempered in the regulatory process, during both the rulemaking and the enforcement stages. The regulatory agency and process were used to minimize the impact of a counterhegemonic strategy. But they were not capable of neutralizing that strategy's impact.

CONCLUSION

The Reagan administration steadily pushed back on prior legal mandates and regulations to protect workers' health and safety and the environment. The environmental movement focused public concerns about hazardous waste to push Congress for a strengthened Superfund law. In the midst of that effort, labor worked to gain a specific set of workplace protections for HAZWOPER workers. The distraction of key industries fighting the main SARA provisions, combined with lack of concern about worker protection regulations by an industry sector reliant on regulation for profitability, created the opening for labor's success.

Political decisions are rooted in the economy, and in existing U.S. capitalism, worker health and safety, as well as environmental protection, are contested areas where human rights considerations must be fought for against ruling-class economic interests. Exploring the roles of unions, industrial managers and owners, health and other related professionals, the state's governance system, and social movements provides a window through which we can see the political economy of occupational safety and health regulation.

The history of the legislative effort and the first 5 years of program implementation reveals a worker protection initiative that straddles the end of the era of liberal reforms and the entrenchment of an era of market fundamentalism. Congress mandated the executive branch's regulatory agencies to implement the regulations, even establishing the specific elements to be included in them. The antiregulatory drive of the new era produced stonewalling that reduced the regulations' scope from what labor had wanted, and reduced enforcement to less than what was needed for optimal worker protection.

These are the political and economic contexts within which an extremely effective worker health and safety training program was established and shaped. A combination of commitment and willingness to collaborate by specific labor unions and public health professionals allied with progressive social movements—especially the health and safety movement—and politically astute government agency leadership has forged two decades of progress within the limits of the law on hazardous waste cleanup and hazardous materials emergency preparedness and response.

ENDNOTES

1. The corporate and financial sectors, as well as the huge number of smaller employers, are certainly not a monolithic force in U.S. capitalism. Many divisions exist, both within and between industry sectors. Nonetheless, they can be spoken of as an employing class with interests generally distinct from those of the laboring classes.
2. See Wooding (1994) for a discussion of the position of health and safety activists as links to labor in the new left, which was not as closely aligned with labor as the old left.
3. In less than a decade after the promulgation of the final HAZWOPER rule, employers, particularly in the environmental consulting sector, were posting help-wanted ads in newspapers stating that preference in hiring would be given to those applicants who already possessed a certificate stating that they had undergone the required health and safety training. Although employers in this sector may not oppose environmental and health and safety regulations, since these are the basis for their work, they are still inclined to externalize their costs for regulatory mandates.
4. Both Curtis Moore and Richard Duffy vaguely recollected some negotiation between Hatch's staff and the IAFF about health and safety protections for ER activities. But neither could remember the content of the negotiations.
5. The EPA has never officially acknowledged its authority to enforce its HAZWOPER standard (40 CFR Part 311). The agency makes it clear that public sector employers must comply with the standard, but various explanations of its lack of authority include the fact that SARA did not authorize EPA enforcement of a worker health and safety provision. (Web access to the regulation at: http://www.access.gpr.gov/nara/cfr/waisidx_03/40cfr311_03.html)
6. During the two terms of the George W. Bush administration, with a Republican majority in Congress, the NIH budgets were reduced as the emphasis was shifted to tax cuts for the wealthy and funding was shifted to supporting U.S. military operations in Iraq and Afghanistan.
7. The environmental justice movement represents a convergence of the labor, environmental, public health, and civil rights movements. As early as 1976, a conference, titled "Working for Environmental and Economic Justice and Jobs," was hosted by Environmentalists for Full Employment, the UAW, the Urban Environment Conference, and more than 100 other organizations. For further discussions of the environmental justice movement, see the following: Dowie (1997); Freudenberg (1984); Gottlieb (1993); Kazis and Grossman (1991); and Szasz (1994). For discussions of the disproportionate exposure to and impacts from hazardous waste sites suffered by non-white U.S. communities, see Bullard (2000); and Commission for Racial Justice (1987).

REFERENCES

54 Federal Register. (1989). U.S. DOL, Occupational Safety and Health Administration: "Hazardous Waste Operations and Emergency Response; Final Rule." *29 CFR 1910.120, preamble to final rule* (Vol. 54, pp. 9294-9336): Government Printing Office.

59 Federal Register. (1994a). U.S. DOL, Occupational Safety and Health Administration. Final Rule, Personal Protective Equipment for General Industry. *29 CFR 1910.132* (Vol. 59, p. 16334): Government Printing Office, from http://frwebgate4.access.gpo.gov/cgi-bin/waisgate.cgi?WAISdocID=185403455079+8+0+0&WAISaction=retrieve

59 Federal Register. (1994b). Hazardous Waste Operations and Emergency Response; Final Rule, Technical amendments to existing Appendix B, and a new non-mandatory Appendix E to both 29 CFR 1910.120 and 29 CFR 1926.65. In U. S. DOL (Ed.), *Occupational Safety and Health Administration* (Vol. 59, pp. 43268-43281). Washington, D.C.: Government Printing Office, from http://frwebgate4.access.gpo.gov/cgi-bin/waisgate.cgi?WAISdocID=185403455079+12+0+0&WAISaction=retrieve.

Barnett, H. C. (1994). *Toxic Debts and the Superfund Dilemma.* Chapel Hill: University of North Carolina Press.

Bullard, R. D. (2000). *Dumping in Dixie: Race, Class, and Environmental Quality* (3rd ed.). Boulder, CO: Westview Press.

Commission for Racial Justice. (1987). *Toxic Wastes and Race in the United States: A National Report on the Racial and Socioeconomic Characteristics of Communities With Hazardous Waste Sites.* New York: United Church of Christ.

Dowie, M. (1997). *Losing Ground: American Environmentalism at the Close of the Twentieth Century.* Cambridge, MA: MIT Press.

Florio, J. J. (1986). Congress as Reluctant Regulator: Hazardous Waste Policy in the 1980s. *Yale Journal of Regulation, 3*, 351-382.

Freudenberg, N. (1984). *Not in Our Backyards! Community Action for Health and the Environment.* New York: Monthly Review Press.

Gottlieb, R. (1993). *Forcing the Spring*. Washington, DC: Island Press.

ICEM. (1996). *ICEM World Conference on the Environmental Services Industries: Report. October 16-18.* Brussels, Belgium: Author.

Kazis, R., & Grossman, R. L. (1991). *Fear at Work: Job Blackmail, Labor and the Environment* (New ed.). Santa Cruz, CA: New Society Publishers.

Levenstein, C., & Tuminaro, D. J. (1991). The Political Economy of Occupational Disease. *New Solutions, A Journal of Environmental and Occupational Health Policy, 2*(1), 25-34.

Mallino, D., Sr. (1997). Interview by author, tape recording, Washington, DC (December 10).

Merrill, M. (1991). An Overview of the OCAW/Labor Institute Worker-to-Worker Training Program in Hazard Communication, Hazardous Waste Operations, and Emergency Response, Appendix A of OCAW proposal in response to NIEHS RFA ES-92-1, Worker Health and Safety Training Cooperative Agreement, January 23, 1992 (1991/9). NIEHS files, RTP, NC.

Szasz, A. (1994). *EcoPopulism: Toxic Waste and the Movement for Environmental Justice.* Minneapolis: University of Minnesota Press.

Wells, J. C., Kochan, T. A., & Smith, M. (1991). *Managing Workplace Safety and Health: The Case of Contract Labor in the U.S. Petrochemical Industry.* Beaumont, TX: John Gray Institute, Lamar University System.

Wooding, J. (1990). *Dire States: Workplace Health and Safety Regulations in the Reagan/Thatcher Era.* Dissertation. University Microfilms International Dissertation Services, Ann Arbor, MI. 366 pages; AAT 9017977.

Wooding, J. (1994). *Labor and the Legacy of the New Left: The Impact on the Conditions of Work.* Paper presented at the annual meeting of the American Political Science Association, New York.

Wooding, J., & Levenstein, C. (1999). *The Point of Production.* New York: Guilford.

Firefighters Responding to the Destruction of the World Trade Center, September 2001.
Reprinted with permission www.earldotter.com

CHAPTER 9

The WETP: Protecting Workers, but the Ground Remains Poisoned

This story is framed by the abundance of toxic and hazardous chemicals in the work environment and the inability to systematically prevent environmental degradation and the public health consequences that result from exposures to hazardous industrial chemical wastes. It is a story of the consequences of production and consumption technologies that are developed and implemented with more regard for economic than for environmental and public health considerations.

The expansive use of chemicals in production, the mid-20th century transition from a biophysical economy to a chemical economy, introduced new production processes and methods that greatly changed the nature and levels of production throughout industry. Chemical inputs could enhance automation and reduce labor costs by limiting the need for skilled workers and facilitating automation-related employment reductions. Throughout industry, the chemical revolution transformed production and work. It also produced massive volumes of hazardous waste.

The health and safety strategies of the labor and health and safety movements from the late 1960s through the 1970s were related in large part to these chemical technologies and their increasing introduction through most industrial sectors. The widespread use of hazardous chemicals, with concern for their toxicity, potential for explosions and fire, and other dangerous properties, led to a regulatory system that established exposure limits, monitoring requirements, and other measures for controlling worker exposure. The approach evolved from the social contract of the post–World War II era, in which decision making about the organization and technologies of production was handed to its owners in exchange for some level of acceptance of unions as negotiators of wages, hours, and working conditions (at least for a percentage of the workforce). That is, the mode of production was not up for negotiation. This tacit agreement was in place for the Cold War economy that put the creation of weapons of mass destruction ahead of affordable housing, national health care, and free higher education for all. It was in place for the building of highways instead of mass transit systems, and for the making of automobiles that relied on pollutant fuels. And for workers employed in industries that relied on intensive toxic and hazardous materials use, any discussion that challenged the decision-making prerogatives of these industries brought fear of economic insecurity. Congressman Al Gore asked USWA Local 12256 President Dennis Virtuoso how he would "balance the . . . conflict between jobs and cleaning up the environment"; Mr. Virtuoso, at least, had the courage to question toxic chemical-based production when he replied, "To me the health of myself and my family is the most important thing. No job is worth your life" (U.S. Congress. House of Representatives, 1979, p. 51).

In the 1960s, the United States acknowledged that it had an environmental pollution crisis, and by the end of the decade it was becoming clear that it included a hazardous waste crisis on the ground—the poisoned ground. A series of ameliorative laws and regulatory measures were implemented in the 1970s, followed by more expansive measures in the 1980s as the crisis grew in size. At every point, it was the public, prodded by the work of the environmental movement, that declared to the politicians that the hazardous waste crisis existed and was unacceptable. In the 1990s, the bubble economy, the entrenchment of neoliberal economic, social, and political restructuring (intensified privatization of economic activity coupled with pursuit of a deregulatory agenda) and the aftermath of decades of environmental injustices led to new strategies and demands in relation to the hazardous waste crisis. The political struggles that hampered the effectiveness of the Superfund remediation effort and its counterparts in the states, coupled with demands to clean up the environments of minority communities whose health and well-being were disproportionately harmed by brownfields, led to a shifting of hazardous waste remediation priorities. The agenda was largely driven by corporations wrestling to free themselves from the yoke of the Superfund principle that the "polluter pays," as well as by developers who thought that the booming real estate market of the 1990s demanded government subsidies to clean up and develop the mostly urban brownfield hazardous waste sites. The crisis persisted into the new millennium. In 2004, the EPA acknowledged that the crisis would continue for the foreseeable decades, but claimed that, at the moment, no new government action was needed.

Labor's approaches to addressing the health and safety of hazardous waste operations and HAZMAT incident ER workers were well crafted, provided strong lessons, and were overwhelmingly successful where applied. Very dangerous work has been made safer, with the added benefit of reducing the public health risks related to hazardous waste management, remediation, and ER activities. Where compliance was either avoided or infeasible due to inadequate resources or political will, workers remained unprotected and the risks to the public increased.

These facts were most vividly obvious in the response to terrorists' destruction of the World Trade Center towers in New York City on September 11, 2001. The initial response force was composed of a majority of workers who, at best, had been inadequately prepared to work in an enormous, chaotic, newly created hazardous waste site of unfathomable dimensions. Video footage from this stage of the event witnessed police, firefighters, public works crews, and many other workers without any equipment to protect them from exposure to the multitude of toxic substances in the environment. Few had had adequate training or proper protective equipment. Sixty-nine percent of 9,442 responders and workers at the site[1] who have since been monitored (in a study being conducted by researchers from the Mount Sinai Medical Center in New York City) reported suffering from respiratory problems, many with a persistent cough that has been nicknamed "World Trade Center cough" (Herbert et al., 2006, p. 1853).

LESSONS TO BE LEARNED

Some important lessons can be learned from this story. The labor, environmental, civil rights, citizen protection, and public health movements worked well enough in consort to organize and mobilize public demands for the corporate sector and government to accept accountability and responsibility for a range of environmental and public health crises. When it came to the hazardous waste crisis, those demands leveraged the incorporation of the "polluter pays" principle into law and a Superfund tax was established. A separate pot of money, the Superfund trust, prevented the public from being held ransom to threats of competing social support needs, at least for hazardous waste site cleanup.

Each set of victories laid the foundation for strategies to work for further achievements. The Superfund trust and CERCLA were expanded to achieve new provisions in SARA—for broad community right-to-know and emergency preparedness and prevention and for the protection of the workers who would take on the task of dealing with the hazardous waste and hazardous materials crises. Not only did the worker training strategy secure a mandate for the fund to be used for a training grant program, but it also secured a mandate for regulatory standards and enforcement—for both private- and public-sector workers.

Because regressive elements in government bureaucracies could always be commandeered to thwart progressive victories, and because one of the prizes of labor's primary health and safety protection strategies, NIOSH, had been compromised by the Reagan administration, the program was placed in a less visible agency with a friendly director. The labor strategists worked with the agency to identify and encourage the appointment of public health professionals with pro-labor and pro-worker perspectives to run the program. All parties agreed to a cooperative design, a partnership between the agency and its new constituencies, for the development and implementation of the program. A network of progressive public health professionals, trained in occupational and environmental health, used the lessons of the past to build a sustainable program based on a foundation of worker-oriented health education principles.

The professionals understood the critical need to build a cohesive program. Participatory strategies were used to bring awardees together around common interests and to achieve buy-in from other stakeholders, particularly in the federal government. They ensured that the program maintained its relevance by addressing emerging issues, such as the need to clean up DOE facilities, the environmental health and protection needs of underserved populations, and more recently the health and safety needs of workers engaged in poisoned environments created by terrorists using lethal weapons or by natural disasters.[2] The WETP revealed the value of designing worker health interventions for specific settings, by industry, community, and type of issue. But it also revealed that the interventions require guidelines and structures that can support iterative and participatory processes promoting agency and awardee interaction.

Familiar with the progressive worker health education strategies developed in the OSHA period, the members of the WETP administration shaped a program that built on the lessons of past successes as well as on more recent losses. They also sought to preserve and protect the network of pro-labor health and safety programs that had been supported by OSHA's New Directions program. Emphasizing excellence, worker-oriented training that was hands-on and participatory, and evaluation, the WETP was organized to facilitate a cohesive national network that interacted well with other stakeholders in government and industry.

In large part, the WETP's successful start-up reflected human agency in a federal bureaucracy—the ability of some individuals to take autonomous action in the face of countervailing political tendencies. But its success cannot be ascribed only to such agency. The WETP also reflected the collective commitment of an evolving health and safety movement that was closely linked with the U.S. labor movement. Even in weakened political positions, the movements ably propelled the policy initiative and guided it to implementation.

OCAW'S PROGRAM

The case study of this program focused on OCAW's health and safety training for workers in the oil and petrochemical industries, which tend to be made up of large industrial facilities that are highly automated, use continuous flow processes, and are inherently dangerous. They generate vast quantities of hazardous wastes and are regulated under RCRA with regard to their on-site hazardous waste treatment, storage, and disposal facilities. The industries have historically had combative labor-management relations, which were exacerbated by restructuring from the late 1970s to the early 1990s. OCAW's members regularly confront the reality of occupational fatalities—on average, one OCAW member is killed on the job every month. The OCAW program has also reflected the union's history of health and safety activism.

By the early 1980s, restructuring had resulted in massive job loss (much more than resulted from compliance with environmental regulations, as the industry threatened). Job loss resulted in a weakened and insecure workforce, cautious about fighting back, fearful about further job cuts. For the long-time health and safety advocates in OCAW, the WETP offered an opportunity for the development of internal organizing strategies, providing health and safety training to members, beyond the control of employers, intended to mobilize direct worker action to improve workplace conditions in resistance to employers' demands for concessions. OCAW believed that the increasing number of accidents, injuries, and fatalities was related to the continued weakening of safety systems due to restructuring and made health and safety issues central to the effort to mobilize the rank and file.

The program that OCAW established under the WETP had additional goals that required the refinement of earlier strategies. It sought to minimize the union's earlier reliance on supportive professionals and instead expand the network of worker-trainers who could help union members understand technical and legal issues. OCAW aimed to develop the capacity for production line workers to become safety systems analysts capable of challenging faults in the system and presenting improvements. The goal was to facilitate the ability of production line workers and their local unions to organize for increased workplace democracy, which would provide for their integration into operational decision making and control at their plants. The OCAW program established the incorporation of workers into production planning processes as an essential strategy for preventing workplace injuries, illnesses, and fatalities.

The Labor Institute developed curricula and delivered a model of training to the union that was an extension of the union's earlier innovative model for health and safety education. Rather than being used as trainers, professionals helped existing workers become trainers. A worker-to-worker program was developed using a small group activity method that was curriculum driven to provide a learner-centered approach. The program aspired to excellence in support of the union's members and in order to demonstrate to employers the value of union-sponsored training. Medical and health and safety professionals were recruited to support technical excellence.

OCAW established itself as a leader in the WETP. Its emphasis on excellence and evaluation helped demonstrate the value of an intervention program. It has repeatedly stressed the importance of giving a voice to workers in order to provide an understanding of the nature of the public health problems and the basis for successful interventions. The program recognized the limits of worker health education as only one aspect of industrial health and safety. It emphasized developing workers' abilities to impact the programs.

THE L-AGC'S PROGRAM

The L-AGC aimed its training program at hazardous waste operations workers. The program came about as a consequence of decisions by LIUNA and the L-AGC to organize the hazardous waste remediation industry. Entrance into the industry, however, brought the realization that construction workers would be at risk of chemical exposures as great as those of any chemical worker. Therefore, health and safety issues became key components in the plan, and the L-AGC and other similarly directed building trades unions built their strategies on those used by some industrial unions faced with significant toxic chemical exposures.

The L-AGC's strategy represented one of the most significant labor organizing efforts based on health and safety issues in the history of the labor movement. Not only were employers required to take broad worker health and safety protection measures, but the union manipulated employer divisions (union and nonunion) within the industry by developing a plan to level the environmental remediation playing field for union contractors. Central to this was establishing health and safety practices as criteria for determining the ability of contractors and workers to perform the work in a cost-effective manner and without jeopardizing public health.

Although much of the L-AGC model is appropriate for any worker who requires training for protection against HAZMAT exposures, the model has been particularly useful in the construction industry, where workers are employed from job to job, rather than working at a fixed facility. The formation of the L-AGC Education and Training Fund in the late 1960s demonstrated a degree of dependence between a union and employers for the achievement of mutual goals.

The L-AGC training program drew substantial support from professionals in health and safety, medicine, law, government affairs, and education, who had strong interests in the needs of construction workers. Knut Ringen, a former NCI researcher who became executive director of LHSFNA, has said that "the health and safety needs of building trades workers are much more severe than those of most workers" (Goodman, 1991, p. 111). Expert professionals maintained a high level of involvement in support of establishing both a strong union health and safety education program and a well-trained workforce. The professionals advocated for the development of worker knowledge and skills that empower workers to enter new areas of employment with the ability to understand their health and safety needs.

The L-AGC developed a network of instructors who, for the most part, had worked originally as construction laborers. Many of them were active in their locals. The instructors have been supported by the L-AGC fund through an evolving instructor development program, which helped some instructors become involved in curriculum development and the training of new and less experienced instructors.

The L-AGC's training addressed the conditions of the construction sector of the industry. The program incorporated a curriculum that was tailored to the learning styles and needs of laborers. The L-AGC understood that construction workers are largely kinesthetic learners—they learn by doing and through the experiences of action and touch. At least 40% of the training course was dedicated to hands-on activities. The union established elaborate mock hazardous waste sites to strengthen the hands-on training.

An initial group of "master trainers" was organized to develop the program and to teach the instructors how to deliver the training. It presented highly technical material that included chemistry, toxicology, exposure monitoring, industrial hygiene, and a host of other issues. The program developed a curriculum plus instruction and support mechanisms that enabled former construction workers to competently deliver the training. The L-AGC strongly believed that workers learn best when taught by others who have done the same work. The initial instructors mostly had histories as construction workers. Since 1998, each new group of trainers has been composed largely of workers from the environmental industry.

The L-AGC cannot dictate the health and safety procedures to be employed by contractors. Nor can it ensure that each of its member contractors maintains a high standard of labor-management cooperation and health and safety program management. Nonetheless, the commitment of contractor members of the L-AGC's board of trustees and the training program's advisory board created a forum for labor and management discussion about appropriate health and safety measures and the expanded influence of the fund. The negotiated cents-per-hour contribution to support the fund promoted the continual expansion of the training centers' activities. The contributions of the LHSFNA further strengthened the likelihood of joint labor-management measures to prevent occupational injuries and illnesses.

The L-AGC has participated actively in the national WETP. L-AGC representatives maintained steady communication with the WETP's administration at NIEHS. They listened to what the administrators needed in order to strongly support the program and told them what the L-AGC needed from the agency. The L-AGC negotiated for resources, willing to compromise but not to go unrecognized. The L-AGC protected the mandate and funding of the program. L-AGC representatives interacted with OSHA, the EPA, and other federal agencies to extend and preserve support for hazardous waste worker protections. They also gained Congressional support to strengthen the law when necessary, for example, increasing the funding and securing a degree of liability protection for the training program. These measures were necessary for the success of the L-AGC's health and safety strategies.

PROFESSIONALS ALLIED WITH LABOR

In each of the union case studies, an emphasis could be seen on providing ways for rank-and-file workers to become health and safety experts in their industry. In each program, progressive professionals allied themselves with the labor movement to help workers secure safe and healthy workplaces. Much of the literature on occupational safety and health professionals and scientists discusses their location within industry as well as their allegiance to management rather than to workers. The story of the hazardous waste worker health and safety policy initiative and its implementation as the WETP demonstrates a broad alliance between labor and professionals. The professionals involved are located in unions, universities, medicine, government, and nonprofit organizations. Many of them gained their educational experience, professional credentials, and even jobs as a result of the successful labor strategies that resulted in OSHA and NIOSH.

NIOSH grants to academic institutions since the mid-1970s have supported the training and research of many occupational health professionals and scientists. New Directions funding helped unions, colleges and universities, and nonprofit advocacy organizations such as the COSH groups to build the necessary competency to maintain health and safety programs. The programs supplied openings for activists and career avenues for college graduates. Critical to the location of these professionals were the OSHA law and the regulations made pursuant to that law. Just as the WETP strategy incorporated training requirements for employers, it also supported health and safety requirements that were essential for supplying an economic basis for the development of these professionals.

SOCIAL MOVEMENTS

The WETP represented the juncture of at least three social movements: labor, health and safety, and environmental. In its implementation, it also has become an area for convergence with a broadening popular education movement, and has included segments of the civil rights movement through integration with the environmental justice movement.

The WETP is a result of successful labor strategies designed to build on the environmental movement's victories. The environmental movement succeeded in achieving legislation that established mechanisms for expanding hazardous waste management. Both RCRA and CERCLA regulated hazardous waste management throughout the economic sectors and forced the emergence of a hazardous waste management industry. Labor sought to organize that industry and to achieve federal health and safety protection for workers in hazardous waste operations and

HAZMAT ER. The successful Superfund reauthorization effort was a victory for the environmental movement, encompassing both the mainstream elements and the more grassroots-based anti-toxics movement. Labor worked closely with environmentalists to achieve the passage of community right-to-know provisions in SARA. Labor also pursued its own initiative, relying on the environmental movement's strength of the moment, which built on its political imperative (in the aftermath of the Reagan administration Superfund scandals and the Bhopal, India, catastrophe) and its successful increasing of the Superfund tax.

The combined movement effort to pass a strong Superfund reauthorization bill was the last major successful effort by the labor-environment network. The neoliberal assault on progressive movements and their earlier gains has effectively weakened the capacity for movement collaboration at a time when collaboration is needed to mount an effective countervailing social force. The WETP exists as a holdover from past victories. Yet, labor's success in riding the coattails of an environmental victory has also been the unintended Achilles heel of the program. Tied to the Superfund, the WETP remains limited to addressing the management and remediation of hazardous wastes. It is not able to risk independent expansion to provide training that would help workers and their unions develop and mobilize around strategies for sustainable modes of production that would optimally limit, if not eliminate, the use of toxic and hazardous substances and their waste products.

The Superfund law remains as an amazing counterhegemonic victory, if for no other reason than its "polluter pays" mandate. The mandate is certainly the reason for the broad coalition of corporate forces that have been successfully lobbying Congress to limit the mandate's use. The radical tendencies in the environmental movement continue to build on the failed initiative established in the Hazardous and Solid Waste Amendments of 1984, which mandated pollution prevention as the priority goal for national environmental policy. Although pollution prevention through sustainable production methods is an essential policy for minimizing the generation of hazardous wastes, and therefore their management, hazardous wastes continue to be major components of industrial production and we are compelled to address effective management. In addition, a global hazardous waste crisis remains, whether acknowledged by public concern or not, with vast numbers of uncontrolled hazardous waste sites posing potential threats to the health and well-being of current and future generations. The management of industrial hazardous wastes and the remediation of uncontrolled hazardous waste sites must remain a priority for the labor, health and safety, and environmental movements.

LESSONS UNLEARNED

In 1995, the 104th Congress eliminated the Superfund tax, eroding the polluter pays principle by putting an ever-increasing share of federal hazardous waste remediation costs onto the shoulders of the public. In 1995, the Superfund's program expenses began to be split between the Superfund trust fund and the general tax fund. According to the General Accounting Office (GAO), the 18% of Superfund Program appropriations were from general revenues in 1995 but 45% in 2002 as the Superfund trust fund steadily diminished. The fiscal year 2004 appropriations from the general fund accounted for nearly 80% of the program's revenues. In addition, total Superfund appropriations are decreasing steadily. The GAO also raised concerns that state programs face fiscal constraints that will weaken their ability to clean up orphaned hazardous waste sites (Stephenson, 2003, pp. 11, 26, and 27).

In 2004, the EPA reported that, from then until 2033, 294,000 hazardous waste sites would require cleanup, at an estimated cost of $209 billion. These numbers included an estimated 217,000 sites yet to be discovered (U.S. EPA OSWER, 2004, pp. viii and C.1-4). In December 2004, *The New York Times* reported that Thomas P. Dunne, EPA assistant administrator for the Superfund Program, had called for a discussion "to balance public expectations for action and budgetary realities that make timely (Superfund) responses increasingly less likely" (Janofsky, 2004, p. 36). The possible solutions Dunne presented included, on the one hand, having private businesses with economic interests pay for cleanups and, on the other hand, just not listing new contaminated sites until existing known sites are cleaned up. The old "what-you-don't-know-won't-hurt-you" routine. At the same time, though, *The New York Times* reported that " the number of sites needing clean-up is increasing by an average of 28 daily" (Janofsky, 2004, p. 36).

The Democrats were calling for the restoration of the Superfund tax. The lobbying effort against this was being led by the Superfund Settlements Project, a corporate coalition that included DuPont, Honeywell, General Electric, General Motors, Ciba Specialty Chemicals, Solutia, United Technologies, IBM, and Waste Management, Inc. And, as the Bush administration stretched the Pentagon's capacity with its wars in Afghanistan and Iraq, the Pentagon released a December 2004 proposal to eliminate the DOD's 1996 directive to display environmental security leadership and instead stress its "national defense mission." *The Los Angeles Times* reported the story and noted that the "Defense Department . . . has more facilities on the Superfund National Priorities List than any other entity in the U.S. . . . 28,500 potentially contaminated sites " (Getter, 2004, p. 31).

THE NEXT STEPS

The obfuscation of the public's mandate to remediate and manage hazardous wastes is unacceptable. Collective social movement action is needed to inform Americans that their trust has been betrayed and that hazardous waste sites still pose dangers. But citizens must also see feasible plans for making a transition to sustainable modes of production and consumption. They must know that the rules have changed, without their consent, to "the public pays the polluter." Restoring the Superfund tax would allow the use of the lessons of the WETP to expand the training program to provide public health education that will promote a national dialogue on how to make that transition.

SARA, including Section 126, was passed during a transition from dominance by liberal policy to priority being given to neoliberal interests. Even the liberal solution favored the development of a market initiative—the hazardous waste management industry—over a national pollution abatement, remediation, and prevention solution. The AFL-CIO addressed the immediate concerns of workers exposed to hazardous waste materials, but did not extend its thinking to say that hazardous waste sites are bad for workers, working with hazardous wastes is bad for workers, a productions system that creates massive volumes of hazardous wastes is bad for workers, and therefore, labor opposes this production system and calls for a national initiative to make a transition to clean production. The environmental movement generally accepted the new hazardous waste management industry and engaged in a strategy of command and control. The anti-toxics movement pushed it further when it saw the right to know as a way to build public support to demand at least proper controls and remediation. But the notions of toxics use reduction and clean production were still not clear and were not discussed as national policy options. Even the Pollution Prevention Act (1990) failed to mandate such a change (Armenti, Moure-Eraso, Slatin, & Geiser, 2003, pp. 249-251).

So the strategies encapsulated in SARA's Section 126 work well when applied and they have made dangerous work safer. The limits, however, of these and the many other strategies for environmental health protection are that they are bounded by Margaret Thatcher's proposition: TINA—"There is no alternative.' To rephrase a popular antiglobalization rallying cry, "This is what hegemony looks like." Without a politically viable way to challenge corporate dominance, the best that social movements can come up with is an incremental improvement of conditions for the working class (which includes a lot of middle-income people). For the labor and health and safety movements, that means building in protections for workers, their families, and their communities. This early history of the WETP exposes hegemony by revealing the efforts by a range of actors to make the system work better, including the collaborative cooperation, although often reluctantly, by employers and their associations.

A national dialogue is needed to debate, define, and call for industrial policy that will support a transition to a just and ecologically sustainable economy. The example of a regulated private-sector hazardous waste management industry strategy shows that a market orientation, even when regulated, is incapable of working for such sustainability. The expectation of 217,000 yet-to-be discovered hazardous waste sites between 2004 and 2033—with a mature hazardous waste management industry—is testimony enough to that.

Americans have a bill of rights, but lack the rights to a clean environment, to freedom of organization as labor, to health and health care, to affordable housing, and to affordable education at all levels. Citizens and policy makers must commit to national pollution abatement, remediation, and prevention initiatives, and to matching that commitment with sufficient funding to take the necessary actions in the shortest possible time. Extensive research to develop technologies, such as green chemistry and clean energy, is needed so that the generation of hazardous wastes can be rapidly reduced without the withdrawal of the materials and equipment on which our standard of living has come to rely.

In 1973, the EPA predicted that an indicator of system failure would be the discovery of uncontrolled hazardous waste sites. The national hazardous waste crisis persists now, nearly 30 years after its acknowledgment by the U.S. Congress, yet public concern has significantly diminished. Perhaps the success of the hazardous waste management industry has been in allaying public concerns to such an extent that the hazardous waste crisis has now gone underground. But do we really want to live and work on poisoned ground at all?

ENDNOTES

1. Approximately 40,000 rescue and recovery workers were involved in activities at the site, and 11,000 of them were firefighters.
2. Although Hurricanes Katrina and Rita caused unimagined damage, their results may arise more from the failure to be prepared for the consequences of infrequent but normally occurring weather events than from what are called "natural disasters."

REFERENCES

Armenti, K., Moure-Eraso, R., Slatin, C., & Geiser, K. (2003). Joint Occupational and Environmental Pollution Prevention Strategies: A Model for Primary Prevention. *New Solutions, A Journal of Environmental and Occupational Health Policy, 13*(3), 241-259.

Getter, L. (2004, December 17). Pentagon Proposes Loosening Its Environmental Policy. *The Los Angeles Times,* p. A31.

Goodman, J. F. (1991). *Working at the Calling.* Hopkinton, MA: New England Laborers' Labor-Management Cooperation Trust.

Herbert, R., Moline, J., Skloot, G., Metzger, K., Baron, S., Luft, B., et al. (2006). The World Trade Center Disaster and the Health of Workers: Five-Year Assessment of a Unique Medical Screening Program. *Environmental Health Perspectives, 114*(12), 1853-1858.

Janofsky, M. (2004). Changes May Be Needed in Superfund, Chief Says. *The New York Times,* Section 1, p. 36.

Stephenson, J. B. (2003). *Superfund Program: Current Status and Future Fiscal Challenges.* Report to the Chairman, Subcommittee on Oversight of Government Management, the Federal Workforce, and the District of Columbia, Committee on Governmental Affairs, U.S. Senate No. GAO-03-850. July. Washington, DC: GAO.

U.S. Congress. House of Representatives. (1979). Committee on Interstate and Foreign Commerce, Subcommittee on Oversight and Investigations. *Hazardous Waste Disposal Hearings: Part 1.* 96th Congress. March-June. Washington, DC: GPO.

U.S. EPA OSWER. (2004). *Cleaning Up the Nation's Waste Sites: Markets and Technology Trends—2004 Edition* (No. EPA 542-R-04-015). September. Washington, DC: U.S. Environmental Protection Agency, Office of Solid Waste and Emergency Response.

Interviews and Correspondence

Allen, Ken. Interview by author, tape recording, Severna Park, MD, May 6, 1998.

Anderson, Joseph. Interview by author, tape recording, RTP, NC, August 1, 1998.

Bergfeld, William. Interview by author, tape recording, May 28, 1998.

Bergfield,, William. Interview by author, tape recording, July 17, 1998.

Brown, Marianne. E-mail correspondence with author, October 29, 1998.

Dement, John, former Director of the NIEHS WETP. Interview by author, tape recording, RTP, NC, October 20, 1997.

Dobbin, Ronald "Denny." Interviews by author, tape recording, Los Angeles, April 10, 1997, and RTP, NC, May 5, 1989 (e-mail correspondence was exchanged as review of interview transcripts, by author, required clarification of statements).

Dodge, Bradley, tape recording, RTP, NC, August 1, 1998.

Duffy, Richard, Director of Health and Safety, International Association of Fire Fighters (IAFF). Interview by author, tape recording, Washington, DC, December 9, 1997.

Elisburg, Donald. Interview by author, tape recording, RTP, NC, October 21, 1997.

Elisburg, Donald. E-mail correspondence with author, February 9, 1998. Responses to a request for clarification or confirmation of information obtained from Samuels and Duffy, and additional questions regarding WETP and Section 126 of SARA.

Elisburg, Donald. Telephone interview by author, tape recording, July 13, 1998.

Erwin, Glen. Telephone interview by author, tape recording, August 7, 1998.

Finklea, Dr. Jack. Telephone interview by author, tape recording, July 27, 1998.

Geiser, Kenneth. Interview by author, notes, Lowell, MA, May 10, 1998.

Kieding, Sylvia. Interview by author, tape recording, Denver, CO, July 18, 1997.

Lange, Sandra. Interview by author, tape recording, RTP, NC, October 15, 1997.

Leonard, Dick, OCAW senior staff member. Telephone conversation, October 7, 1998.

Leopold, Les. Interview by author, tape recording, New York, July 9, 1998.

Mallino, Sr., David, Legislative Director, Connerton and Ray. Interview by author, tape recording, Washington, DC, December 10, 1997.

Matheny, Carol, retired Grants and Contracts Manager for NIEHS WETP. Interview by author, typed responses by interviewee, and notes from interview, Durham, NC, July 29, 1998.

Mazzochi, Tony. Telephone interview by author, tape recording, August 8, 1998.

Melius, Dr. James, former Director of the NIOSH Health Hazard Evaluation Division. Telephone interview by author, notes, February 18, 1998.

Merrill, Michael. Interview by author, tape recording, Princeton, NJ, July 9, 1998.

Miller, Richard, OCAW senior staff member. Telephone conversation, October 5, 1998.

Mirer, Franklin, Director of Health and Safety, United Auto Workers Union. Telephone conversation, July 14, 1998.

Moore, Curtis. Interview by author, tape recording, McLean, VA, January 15, 1998.

Moran, John. Telephone interview by author, tape recording, July 27, 1998.

Morawetz, John, ICWU Training Center Director. E-mail correspondence, February 9, 1998.

Morris, Sharon, former NIOSH Legislative Officer. E-mail correspondence, March 16, 1998.

Oliver, Dr. Christine. Former OCAW medical intern. Telephone conversation, May 11, 1998.

Ortlieb, David, Director of Health and Safety, International Union of Paperworkers. Telephone conversation, February 23, 1998.

Powers, Marilyn, former OSHA New Directions Program Administrator. Interview by author, notes, Denver, CO, July 19, 1997.

Rall, David, MD, PhD. Interview by author, notes, Washington, DC, December 10, 1997.

Randall, Jacky. Telephone interview by author, notes, March 27, 1998 (Ms. Randall, formerly Ms. Simon, worked closely with Dr. Rall at NIEHS in the mid-1980s).

Reimherr, Joyce, former Director of the National Clearinghouse for Hazardous Waste Worker Health and Safety. Telephone interview by author, tape recording, February 28, 1998.

Rice, Carol, Director of the Midwest Consortium. Telephone conversation, September 1997.

Robbins, Dr. Tony, former NIOSH Director. Telephone interview by author, notes, March 10, 1998.

Samuels, Sheldon. Interview by author, tape recording, Solomon's Is., MD, January 16, 1998.

Sassaman, Dr. Anne. Interview by author, tape recording, RTP, NC, October 16, 1997.

Seminario, Margaret, Director of the AFL-CIO Department of Safety and Health. Interview by author, tape recording, Washington, DC, December 10, 1997

Seminario, Margaret. Telephone conversation, notes, April 3, 1998.

Thursby, Neil. Interview by author, tape recording, June 22, 1998;.

Wages, Robert. Telephone interview by author, tape recording, August 11, 1998.

Warren, James M. Interview by author, tape recording, May 28, 1998.

Weisberg, Stuart, former Staff Director of the Subcommittee on Employment and Housing, House Committee on Government Operations. Telephone interview by author, notes, April 3, 1998.

Index

In Praise

Environmental Unions is a fascinating inside look at the politics, science, and strategic decisions that produced an important workers' health and safety initiative—worker training for workers at hazardous waste sites. It situates the worker training projects in the political economy of the U.S. chemical industry in the late 20th century and the efforts by unions and health and safety advocates to reverse the poisoning of both the environment and the workers. The author was a participant and a keen observer of this work, who drew wise lessons that will have broad relevance for years to come.

Richard W. Clapp, D.Sc., M.P.H.
Professor, Boston University School of Public Health

The worker training program is one of the most far-reaching public health initiatives of the late 20th century. The education, training, and empowerment of workers to reduce workplace exposures will have a continued impact on improving health for years to come. This detailed chronicle of program development and the subsequent lessons learned is a credit to Dr. Slatin's diligence and is a valuable resource for the design of future initiatives by labor and government. The book documents history, but the content must not become history. Dr. Slatin's work challenges the nation to expanded education and training in health and safety so that health is preserved at work.

Carol Rice, Ph.D., C.I.H
Professor, Department of Environmental Health
University of Cincinnati

Environmental Unions: *Labor and the Superfund* is specifically about labor's multiple policy initiatives that led to the setting up of the Workers Education and Training Program, particularly during a time when labor's own power was declining. In a broader sense, it is a story about the strengths and weaknesses of labor, and how unions responded to the rise of the hazardous waste management industry, with its inherent dangers for workers, by pursuing both public and private sector measures to protect their members. The WETP exists because of labor's ability to perceive the need for worker protection strategies related to the state's responses to demands from the environmental movement. Dr. Slatin has provided a critical framework for understanding the historical relevance of movements as actors in the political economy of the work environment and occupational safety and health regulation. This story of how unions were able to develop coalitions with environmentalists demonstrates the potential for labor and other movements to join in promoting policies that may lead to a more sustainable future. It is an important model for anyone interested in changing traditional ideas and practices as we pursue new strategies for achieving the advancement of workers' rights and global democracy.

Karla R. Armenti, Sc.D.
Chief, Health Statistics & Data Management
New Hampshire Division of Public Health Services
Adjunct Professor, M.P.H.Program
University of New Hampshire

A thoughtful, well-written account of a unique collaboration (20 years and counting) of government, labor, universities, and environmental justice to deliver excellent training to thousands of hazardous material workers.

John S. Morawetz
Director, ICWU Health and Safety Department

Craig Slatin tells an important story at the intersection of labor unions and environmental cleanup of hazardous materials. If organized labor is to grow again in the U.S., the labor–environment–clean energy nexus is one of the critical paths that such growth must follow. Slatin's focus on occupational health and safety education and training in the Superfund program brings to light a little-known history with valuable lessons for labor and environmental advocates and educators.

Steven Hecker
Senior Lecturer, Department of Environmental and
Occupational Health Sciences
University of Washington

Craig Slatin relates a compelling story here. As a chemical worker for twenty five years, I experienced firsthand the positive impact of the program he describes. But this telling is more than just an academic account of an important chapter in the occupational health and safety movement in this country. Slatin places his analysis within the framework of the political economy at play at the time, thereby grounding the events in a larger social context. This is important because these very forces continue to affect our ability to provide additional needed protections to workers, the community, and the environment we live in, from the toxic hazards that continue to surround us.

Paul C. Renner, J.D.
Associate Director, The Labor Institute
New York

Environmental Unions: Labor and the Superfund is essential reading for anyone interested in the history of health and safety training in the U.S. from the mid-1980s to the present. Slatin deftly details the interplay of political and economic forces that led to the establishment of and shaped the nation's most successful and enduring government-sponsored worker safety and health training program since the demise of the OSHA New Directions Program. Through interviews with key union leaders, government officials, and safety and health professionals, Slatin outlines the issues of public policy that were fought out in the legislative sphere, the compromises resulting from conflicting interests, and their implications for the health and safety of workers. Through case studies of programs instituted by the Oil Chemical and Atomic Workers and the joint labor-management program of the Laborers Associated General Contractors, Slatin details how hazardous waste training empowered workers and affected these disparate unions.

Joel Shufro, Ph.D.
Executive Director, New York Committee for
Occupational Safety and Health

In the 1980s, diverse movements of labor unions, community organizations, public health professionals, and environmental activists took action to confront the tragedy of exposures to chemical and hazardous material waste sites, spills, emissions, and accidental releases. This loose alliance fought for reauthorization of the federal Superfund program and, as part of it, demanded the creation of a worker health and safety training program to prepare the workers who must clean up uncontrolled hazardous waste sites and those on the front line of emergency response. In 1986, the National Institute of Environmental Health Sciences established the Worker Education and Training Program, now a network of more than 100 organizations. Dr. Slatin, a key participant in the WETP for much of its existence, has written a fascinating and informative history of this effective union of federal resources with private and public nonprofit organizations. I recommend it to anyone interested in learning more about the challenges and rewards of a unique and effective public health intervention. The WETP has had to adapt in dramatic fashion to address the growing levels of man-made and natural disasters and has saved untold numbers of lives. Slatin captures that history and, more importantly, relates how this network remains true to the principles that shaped it.

Paul Morse
Project Director, The New England Consortium
University of Massachusetts Lowell

A SELECTION OF TITLES FROM THE

WORK, HEALTH AND ENVIRONMENT SERIES

Series Editors, *Charles Levenstein, Robert Forrant and John Wooding*

AT THE POINT OF PRODUCTION
The Social Analysis of Occupational and Environmental Health
Edited by Charles Levenstein

BEYOND CHILD'S PLAY
Sustainable Product Design in the Global Doll-Making Industry
Sally Edwards

ENVIRONMENTAL UNIONS
Labor and the Superfund
Craig Slatin

METAL FATIGUE
American Bosch and the Demise of Metalworking in the Connecticut River Valley
Robert Forrant

SHOES, GLUES AND HOMEWORK
Dangerous Work in the Global Footwear Industry
Pia Markkanen

WITHIN REACH?
Managing Chemical Risks in Small Enterprises
David Walters

INSIDE AND OUT
Universities and Education for Sustainable Development
Edited by Robert Forrant and Linda Silka

WORKING DISASTERS
The Politics of Recognition and Response
Edited by Eric Tucker

LABOR-ENVIRONMENTAL COALITIONS
Lessons from a Louisiana Petrochemical Region
Thomas Estabrook

CORPORATE SOCIAL RESPONSIBILITY FAILURES IN THE OIL INDUSTRY
Edited by Charles Woolfson and Matthias Beck